Once a reporter for Independent Television News, Gerald Seymour is the author of eighteen bestselling novels, including *Harry's Game*, *The Glory Boys* and, most recently, *Holding the Zero* and *The Untouchable*. He lives in the West Country. One of his novels, *The Waiting Time*, has recently been adapted for Carlton Television.

THE JOURNEYMAN
TAILOR

Gerald Seymour

CORGI BOOKS

THE JOURNEYMAN TAILOR
A CORGI BOOK : 9780552147248

Originally published in Great Britain by Harvill

PRINTING HISTORY
Harvill edition published 1992
Fontana edition published 1993
Corgi edition published 1999

5 7 9 10 8 6 4

Set in 10/12pt Palatino by
Phoenix Typesetting, Ilkley, West Yorkshire.

Corgi Books are published by Transworld Publishers,
61–63 Uxbridge Road, London W5 5SA,
A Random House Group Company.

Addresses for Random House Group Ltd companies outside the UK
can be found at: www.randomhouse.co.uk
The Random House Group Ltd Reg. No. 954009.

Printed and bound in Great Britain by
CPI Cox & Wyman, Reading, RG1 8EX

The Random House Group Limited supports The Forest Stewardship
Council (FSC), the leading international forest certification organisation.
All our titles that are printed on Greenpeace approved FSC certified paper
carry the FSC logo. Our paper procurement policy can be found at:
www.rbooks.co.uk/environment.

To Gillian, Nicholas and James

Chapter One

All through the day they had left him to his own thoughts, his own moods.

It was as if the soldiers and the policemen were nervous of him and believed they should give him room, as if they thought his building anger might explode against them.

He stood, alone, in the centre of the lane, and all the time he stared up the rising length of the potted road towards the crest of the hill. In the middle of the day, as they had the day before, they had offered him a hot mug of coffee and a sandwich wrapped in clingfilm, and both times he had declined the chance to eat or to warm himself with the drink. It had been a good morning, low dreamy winter sunshine and a sharp wind, enough to dry the heavy oiled coat closed tight across his body that had taken a drenching from the driving rain of the previous day. The light was falling now and a rain blanket had gathered over the distant mountain summit that was beyond the horizon of the top of the lane. The cold cut through the protection of his coat, and whipped his trouser legs. He shivered. To either side of him, beyond the uncut hedgerows of thorn and holly and hazel, were the rain-soaked fields. There were song birds in the hedgerows, feasting on berries and grubbing for worms. Away out in the fields, amongst the rushes that grew in the bog land, ignoring the sheep that had cropped the grass short, the black crows and arrogant magpies strutted in their search for carrion. Hovering above the lane, occasionally masked by the low-flying cloud, was the helicopter.

The helicopter had been up all through the day before and all of that day, and for most of the night it had pierced the darkness of the lane with the power beam of a searchlight. The noise of the helicopter's engine blasted out the sweetness of the birds' excitement in the hedgerow, killed the low voices of the soldiers and the policemen.

Slowly he gazed around him. There were young soldiers from a Fusilier regiment kneeling in the water-filled ditches beside the lane, aiming their rifles and their machine guns out towards the further hedgelines that were now blurred by the first rain spits of the squall that rushed to meet them. There were policemen, encased in their all-weather clothing, clutching their clipboards and Scenes of Crime notebooks, and talking with urgency into their radio sets. There were the small white bungalows further up and further down the hillside, with closed front doors, and peat smoke streaming from the chimneys, where the answer of the farmers and their wives and children would be that they had seen nothing and heard nothing and knew nothing. There were two men, huge in the body armour that they wore under their camouflaged combat uniforms, walking back down

the lane, and the one passed the other a bright cigarette packet and dropped the cellophane and gold
paper wrapping onto the tarmac, and took a box of
matches from his colleague. He saw it all and he hated
it all.

There was a stirring of the soldiers and policemen
in front and behind him.

The cold bit into him. He had wrapped his scarf
tight around the lower part of his face and pulled his
flat cap down over his forehead, not against the
weather but so that his identity and his features
would not be seen by the priest who had earlier been
allowed to go forward up the lane to whisper the Last
Rites and the Act of Contrition into the ear of the body.

It was three days now since the report had reached
his desk of the finding of the body. He hated everything that was around him. He knew, of course, the
name of the man who lay dead halfway between
where he stood and the horizon of the lane. The fields
on either side of the lane had long since been swept
by the electronics that the military used, and the
hedgerows had been pronounced clear of booby-trap
explosives and command wires. The helicopter's
vantage point ensured that the high ground to the
right of the lane and ahead was free of snipers, and
now the bomb men, ambling back down the lane, had
passed the body as safe for inspection.

The body was of his man. He had felt it necessary
to be there. For the first time in his life he knew the
responsibility for the death of a man. He would not
have wished to have been anywhere else.

There was the stamping of feet around him, to
inject warmth, and shrill laughter, to pretend that it

9

didn't matter and that life went ahead for the living, and coughing and spat phlegm, to clear the lungs before the walk up the hill to inspect a body that was not wired to a detonator and a pressure plate and explosives.

They had two hundred yards to walk up the lane.

He stepped out briskly. There was an army major leading and two police officers and their photographer were behind him. The rain was in earnest. It fell from the brow of his cap, dripped onto his scarf, ran at the collar of his coat, clung at his trousers, squirmed in his feet.

It was eighteen days since he had last seen his player. A meeting like most of the others of the last year. The dark side of a car park, well away from the front entrance of the hotel, at least a dozen miles from the player's own neighbourhood. The player had been fine, had chainsmoked but that was normal, had talked and even made what passed for a joke – and that wasn't normal. He'd got nothing dramatic, nothing that was going to win the war, but nothing either that indicated any specific anxiety. The player had taken his money. He had slapped his player's back, as he always did, to give him confidence. He had waved the poor bastard away, seen the rear lights of his car head off into the dark.

When they were close to it, almost upon it, he saw the white of the flesh of the shoulder and the glistening black of the dustbin bag.

And then, ten nights ago, he had sat in the car with his colleague for more than two hours, and he had cursed the player for not showing, and cared not to remember that it was the first time in a year that his player had not been on time for a meeting. His temper had been short because of his own fear. Sitting in his car, his weapon loaded and cocked, wondering as the minutes passed whether he and his colleague were compromised and not daring to wonder aloud whether the player was lost. A ghastly two hours until he had thrown in the towel and got the hell out. And all the drive back he had known in his gut the terrible fear that came from his feeling of responsibility for his player.

There were the fiery white flashes from the camera, startling in the coming dusk. The rain buffeted him. The photographer stepped back. The body was half on the grass verge of the lane and half in the ditch. The head of the body, hidden in the dustbin bag that was loosely tied at the throat with orange bale twine, was deep in the ditch and damming the flow of the rainwater. The body was naked to the waist. The trousers were sodden. There was more twine binding the ankles, and the bare feet on the road.

When he needed it, he could get a police or an army uniform. The morning after that failed meeting, he had been with a search party of troops that had raided the player's home. A small terraced house, full of bawling kids, on the edge of a barren housing estate. He had stood by as the lieutenant who led the search party had questioned the player's wife. He knew all about the woman. He knew what she had been given for her birthday, and what she was to have been given for Christmas. He knew the names of all her children. He knew where the roof dripped, and which central heating radiator leaked. Where was her man now? When was he last at home? When was he coming back? Who had called by for him? Good woman, the wife of the player, a good woman because she thought she was married only to a volunteer in an active service unit of the Provisional wing of the Irish Republican Army, and there was no way that she was going to utter a single word to betray the Organization. Tough woman, too. She hadn't answered anything, but her eyes that were red from weeping had told half the story, and a sergeant who was a family man had extracted from the seven-year-old out of sight on the stairs that her Da had been taken out of the house fighting and kicking and crying for his life. And that had been the start of the waiting time.

By the time the woman saw her man's body she would know what he had been, what he had suffered.

He knelt at the edge of the tarmacadam and carefully turned the body over. The player had seemed a slight man when they had met in car parks, behind pubs, at railway stations and supermarkets. But he was dead weight now. The cigarette burns were bright on the pale chest amongst the sparse gingery hairs. The handler shuddered. They had had him for a week, a good clear week since the big men in their combat jackets and their balaclavas had bullocked into his house. A week before they had hooded him, trussed him with twine, put him into the boot of a car or the back of a van, and driven him to the killing ground. He saw that the hands were tied together at the wrist and seemed to clutch at his privates, as if even at the moment of death he had flinched from another kicking. He heard the sigh of impatience from the major behind him and the fidgeting of the

12

policemen. He couldn't blame them, couldn't blame anyone for wanting to be off this bloody awful hillside before darkness came down.

In time the player might have become seriously important. As it was, he had only been useful. He had wanted to please. That had been the worst thing about him. Pathetically eager to please. Perhaps they had rushed him. He had told the player often enough that his life was sacred, that no risk would be taken with his safety. And he would never know how his player had been discovered. It could have been because of his knowing of the movement of the two Kalashnikovs in the car that had been stopped a month back at the apparently random vehicle check-point at which two volunteers had been arrested. It could have been because he had flashed his money in a bar when the whole estate knew he hadn't been in work since he came out of gaol. It could have been because he'd taken drink and the adrenalin of the double life had pushed out some careless remark. Whatever the reason, the player was dead, and the player's life had been his responsibility.

They always hooded them. They always took the shoes off them; in that community it was the ultimate shame to die barefoot. He took the black plastic in his hands and ripped it. He saw the bruising on the face, and the left eye puffed shut, and the front tooth missing. He saw the blood mess of the bullet's entry wound.

He nodded. It was his player. He pushed himself up from the grass. As he had stepped away they were already bringing the stretcher forward, and moments later the Scenes of Crime men were starting a check of the ground on which the body had been dumped. It had happened before, it would happen again. The handler gazed down into the mutilated and tortured face of his player, and then the face was lost to his view by the slashing zip of the bodybag.

He walked fast back down the lane towards the knot of soldiers and policemen. No-one spoke to him. He was the handler who had lost his man to the enemy for a week. His man had been beaten and kicked and burned until he shrieked his confession onto the slowly turning spools of their tape recorder. The enemy would know everything of him that Eddie Dignan, codename Tallboy, had known.

Through a farm gateway, he sheltered by the hedge from the wind. He wanted to be out on the first of the helicopters, with the major and the senior police officers and the body of the informer. He had thought himself a hard man and the tears ran down his cheeks. He would never work in the Province again. Never again play God, hold in his safekeeping the life of an informer. Good riddance. Send in some other bastard, and good luck to you, sunshine.

In the barracks where the helicopter put down, he walked at once to his car. He had to wait at the main security gate because the sentries gave precedence to the hearse coming in. On an empty road, in the darkness, he drove back to Belfast to write his report, to pack his bag, and to get on a flight home. Two and a half years of work come to an end, with his player in a ditch.

'There was this preacher, might have been Paisley and it might not, real red hell-fire merchant, and up the

14

Shankill he's given them two hours of sermon, frightened the wits out of them. First time in two hours and he draws breath, mops his forehead, sweat like it's raining. "Are there any questions?" Little wee lady, clutching her brolly, at the back, pipes up, "Do angels have wings?" Big fellow in the front, fast as light, says "Do they, feck . . ." And the preacher he shouts back, "One question at a time . . ." Got it?'

Jon Jo laughed out loud. He always laughed at that story, whether he heard it or whether he told it himself.

He thought the driver was all tensed up and needed to wind down. The driver had missed the last set of lights, gone straight through on red. The joke was to calm the driver. And round the next bend there had been a police car, just cruising. Even Jon Jo, and it was hard to get his temperature up, had felt his heart racing when they had gone past the police car after being tucked in behind it for a full minute when the police car had slowed right down. And over the next mile as the police car sat on their tail.

'I heard it already,' the driver muttered, through gritted teeth.

'Did you now?'

'And it was told better the last time.'

'Was it now?'

And then the police siren exploded on them and the driver moaned and jammed on the brakes, but the police car was past them, blue lights twirling, and they sat still with the engine off for several minutes, saying nothing.

He had never seen the driver before. He had been given over the telephone the colour and make of the

15

car, its registration number and what time it would pick him up by the taxi rank outside the underground station when he came off the last train of the night. He cuffed the shoulder of the driver to encourage him. The drivers weren't as good as they had been the year before, nor the couriers.

'So just watch the road.'

'I will.'

The driver's accent was Dublin. Jon Jo Donnelly didn't rate these youngsters from down south. Given his choice, and he wasn't, he would have had boys from his own place, but they sent him drivers and couriers from the south now because they were the ones who weren't on the fingerprint files.

Jon Jo had the map spread across his knees, and he used a torch to track their route into the sprawl beyond Wimbledon. He was wearing pink plastic washing-up gloves. The last thing that he had done before he had identified the car had been to pull on the thin, clammy gloves. It was past one in the morning. He thought the driver was scared out of his mind. He gave the directions quietly and he tried to breathe his confidence back into the kid. They came to the road, the headlights caught the name of the road.

'Well done, that's great.'

The driver did not reply.

The road was poorly lit, long stretches of blackness between the street lights. Along the avenue of mock-Tudor homes a very few still showed an upstairs light, and one only had a ground-floor light on. The suburb was asleep. He had walked down the road and round the right-hand bend, just before the target's house, in the morning of the day before. He had walked fast

16

and not slackened his speed when he had passed the house that concerned him. The house needed new guttering at the side above the garage, and he had noted the car parked by the front door, and he had seen the bright new burglar alarm box high above the windows on the first floor. There were no lights now in the house. They drove down the avenue, and then did a figure of eight in the streets at the end. No cars passed them. They came back down the road again.

Two streets away there was a railway station with a sporadic service through the night from Waterloo. The driver parked there, away from the lights. It was the time of night that fathers and brothers and boyfriends would wait outside a station to pick up a girl to save her walking home. Jon Jo rehearsed the driver in his role and then he said, 'Ten minutes, could be fifteen, but you wait for me.'

'Good luck.'

'Won't be me that's needing luck. You wait, you don't crash out unless there's sirens in my street, you hear me?'

The driver said, 'Get the pig.'

'You just have the car good and ready.' Jon Jo switched off the car's interior light, checked that the car park was empty and slipped out through the door. He closed it quietly behind him. For a moment he saw the driver's face. So bloody young. He walked away from the car carrying a dark brown shopping bag, heavily weighted.

He hugged the shadows. The night was his friend, and had been ever since he could remember.

He was a little over six foot in height, broad and strong because all his life he had known physical labour. He was made more formidable by the quilted charcoal anorak that he wore and the black woollen cap that was pulled down to hide his hair line. Dark clothes, nothing that would catch the eye of a woman letting her cat out, a man taking his dog for a last walk, a taxi driver idling for a fare.

He crossed into the target's road. He was very calm. He knew that because of the even pattern of his breathing, and because there was no tightness in his legs.

The house was well-placed for him, almost exactly halfway between two street lights. A white Metro was parked in the driveway behind the low wrought-iron gates. The car was backed up against the green-painted garage doors. He moved silently along the pavement in his worn old trainer shoes. When he was beyond a street light's reach and still short of the target's house, he dropped to his knees and retied his shoes' laces. He turned and his eyes swept the road behind him. No dogs, no cats, no taxis. He stood again and looked up the road. He was against a fence and the hedge above it. He stood very still.

He heard the door open.

He heard, 'Go on, you little bugger, get on with it.'

He heard the door pulled shut.

Jon Jo went forward. He moved fast now. He came to the wrought-iron gates and swung his leg and his bag over, steadied himself, then brought the other leg over, and came down, lightly, onto the tarmacadam driveway. He crouched, waiting. No sound. No light. He walked to the deeper shadow of the passageway between the house and the garage.

The target's car was a Volvo. It would be inside the

18

garage. The Metro would be the wife's. It would make just as much pain to blow the wife away, very influential people British establishment wives, and if they lost one of their kind it might raise the panic scream a ratchet higher. But the target was the driver of the Volvo. Forty times harder to get at. And the Army Council would have the skin off his back if he took the easy road, the Metro.

He reckoned the target would have believed himself at threat and that precautions would be in place. The best location for an electronic beam inside the garage was across the doorway. That's where he thought they'd have recommended putting it. He used a short heavy screwdriver to prise open the small window to the garage set high in the passageway. The surveillance had said that the window was big enough for him. He took the shopping bag in his teeth, so that it half seemed to pull his jaw away and he heaved himself up onto the ridge, holding the window open with one hand, balancing himself, and reaching down inside for a hand-hold with the other. His anorak snagged on the window's fastener, and he believed that the noise he made would have raised half the road. His fingers found a spade handle. It took his weight. He eased himself over the ridge and down, and his foot caught the box of a lawn mower and upended it. He hung on to the window and he lowered himself inch by inch until his feet were firm on the ground. He listened to the silence of the night echoing in his ears.

There was little space for him to move between the lawn mower and the car. He knelt, with his back to the window and took from the plastic bag a box which had once held two litres of vanilla-flavoured soft-scoop ice cream. It was bound tight with adhesive tape, and under the tape across the lid were two circular magnets. With his torch in his teeth, he stripped open the box. His fingers, awkward in the plastic gloves, fiddled to clear the rubber tube that covered the contact pin. He set the clock, from a kitchen timer, for thirty minutes. He checked the wiring of the detonator, the clamps on the battery, the leads to the mercury tilt switch that lay across the mass of the explosive. He wound the tape back across the box.

There was the sharp sound of the magnets thudding onto the underbody of the car. He checked that he had dropped nothing.

In thirty minutes the hand of the clock from a kitchen timer would be stopped against the contact pin. The bomb of four pounds weight of Semtex explosive would be live. Detonation would follow immediately after the mercury tilt switch was jolted and the battery-powered circuit completed. He picked up all the tape and the box, which he crushed, and the plastic bag, and put them in his anorak pocket with the torch and the screwdriver. He set the lawn-mower box upright and rubbed the window catch clean – unthinking instinct, unnecessary because he wore the rubber gloves, care his life style – and then stood still beside the window, listening. When, for a minute, he had heard nothing, he climbed back out and eased the window to its closed position.

Jon Jo went back the way that he had come, in shadow. The car was as he had left it. He dropped down into the passenger seat. The driver looked at him, questioning, and Jon Jo nodded. The excitement would be later, at that moment he felt only the extremes of exhaustion. They drove away.

He had never seen his target, not even a photograph. All he knew of him was his occupation and his address and the make of his car. The occupation was enough to make him a target.

The streets were dead. They went over Putney Bridge and through central London. He dozed, and hazily he heard the murmur of the driver's song. It was an Irish song of the heroes and the martyrs of the Organization, a song that he might have heard in any of the bars that were on the mountainside that was his home. So long, near to a full year, since he had last been home. The car stopped beside the entrance to the mainline railway station.

He opened his door, then in play punched the shoulder of the driver. 'Thanks, you were fine.'

The words gushed. 'You're Jon Jo Donnelly, right? We all talk about you. You're feckin' brilliant. Without the likes of you, this war's over. It's been my privilege to meet you, Mr Donnelly . . .'

The words were strangled. He held the driver's throat in his hand.

'Don't ever speak my name again. Don't ever think of going careless with my name. You ever do that and I'll gut you.'

He slammed the door and strode away into the shadows, stripping off the gloves. He left the station by the exit on the other side and walked eight blocks to find a rubbish sack to stuff his bag and the gloves in, then more slowly back to the station and onto the concourse to find a bench not yet taken by a dosser

21

where he could stretch himself out until the time of the first train of the morning.

When he had come on duty he had immediately been aware of an atmosphere of minor crisis ebbing in and out of the Section Head's office. Had to be a crisis for Wilkins to have stayed on as late as nine, and his P.A. had been there, and Carthew and Foster. Behind the closed door there had been the clatter of glasses. Then it was all over, Carthew and Foster slipping away like ghosts in the night, the P.A. sliding an empty scotch bottle into her waste bin and leaving as if she'd stood up a date in a restaurant for a couple of hours. Wilkins had just said, as he was shrugging into an overcoat, that he would be at home if a 'Priority' came through. And that had been that. The crisis must have been contained, because no trace had spilled over into the Night Desk Officer's vigil.

Two faxes on the secure line from Belfast, neither of them remotely 'priority', a phone call from SO13 at the Yard asking for a trace on a building worker from Limerick, the usual job of getting the Sit Rep ready for the Section Head's desk for when he came in at one minute to nine o'clock.

The first girl into the typing pool whispered something inaudible to the second girl, and she looked at him and giggled. The office area had begun to fill up. The kettle was on, the telephones had begun to ring.

It was a Friday morning.

The voices played around Bren. He filled his brief-case. Just the box for his sandwiches, his flask and the mug that he had washed up when he had shaved, and the envelope from Personnel with a flimsy on Security

Service pensions. He heard all that was said, but he knew that he was an outsider.

The chatter had started.

The talk was of the weekend.

'You be careful down at Archie's. All he gets people down there for is two days of mucking out his bloody stables. It's slave labour. First thing you'll be given is a pitchfork, all the exercise you'll get is carting manure . . .' 'Sybil and I are going to Budapest. No, just for the weekend, out tonight, back at sparrow-fart on Monday morning. She says we'll get all the Christmas presents there for half of what Regent Street'd cost . . .' 'Yes, with Roddy, somewhere in Northants. It's his sister's twenty-first. I had to buy a new dress, four hundred bloody pounds. Some D.J. oick from the Beeb's doing the disco . . .' 'No, really, we're camping. Fiona's into that sort of thing. Exmoor in November, Christ! I said I'd be sleeping in longjohns with the sleeping bag tied at my neck. She's a tough little vixen . . .'

Bren was going nowhere for the weekend. He was going nowhere because he had not been invited anywhere.

He was at the door. No-one seemed to have noticed that he was leaving. Bren stood aside to make way for his Section Head.

'Just off then, Bren?'

Well, he was at the door with his raincoat on and his briefcase in his hand . . . 'Just off, Mr Wilkins.'

'You didn't call me.'

'Nothing came through that was Priority.'

'Thank the good Lord for that.'

'I checked through the statistics, sir. It's the first

week in the last ten that we haven't had either a shooting or a bombing, or even a failure. Good morning, then, Mr Wilkins.'

He looked back at his desk, to be certain that it was cleared, that all the sheets of paper that he had headed DONNELLY JJ had gone to the shredder. There would have been a small frown from Mr Wilkins if he had left any vestige of his night's work on the desk. It was what he wanted, what he prepared himself for, to be taken onto the team working on DONNELLY JJ. He had spent two and a half hours after three o'clock trying to extract from the computer database any pattern in the present campaign of attacks. It was about all that he had come up with, that there had not been a shooting or a bombing for seven days, the longest clear time in ten weeks.

'You are home over the weekend?'

'Yes, Mr Wilkins.' There was a gym near his flat and if he left home over the weekend he would go there, pump weights; he would fight the heavy bag on Saturday for two hours and he would do a half-marathon on Sunday.

'Not escaping to the country?'

'No, Mr Wilkins.'

'Thank you, Bren . . .'

Old men with nothing more in their lives to fear came out to walk behind the hearse to the parish church, and women who had slipped into their shopping coats against the cruel wind, and a few children with them. Not more than 150 souls took it upon themselves to accompany the family of Eddie Dignan, the informer, to the funeral Mass. Most of that tight community in the housing estate stayed indoors, or gathered at their front gates. He was the man who had betrayed his own. Eddie Dignan had taken the Crown's gold. His widow, and she was much liked by her neighbours, walked with her children around her, and those that knew her best said afterwards that her face showed more shame than grief. They walked behind the hearse, the widow of the tout, the children of the tout, the friends of the tout. A little tide of hard, pain-etched faces went slowly past the news cameras, and up the steps into the church.

Across the plain coffin, over the small bunches of fresh flowers, over the heads of the widow and her wee ones, over the bowed shoulders of the few inside the great church, the priest said, '. . . Eddie was trapped between two groups of unscrupulous men, one of which – as covert agents of the state – has a skein of respectability masking its work of dark corruption. They too work unseen, seeking victims like Eddie whom they can manipulate for their own ends . . .' As they waited for the widow and her children to ride away in the big black car from the graveside, it was muttered that the greater blame lay with the bastard British who had used Eddie Dignan, not with the Provo gunman who had shot him dead.

It was a more comfortable thought.

He had slept on the bench at Paddington railway station, and then he had gone to the Left Luggage and collected the grip bag with his clothes and the canvas holder that held his carpentry tools. He had bought his ticket, paying cash, and taken the early train to the west.

Jon Jo stood on the platform at Newton Abbot. It was near to nine o'clock. The cold morning air seemed to blast off Dartmoor and swirl across the open space of the station. He had come off the fast train, and the slow train was running late. It was nearly nine o'clock. After a hit, there was a room in London that he could use, in Hackney. There was another always available to him in a Victorian house divided up into bedsitters in Guildford. A third room in Reading, west of London, had also been rented for him. Those rooms had been chosen and paid for by deep cover operatives. The room in the Devon summer resort town of Paignton, he had found for himself. It was where he felt most safe.

Jon Jo took a Walkman from his grip. Methodically he untangled the wires and tuned across the babble of the stations until he caught the chimes of nine o'clock. There was the abbreviated news bulletin. The Gulf, the trade figures, the storm force winds approaching the northwest, the still unsuccessful hunt for a missing child, a soccer transfer record for a central defender . . . The introduction to a phone-in broadcast on Equal Opportunities . . . He tore off the earphones, and buried the Walkman back in his grip.

What the feck had happened? Every morning, winter and summer, the target left for work at twenty minutes past seven. The surveillance report had been definite on that. If the gouging of the window with his screwdriver had been spotted . . . Or if the target had sat so heavily into the driver's seat as to shake off the magnets, and the fall had not thrown the tilt switch. If . . . But the road of the target house would have been swarming with police. There should still have been, 'News is coming in of . . .'

For the first time since he could remember, the first time since he had crossed the water, he felt the sweat of the fear of failure run in the pit of his back.

The platform was crowded. Men and women and school children jostled their way onto the two-carriage train going south and west to the coast towns. Jon Jo was amongst them, his bottom lip white between his teeth.

His PA had been sent with a fistful of loose change to the shop across Curzon Street to buy the sand-wiches and two large bottles of Perrier. They were talking through the lunch break because Wilkins knew that Carthew would be off at three to meet his wife at the airport, and Foster would be wanting to get away early so that he could get onto the M4 before it seized up at the start of his drive to Exmoor. Carthew was certainly work-shy, and Foster might just be certifiable if he intended to pitch a tent against the elements at this time of year.

'So, it's Brennard, is it, until we can get Ferdie back?'

Foster said, 'He's the obvious one, the one we'd miss the least.'

Carthew said, 'He's a prickly little beggar.'

Foster said, 'Prickly is an understatement.'

Carthew said, 'You know, when he first came, and I called him Gary, I thought he was going to do me Criminal Assault.'

'He's the one that I would think most suitable,' Wilkins said quietly. 'It had crossed my mind to move him to the Donnelly team, give him something

27

tougher to cut his teeth on. I'd say he was a little frantic for some meat, in rather a hurry, oh yes. He deserves the chance . . . but I would be less than honest if I did not make plain my disappointment with the reaction of other members of our section . . .'

Foster said, 'I thought Bill was going to have a coronary . . .'

Carthew said, 'No-one in their right mind actually *wants* to go . . .'

Foster said, 'Trouble with Charles is that he's got the private means cushion to fall back on. I think if he were posted he'd quit. Be a waste if we pushed him too hard.'

Carthew said, 'Ulster's hardly the place for a pressed man . . .'

Foster said, 'The only other one that I could think of was Archie. Quite simply, he declined. I suppose it's because he's taken on that place in the country. The problem is, Ernest, that no-one who has a halfway normal life to lead is going to be ambitious for a posting in that dreadful country.'

Carthew said, 'Brennard's particularly well-suited . . .'

Objectively, of course, it was not satisfactory to put in a raw young man, but it was temporary. Foster would check out the position on Ferdie Penn, when he could be recovered from the training programme he was running down in Nairobi. Might be a month, might be two . . . Brennard wouldn't need to be told that it was just a temporary thing because that would be demotivating.

They chewed at their sandwiches. Wilkins mused, 'It's a life that none of us older men were trained for.

Alright, we have our Watchers, and we do that well, but for the most part we are a collating agency. All of this frigging around in ditches, carrying sidearms, running sources, it's a new science . . . You don't think Brennard will let us down?'

Foster said, 'Be working under Parker, won't he?'

Carthew said, 'With Parker in charge, you could send a babe in arms.'

And so, over beef and salad sandwiches and mineral water, it was agreed by the Section Head and his two principal Higher Executive Officers that Gary Brennard should be invited to offer himself for a posting to the Security Service unit working in the province of Northern Ireland. It was further agreed that the invitation should be made quickly, in order that the vacancy left by the compromised Faber should be filled as soon as possible. Faber's return, regrettable though its cause was, would be an asset to the Desk.

'Don't you trouble yourself about young Faber,' said Carthew. 'He's as tough as old boots. Put him straight to work, that's my advice. Give him any sort of break and you'll be doing him no favours.'

Wilkins talked on about the difficulties with Finance. Carthew defended the quality of the glass that could be bought in Hungary. Foster recalled that every stitch of his and Marjory's spare clothing had been stolen from a camp site near Nice last summer. They were civilized men. They enjoyed each other's company and conversation. Ireland, the abscess that governed their lives, was, temporarily, forgotten. The laughter was warm.

His PA stood in the doorway.

'Bomb in Motspur Park, probably Irish. One woman, two children, both girls, fatals.'

He was the familiar figure.

The Commander of SO13, the Anti-Terrorist Branch of New Scotland Yard, had travelled to the location of four shootings and five bombings that long autumn. He thought he should be seen to attend the site of every atrocity. He regarded the British public as his last and best hope of defeating the terrorist scourge now visited on the Home Counties. The landlady of the block of letting rooms, the curious neighbour behind her lace curtains, the inquisitive salesman in the second-hand car yard, the Commander regarded them as his most reliable allies. If he could not be bothered to abandon his schedule and turn out, then he could not expect the watchful and the curious to telephone the police with their suspicions.

He still experienced the sledgehammer blow of shock. He reckoned he always would. He stared grimly across the scene. He had been told in the car coming down that James Tennyson, late of the Northern Ireland Office, now with the Department of Trade and Industry, had been warned that his name was on a list passed from Dublin nine months before, and told also that a local Crime Prevention Officer had been to his home to make recommendations on a security system that wouldn't eat half of a senior civil servant's salary. And he had been told that the man was ill, too ill to go to the office that day, that his wife had taken the Volvo rather than her own smaller car to go with their two children to collect some others for a music class. Tennyson had been taken to a brother's house in Kent.

It was pitiful, they were so naked, these men and their families. The Commander stood alone. He was tall, straight in the back. He tugged continually at his heavy moustache.

The car, metallic grey, was just recognizable as a Volvo. The two nearside doors were completely off. The roof, with the splintered sun hatch at the apex, had expanded to a jagged pyramid. The bonnet was nowhere to be seen and a far-side front wheel was gone. Close to a window frame was the chalked outline of a small body shape and a buckled shoe and one half of a violin case.

The car had cleared the drive, probably bounced in the gutter, and been almost in the middle of the road when the device exploded. The garden fence was flattened back onto the flower bed, the gates were off their hinges and mangled, a bare cherry tree was snapped off at its roots. The front windows of the house were blown in, but the curtains were now drawn and flapping in the wind. He knew the age of the girls, and the name of Tennyson's wife . . . He wasn't even important. He had once been a civil servant doing whatever civil servants do, but in Belfast.

There were neighbours across the road who stared at him. They stood with defiantly folded arms.

A Chief Inspector was at his shoulder.

'The garage had an alarm, and he could have expected that. He still went into the garage. He was prepared to take a hell of a risk . . .'

31

'So, was he stupid?'

There was the grate, now, of the shovels gathering up the fragments of glass and the metal mess from the roadway to tip into the dustbins. They moved across to the pavement to allow the recovery vehicle to pass by with the winch to drag the Volvo onto its trailer.

'Ruthless, I'd say, determined to get it right. He used a heavy tool to get the garage window open . . .'

The Commander said, 'Sounds like him.'

'Probably a big screwdriver.'

'That's my old love, Jon Jo, taking risks again.'

When he couldn't sleep, as he hadn't slept in the last ten weeks, when his wife chucked him out and into the spare room at the back of their house, then the face that filled the Commander's mind was that of Jon Jo Donnelly.

'Brennard? Hope I didn't wake you. Ernest Wilkins here . . . Something's come up that I'd like to discuss with you. I can't talk about it on the phone. I hope you haven't anything that can't be switched on Monday morning . . . Let's say before the chaos starts, eight o'clock. Goodbye, and have a good weekend.'

Chapter Two

It was the story that the child loved best, the story that had no ending.

'They called him Shane. He was from the family of the Donnellys, and they had a small castle at what was then called Ballydonnelly that had been built beside the Torrent river, where there was a ford. People could cross the ford, wade across the river, at that place, so it was right for a castle. Shane was one of the young men of the family of the Donnellys. His father was Patrick Modardha, a funny name because it means that he was called Patrick the Gloomy. It is 350 years ago that this all started. They were the Catholic people, they owned the land, and the English set themselves to drive them off that land just because they were Catholics and to put their own people, thugs and scum, onto that land . . .

'Patrick led his men in the attack on the castle of Lord Charlemont at Moy. They sacked the castle, drove the English away. That was when Patrick was a young man, and before Shane was born. The years passed, and for a while the Donnellys at Ballydonnelly Castle were left to themselves. Shane was born. He grew up to be a fine young man, good to his neighbours, kind to the family's tenants.

Even when he was small he had learned to ride a horse and to shoot and to hunt so that he could live off the land on the Altmore mountain. When he was just twenty years old, the English came again. The Englishmen were led by Sir Toby Caulfield, who was a harsh man. The English came with overwhelming force and they killed Patrick Modardha, and they captured the castle at Ballydonnelly. Shane fought as long as he was able and then slipped away and climbed high up onto the Altmore mountain. From there he could see the burning and pillaging and thieving of the English soldiers and the 'gallowglasses' who were paid to fight for them. On that first evening, as he saw far below him the climbing smoke from the Donnelly home and their cattle barns, Shane swore to himself that he would take his revenge of the English for what they had done. At first he joined the rapparee band of Redmond O'Hanlon of Armagh, who was called Terror of the Fews, and then, when Redmond had been killed, he formed his own band of free men. He lived wild on the mountain with them. All his teeth fell out, and he was known as Shane Bearnagh, which is Shane Gaptooth. In all of the band he was the most powerful man, and it was said of him that his toothless gums could bite through a thin plate of iron as if it were gingerbread. The band of Shane Bearnagh became the most famous group of resistance fighters in the whole of Ireland. Down in the valley, Ballydonnelly was now renamed Castlecaulfield and Sir Toby Caulfield lived in Shane's castle, and had taken all the land that had belonged to Shane's family . . .

'The revenge of Shane Bearnagh was on the mountain, but the fear of him spread far and wide. Some of the Englishmen, cowards, paid Shane Bearnagh with money and beef and bread, in the hope that he would leave them alone. He lived in the caves of the mountain, and close to

34

*the main coach road that ran between Dungannon and
Omagh was where he was happiest. At the very summit of
the mountain was a heap of rocks that is to this day called
Shane Bearnagh's sentry box . . .*

*'His friends in Dungannon would light fires when the
coaches left under cover of darkness from Dungannon to
make the run to Omagh. They thought the night would help
them, but they were wrong. Shane could see down to
Dungannon, and the fires that were lit for him, and he and
his men would stop the coaches and take back from the
Englishmen what had been stolen from the Irish people. The
English feared him more than any fighter in all of the island.
They built a barracks on the mountainside, near to the top,
and garrisoned it with their soldiers, and the barracks and
the soldiers were there only to chase and hunt Shane
Bearnagh. They hunted him and they chased him, because
he was the bravest free man in all Ireland . . .'*

'Did they catch him, Ma?'

It was the story that had no ending.

She told him that it was time for them to go together
to feed the stock cattle in the barn.

A whispered voice spoke into a dictaphone.

The machine fitted snugly into the gloved hand and
was held against the lips. The other hand moved the
two inch-long joy-sticks that controlled the zoom on
the camera and the focus.

The camera was 200 yards forward of the hide and
set in a hedgerow above a steeply sloping field. The
camera was well placed. On the close-up it could
monitor the farmhouse and on the wide-angle it
could take in the Nugent bungalow. The bungalow,
set close to the narrow road leading up the mountain

towards Inishative, west of the village, was sixty paces nearer the camera position than the small farm and its rusted metal outbuildings.

The camera and the cables that controlled its zoom and focus functions had taken two weeks to get into position. It had been in operation now for a month. It was the best that the technical support could manufacture. The camera, twenty-five inches long and with the capability of night vision, was concealed in an old log that had been removed under cover of darkness from the hedgerow, taken back to the Mahon Road barracks in Portadown, hollowed out, and replaced before dawn. In the course of six more nights the control cable had been buried. The ground under the hedgerows had been eased back with the sort of tool normally used for edging lawns, a half-moon blade, and then the slit had been painstakingly pushed back together by hand. Only after that, back up the mountain slope, had the hide been dug out and the command panel installed.

The positioning of the camera, its army serial numbers removed, was regarded as of major operational priority.

Day and night, through close-up and wide-angle, the camera oversaw the comings and goings, and the movements at the Donnelly farm and the Nugent bungalow.

It was easier to speak into a dictaphone than to write the log in the lightless cramped hole that was the hide.

A faint voice, 'Attracta and Kevin, taking a bale from the barn to the cow shed, zero nine forty three.'

There was the bare click of the dictaphone being

switched off, then the faint rustle of a sheet of tin foil being unfolded.

With the penknife that she took from her apron pocket she sliced the twine binding the bale and then reached through the railings to loosen the hay. There were eight bullocks in the shed. In the building next door, before it was light, she had already milked the four cows and then manhandled the churn, rolling it round on its base, down the centre of the lane where the tarmac had not been destroyed by the tractor tyres, and left it for the tanker at the junction with the road. There would have to be one more journey for another bale for the three cows that were in calf in the bay beyond the fattening bullocks. She needed Kevin to help her.

Attracta did not know where her man was. She knew where he had been because she had seen the news the night before. Kevin long since asleep, she had been alone in the small front room, sitting beside the chair that had been empty for almost a year. She had been about to put more logs on the fire when the news had started. She had good pine logs, well seasoned, that her father split for her. She had seen the shattered Volvo and the wedding portrait of the wife, and the school photographs of the two children. The younger of the two was Kevin's age. She had switched off the television and gone to bed. It was the bed in which she had been born, the bed in which she had been alone for almost a year.

There had been a bombing or a shooting every week since before the autumn had set in. Now it was winter. She trudged back across the mud-filled yard for the

37

second bale. It was man's work to clear the mud from the yard. The police and the army had come after the third kill and searched the farm, and called her man a murdering cunt. Later, they had sealed off the road on either side of the lane, stopped her when she had taken Kevin to the school at the village, searched her and the car so thoroughly that the child had been forty minutes late for his classes. They had called her a Provo's whore, and they had called her son a Provo's bastard.

She never spoke of the war that her husband fought, not to her Ma, not to Siobhan Nugent who was her only neighbour, not to the women at Mass, not to the mothers who gathered at the school gate in the afternoons.

Even in her loneliest times, when Kevin was asleep and when the wind hit the chimney and sang on the electricity cable, she never criticized her man and what he did. She insulated herself with silence.

With her son trying to help she carried the second bale from the barn to the cow shed.

If they trapped him, finally, with a gun in his hand then they would surely kill him. If they hunted him down and he surrendered with his hands raised then they would surely lock him away until his youth and his middle age had been squeezed from him, until he was old.

The voice murmured, was lost in the wind beat on the russet bracken around the hide.

'Mossie off out. Right, and right again onto the village road, thirteen zero four.'

The screen in the hide, beside the box that could

make a video recording of the picture if that were necessary, blurred at the change of focus. The Nugent bungalow was gone, replaced by the Donnelly farmhouse, seen end on. The dog was clear on the screen, curled up in its kennel. It had good teeth and a persistent yapping bark. If the dog was out in the yard, or quartering the lane to the front of the house, then it was impossible to get within fifty yards and remain undetected. Because of the dog it was necessary to use the surveillance camera. The dog was regarded as a bloody nuisance. There were two policemen from Dungannon who had needed stitches in their arms and anti-tetanus jabs in their backsides because of that dog.

The angle of the house to the camera meant that the back yard and the farm buildings could be seen, and also the lane at the front and the pathway through the small and tidy front garden. It was only the last yard or so to the front door and the kitchen door into the yard that were masked.

In the tiny cramped space of the hide, the dictaphone was laid down next to the camera controls and the recording box, beside the loaded pistol.

Charlie One was Stop and Search. Automatic, no point in arguing it. Out of the car, side of the road, anorak off, coat off, shoes off, and the army or the police, or both, going over his car.

Mossie could live with it. He had known a long time that he was categorized as a Charlie One.

The roadblock was on the hill leading down into the village. He couldn't tell whether they were British or Ulster Defence Regiment. If it was the British he might be away in ten minutes, if it was the UDR then he might be away in an hour. They had his face and they had his car registration. His was a face that was memorized at every patrol briefing, and the number of his old Cortina.

He passed the machinegunner, lying on his stomach, aiming back up the road. He passed the rifleman kneeling in the ditch, up to his waist in water, aiming back up the mountain. There was a chain with tyre-shredding spikes in it in case he had tried to accelerate through. It would have made their afternoon, getting a Charlie One. He thought they looked all excited, they always were when they waved down a Stop and Search, they couldn't believe they'd find less than a rocket-launcher and warhead under the passenger seat. The face was at the window, cheeks and forehead smeared in camouflage cream.

British accent, 'Hello, Mister Nugent, have a little word, shall we?'

'Why not?'

Mossie climbed out of the car. Best that way, best to get out without them pulling him out. Being the Saturday he didn't have his work gear on board. Six weeks before he had had his work gear, the tins of paint, and he had been slow getting out, and they had emptied each last one of the full tins into the ditch, and had a hell of a laugh, and said that the bottom of a tin of paint was just a pretty obvious place to move a firearm or ammunition . . . His coat came off, and his shirt. They were dropped on the verge. A soldier bent and tugged his shoes off. Another was talking into his radio, another was inside the car and ferreting, another had the bonnet up and was peering down into the engine.

The sergeant sneered, 'Off down the pub to get pissed up?'

'No, I'm not.'

'That's the Paddy weekend, isn't it, getting arse-holed . . .'

'I'm not drinking, I'm driving.'

'. . . Then, when you're all pissed up, all arseholed, all brave, going out and blowing away a few kiddies, a few little girls. That's the fucking Paddy weekend, eh?'

It was the wind-up, nothing new.

'I'm going down the shop.'

'You're real brave bastards, aren't you? Blowing up little kiddies. Watched it on the news, did we, Paddy, with the Missus and all your own little kiddies? Right fucking heroes, Provo shit.'

Mossie Nugent was too old to be wound up. He was thirty-seven years old. Twenty years ago he might have stuck one on the sergeant. Just what they wanted. Grievous Bodily Harm or Criminal Assault, anything they cared to think up. He held onto the seams of his trousers, kept his hands down. The cold whipped through his cotton vest, and the damp seeped in his socks.

They were bored by the time that Pakkie Henty came along with his tractor and a load of silage, so they let him go. He dressed. He climbed back into his car and drove on.

Mossie Nugent was the Intelligence Officer of the mountain-based Company that was the driving force inside the East Tyrone Brigade. The men from

Altmore mountain dictated everything that went on in East Tyrone. And the Intelligence Officer would never have been stupid enough, knowing that he and his car were Charlie One, to carry a weapon, explosives, ammunition, or documents. He had been going to meet his OC. They were careful now, all of them, the officers and the volunteers on Altmore. Too many roadblocks, too much military presence. He had been going for a talk. Not any more, not once he had been through a vehicle check point.

He drove to the shop in the village. He bought three tins of baked beans, and a sliced loaf, and a pound of sausages.

And he was stopped again and questioned again on his way back home. When he was let through, he waved to Pakkie Henty whose silage trailer was still being searched.

The Commander sat straight in his chair, a cup of tea on the table beside him.

'What I can tell you, sir, is that every resource available to me is currently deployed in the hunt for this man. There is absolutely no complacency in SO13. What it comes down to is patience . . .

'. . . Over the last three years we have recovered four lists of targets, and they added up to 210 persons and locations. Currently I have 172 of those under some form of surveillance. As I told you at the time, when your Parliamentary colleague was killed, he had attended a public meeting without notifying us. Two of the earlier bombs were against targets that had not figured on any previous list. Mr Tennyson was on one of the lists, but was not provided with protection

42

have topped himself if he'd gone back inside. The money was just gravy, it was the threat of going back inside that held him to us. And then he'd begun to get quite good. It wasn't high-grade stuff because he was only a bottle washer, a volunteer, but he knew what was going on and he drove a bit for them, moving stuff. That's when it starts to get really bloody, when he has something to tell you. It's my fault, you see, I put the report in to Task Co-ordinating Group. Parker wasn't there. God knows where Parker was. So I gave the report to bloody Hobbes, and Hobbes chucked it onto the TCG table. They were going to do a hit. Eddie knew the guns were being moved, but he didn't know the target. It wasn't discussed properly, it was all too fast. They were moving the rifles the next evening, and a VCP was set up. The police wanted arrests. It must have been something said by one of the detectives who questioned them at Gough RUC. Somebody slipped up, because as soon as they saw a solicitor the word was back into the system that it hadn't just been an accident. The tout hunt started. The QM knew they were moving the firepower, and Eddie knew because he'd collected them from the cache, and the two guys in the car. It all pointed to Eddie . . . You know what Hobbes said? Sorry, but he's such a prick, that man. He said Eddie was nothing more than a terrorist, and not worth crying over.'

Late Saturday afternoon. The street lights on. Curzon Street deserted. He watched from the upper window of Leconfield House as Faber came out of the main entrance and walked away to find a bus or an underground train.

He shrugged into his anorak. So difficult, Ernest

Wilkins thought, to find men who were not degraded and disgusted by the Belfast work.

He came out of his office, closed the door and locked it, and walked past Brennard's clean, cleared desk. So extraordinarily difficult to find men who could cope with the Belfast work, and not be scarred.

He was out to whist that evening and should hurry himself if he was not to miss the first rubber.

'. . . What I was told to say was that there's a powerful anger here about it. There's people talking on the radio about being ashamed to be Irish. Army Council, Chief of Staff, nobody likes that.'

The woman was making the call because the man who would otherwise have made it believed himself to be under close surveillance. They were uncertain in the Organization as to the capability of the telephone engineers working for Five to trace calls made from pay phones.

There was a queue waiting to use the box. She had turned her back on them so that she could not see their impatience.

'. . . And I was told to say that next time round they're expecting you to be double certain that it's the target, not his wife and not his kids. They said to tell you they're going to put an apology into *An Phoblacht*. They said you should know that they don't *like* having to do that . . .'

She didn't know the face or the name of the man, and he had said nothing beyond the codeword.

'. . . They also said that what you done up to this last one was just brilliant . . . Oh, and the new money's coming through, and they said like can you spend it a bit slower. It's difficult to come by. That's all that I was to tell you.'

She put the telephone down and the handle of the receiver glistened. She felt the sweat in her palm. She was nothing in the Organization but her brother was in his twelfth year of a life sentence and she was happy to be used. She was sweating because she had had to allow the telephone to ring out at the far end for a full two minutes before it was picked up, before the code-word was given her, and then she had to repeat the message that they had given her. As far as she was concerned, any man who had worked on the main-land was a hero. She thought it quite wrong that he should be slagged for what he had done. She walked away up the Andersonstown Road of West Belfast.

His enemy were the retired and the elderly who walked on the esplanade with their lap dogs that were wrapped against the sea weather with little mono-grammed coats, and the teenagers who smashed what they could not steal, and the fishermen off the trawlers who were waiting for the doors of the bars to open, and the driver who took the empty bus from Torquay to Brixham, and the man who stood beside the heaps of his Sunday newspapers that were covered against the spray by plastic sheeting. They were all his enemy. He had chosen this out-of-season resort town, and it was the only place he felt safe. Never truly safe, God knows, and among his enemies he would never be content. And on Sunday always more alone, more keenly missing his Kevin and his Attracta. In far too long he had had no word from his Attracta, not heard her voice. He felt such an ache of homesickness, of

47

longing to be with his boy and his Attracta, it was a physical pain.

The newspaper seller was smiling at him, friendly. He pointed to the papers that he wanted and he searched out the exact change from his pocket. He spoke as rarely as was possible, and never engaged in conversation with anyone he didn't know. He could change his face and his hair and his clothes, his accent he could not alter. The newspaper seller, his enemy, wished him a good morning and thanked him, and made a remark about the weather brightening from the west. He read the headline of the paper on top, and saw the photograph of the destroyed Volvo. Under it was a quote from a retired Secretary of State, one of the worst of the bastards: 'These terrorists are addicted to the adventure and thrill of killing.'

His fingers were clasped tight. They knew nothing of him, the pensioners and the yob kids and the bus driver and the newspaper seller, and they would lap up the shit that he was 'addicted to the adventure and thrill of killing'. They knew nothing . . . And they didn't know much in Dublin and Belfast, the bastards who had a bit of a girl speak to him on the phone like he was a wee brat who had messed his pants on the first day at school and a complaint had been made by the nuns to his Ma, and he a man on their business hunted by every policeman in their enemy's country, by all the detectives of the Anti-Terrorist Branch and the Special Branch, and by the faceless bastards of MI5. That was close to pleasure, the knowledge that they all hunted him, and failed. He would never be complacent, no. But if he were not complacent and never careless then he believed himself impregnable. But the shits in Dublin, they were something else. So, the kids had got blown away . . . What was the big deal? Legitimate tactic of war to spread fear in the enemy. Let them show him the army officer, the civil servant who hadn't cringed over his morning paper, or the wife or mother of an army officer or civil servant who wouldn't have been shaken rigid by what the zombies in Dublin and Belfast were going to issue an apology for . . . Jesus!

A lone figure, wreathed in the mist of the sea fog, wet from the spray of the climbing waves that broke on the sea wall, walking back to the room that he rented behind the open-air swimming pool that was drained for the winter. It was a terrace of old houses. The Bed and Breakfast and the Vacancies signs rocked in the wind. God, and he missed his Attracta . . . He let himself in. As he closed the door she came out of the kitchen at the back of the hall. She was small, she would have been blown away with a slap. She was his landlady.

'Oh, Mr Robinson, I'm so glad you're back. Would you do me a favour? It's the back door, brand new this summer, and I suppose it's warped. I'd be ever so grateful . . .'

'I'll get my tools,' Jon Jo said.

'You're very kind. And there's something I'd like to say to you. This business in the papers, about the Irish, about the bombs and things. I just wanted to say how sorry I feel for all of you good and decent Irish people. I don't lump you all together. I have a great respect for all of you hard-working Irish people who are prepared to come over here to find work so that you

49

can keep your families, a very sincere respect. To me, they are the real Irish and not these awful guerrilla creatures. I just wanted you to know that.'

'I'll bring my tools down.'

Everybody on the mountain had a brother, cousin, friend, neighbour, who was skilled as a brickie or a sparky or a chippy or a painter/decorator. There was never money involved. A brother, cousin, friend, neighbour, did the work that was his trade, and the work was paid for in kind. Mossie Nugent was a painter/decorator. He had repapered and repainted the two big bedrooms and the living room of the farmhouse, and he hoped that by Christmas he would have little Kevin's room done. In the freezer, in the garage beside the bungalow, he had the greater part of a quarter of a beef bullock from Attracta Donnelly's stock, and each week Siobhan was given free-range eggs. It was the way of the community.

Siobhan had her eggs, and if she didn't like him going down, most Sunday afternoons this past year, to the Donnelly farm, then she could go feck herself.

She was a great girl, Attracta Donnelly and pretty still, and going short because her man was across the water. Up his ladder, scraping off wallpaper, he listened to her quiet song as she washed the plates and saucepans from her lunch.

> 'An outlawed man in a land forlorn,
> He scorned to turn and fly,
> But he kept the cause of freedom safe
> Up on the mountain high.'

He had thought her a great girl since the afternoon that he had finished the first room, her bedroom, and she had climbed the step ladder, stood above him, and stretched up to rehang the curtains. Ankles, knees and the back of her thighs and her blouse riding up the small of her back. And he had known Jon Jo Donnelly all his life. Jon Jo had been better at school. Jon Jo had been in the gaelic team, always on the bus for away games when Mossie had been left in his day on the substitute side-line, won more praise from the Father. Jon Jo had been big in the Organization since he had left school and taken on the farm because of his father's arthritis when Mossie was in the Kesh and serving two and a half years for possession of firearms, won more praise from the big men than ever Mossie had had. And Jon Jo had Attracta, who was a great girl, and Mossie had Siobhan who was a hard bitch.

'It's your decision, of course, Bren.'
  'Yes.'
  'You are under absolutely no pressure to accept.'
  'No, Mr Wilkins.'
  'It's really a rather good career opportunity for you.'
  'I see.'
  'It's the sort of place a young officer gets noticed.'
  'I appreciate that.'
  'Every older man in Five, who's on a plateau, wishes to God that he could roll back the years and do a real job like this one.'
  'Do they?'
  'You'd be on secondment from us to the Belfast end.

51

Hobbes runs things over there . . . Day to day you'd be working with Parker . . .'

'I don't know Parker.'

'You'd be directly involved with our Source Unit, which means that you'd be running informers, the Provisionals that we pay for information. It requires very considerable commitment. And, I repeat myself, you'd be noticed, Bren.'

'I've no experience . . .'

'We'll take care of that, and Parker will show you the ropes.'

Bren wondered who was Parker. There were men who worked in the next office, who he passed several times a day in the corridor and he did not know their names, nor what they did. Perhaps if he were invited for the weekend in the country he would have known who was Parker.

'If you think I have . . .'

'No doubts whatsoever. And let me tell you: there are far too many people in this department who exaggerate the danger of working over there. Oh yes, listen to half the old stagers in this office, and you'd have the impression that you only have to put your nose out of the front door over there to get it blown off. That's rubbish . . . A sensible officer, one who keeps his wits about him, will not only enjoy himself in Ulster but will certainly do his career no harm at all. But let me answer your question. I am quite certain you have the qualities to make a very good fist of Northern Ireland operations.'

'I'll do my best.'

Wilkins smiled and shook Bren's hand. He said that he would phone Hobbes that morning. He suggested that Bren should take forty-eight hours off, get his affairs in order, do something about his flat. He said that he would arrange a fast refresher course with Training Section, his PA would give Bren directions. He should report on Wednesday morning.

'Good, that's it then.'

'Thank you very much, Mr Wilkins, for thinking of me.'

Chapter Three

Mrs Ferguson heard the crunch of the car's tyres on the drive. She was upstairs, in the east wing of the house and making up a bed in one of the single rooms. Now that four lorry loads of fresh gravel stone had been spread out over the length of the drive, hiding most of the weeds and grass, she always heard a new arrival's approach. She busied herself down the narrow corridor that linked the east wing to the main landing and called sharply for George, to warn him. George was in the library, painting the skirting boards. She heard his grunt of acknowledgement, echoed from far below. She wore a new dress and a new apron, and they had been new sheets and pillow cases that she had put on the bed, and George, even in the overalls he wore for painting, was smarter, as any of the visitors who had met him as little as a year before would have agreed. The house itself was much altered because Century House, Six, had agreed with extreme reluctance to share the facility with Curzon Street, Five, and the men who held the purse strings had made the decision and forced it through in the teeth of opposition from the Secret Intelligence

Service. MI6 alone could no longer afford the upkeep of the building so MI5, the Security Service, was now a half partner in the running of the house. There was new gravel on the drive, new paint and wallpaper in the common rooms, a new oil-fired Aga in the kitchen, new sheets on the beds . . . But Mrs Ferguson, the housekeeper, remained. George, too, had survived the cyclone, handyman and gardener. The Rottweiler, older and ever more temperamental, still needed to be shut away behind the stout kitchen door when a newcomer arrived.

The men who came now to the house were *different*. Mrs Ferguson would have said a little less refined than the men from Century – they had even made a formal complaint about her cooking – but since she was not yet ready to retire she kept her peace. The dog had heard the car and the pounding behind the kitchen door billowed up the wide staircase. She looked down from an upstairs window as the car came to a stop beside Mr Ronnie's Sierra. And that was another thing that she disliked about the Five people, they never gave her their full names, so they were Mr Ronnie and Mr Frederick and Mr Ernest . . . Well, that was just childish.

She was agreeably surprised. A pleasant-looking fellow, well built and as tall as her late husband when he was that age. Neat dark hair with a clean parting. A grey suit and a sensible mackintosh for the time of year. She had been told his name. In the old days she would just have had a call from nice Mr Carter and all the arrangements would have been made on the telephone, now her instructions came ahead by the facsimile machine. It was all laid out who would be arriving and when, how long they would be staying, which room they should have, what meals would be needed. It was a Mr Gary who walked now to the front door, but she had been notified that he was to be called Mr Bren.

They were in the sitting room. The paint was new and the settees were old. They sat either side of the freshly-lit fire. Ronnie stopped in mid-sentence. A big and elderly man, a little bowed at the shoulders, shuffled in with a fresh bucket of coal, tipped it into the scuttle, wheezed, and backed out. Not a word. The door closed heavily behind him. Bren smiled, and there was a soundless curse from Ronnie.

Ronnie said, 'I'll get this bloody place sorted out if it's the last thing I do . . . They're used to Six's pansies. I'll get a bloody grenade up their arses . . . Where was I? . . .'

Bren didn't reply, it was his style not to speak when he didn't know of anything useful to say. He had thought Mrs Ferguson like any of the other grandmothers who lived in his parents' road. He had heard the dog, its whine behind the kitchen door, and then the clatter of its paws. He had met George, who had said, straight off, that he should always knock before coming into the kitchen and that he shouldn't walk round the grounds after dark unless he knew for certain the dog was shut away.

'. . . Yes, right, now that our gracious coal man has called . . . Over there is the nastiest and most dirty little low-intensity war that you will ever have the misfortune to blunder into. You make one mistake and you'll get your informer shot. If you're cleverer and you

56

make one *big* mistake then it'll be you that goes into the box. You're being sent – I say "sent" because if you volunteered then you're addled in the brain – after a small mistake was made and an informer was taken by the opposition. He was missing for a week. He was tortured, we assume he told them everything he knew about his handler, he was then shot and dumped. The handler was most likely compromised and we've pulled him out. A great deal of effort and time blown away by one small mistake.'

He had been born in November 1963, and on the day that his mother had come out of hospital the President of the United States of America had been assassinated. He had been brought up in a small street of houses in Bristol near the factories at Filton that were now occupied by British Aerospace. They were Aerospace people, his father and mother. His father drove a minibus, eight hours a day, five days a week, round the works complex, while his mother did the same hours and the same days in the canteen kitchens. They understood so little of their son, an only child, as to make contact points minimal. So little under-standing, so few contact points, but throughout all of his schooling they had tried so hard to help and encourage him with his books. They were barely a part of his life now.

'Why me?' Bren said.

'God knows. Presumably, better qualified people are not in position.'

'I'm not complaining.'

'Well, don't damn well sound like it . . . and don't, please, since time is short, interrupt me again . . .

'Informers are our eyes and our ears. Without the

57

informer I doubt we'd still be in there kicking. We know that, and so do they. That's how important it is. But informers don't grow on trees. Take some figures . . . We approach a hundred men, men we have some leverage on, we work very hard on them, pull all the strings and still we might only get five who turn our way. Work on the five and we might, if we are bloody lucky, get two who are halfway useful. Work on those two, and we might just get one who in time will be close to the centre of operations. That is a valuable commodity.'

He'd hogged those books, and done the Scouts and the CCF, and he'd gained the necessaries from his examinations. Gary Brennard had won admission to the University of Surrey at Guildford. There were boys from Esher and Haywards Heath and Wentworth, and girls from Horsham and Cheam and Virginia Water. He met money. For a 'Gary' there was no access into money. Money marked out the kids who were going far because they had the launch pad of connection and opportunity. Within three weeks of starting his first term, Modern History as his major, he had let it be known to anyone who cared to speak to him that his name was 'Bren'. 'Gary' was buried, a terraced house in Filton went down the drain, a father who worked as a minibus driver for British Aerospace and a mother who loaded the dishwasher in the canteen were off-limits. He joined the Conservative Club, worked bloody, bloody hard, and went home less and less frequently. He was further distanced from his parents, saw them more rarely, didn't know how to cope with it, took no pride in the estrangement.

'. . . A dead informer is bugger all use to us. Your

job is to keep him alive. It is very hard to think of the circumstances that make it worth sacrificing a tout in place . . . The very suspicion of a live one causes a high degree of chaos and demoralization. The Provisionals are paranoid about what they call touts. When they have a tout hunt underway – always undertaken by a special unit of the worst killers – then everything else is dropped. It's an obsession with them. The worm eats into the terrorist who's been arrested. He cannot get it out of his head that he's rotting in prison because of the man he thought was his brother in arms. The volunteer who's going to the cache to collect his weapon or his bomb, the guy who's heading for the home of a UDR part-timer or a policeman, he doesn't know whether he's going to get malleted by the Special Forces. Betrayal from within really hurts them. It's about the only thing that does . . .'

He had never been quite sure how he had been recruited. His tutorial lecturer had had something to do with it. A remark by Bren, over a cup of coffee, about the Civil Service, something more about the Home Office, a vague aside about wanting work that was worthwhile. He'd sat the Civil Service exam, and a letter had just appeared through the post at the Hall of Residence, an invitation to an interview. Stressed the Scouts and the Combined Cadet Force and the Conservative Club, emphasized the desire to serve in areas that could benefit his country . . . Quite incredibly easy. Afterwards, he'd reckoned they must have just agreed a programme for livening up the intake, getting more graduates in and less officers from Army Intelligence who wanted a civilian life.

'. . . Sometimes when you move on the ground you

will be alone, sometimes you will be with a colleague. There will be long periods when you will be beyond the reach of a Quick Reaction Force. If you get into trouble it'll be up to you alone to get out of it. Now, just in case we've any nonsense in our little heads about Queensberry Rules, cast your memory back to the two corporals who drove into the funeral procession in Andersonstown. They were kicked, beaten, stripped, pistol whipped and shot. That's what they'll do to you if you are ever unlucky enough, or daft enough, to offer them the chance. But remember, the Provisionals will want you dead, the army won't give a toss for you, and the police would like nothing better than to see you fall flat on your face . . . And all the time you have one thing above all else in your mind: your informer is gold dust. Well, are you up to it?'

Bren felt pounding excitement. 'I don't see why not.'

'I've painted it black because that's the way it is.'

Five minutes before eleven o'clock in the morning, the first morning. Ronnie went to the cabinet, unlocked it with a key from his pocket, muttered that if the drinks weren't locked away then the old beggar in the house would have cleared them, poured a good glass with no water offered, handed it to Bren.

'Thanks.'

'I've scared you, but unless you're frightened over there and learn that sense of survival, then you won't win. You'll catch on, just listen to what Parker tells you.'

He made his way quietly down the stairs. He liked to be able to come and go without his landlady knowing.

Had to be bloody quiet . . . Jon Jo had his fingers on the handle.

'Off back to London?' She was at the kitchen door.

'Time to be getting back to work.'

'When'll you be back?'

'Depends on what I find. Dockland's still got a bit. Might be a week, let's hope it's two or three.'

'I'll air the bed and change the sheets . . . oh, and the door's so much better.'

'Bye then, Missus.'

He let himself out.

While he was away she would change the sheets and have a thorough search through everything that was his. She was that sort of woman. But she would find nothing. He had built the place when she was out shopping. His plans, his maps, his lists were under the carpet and under the old wood flooring, in the box that he had made. Unless she pulled the carpet back and took a heavy jemmy and dug about a bit under the floor, she'd find nothing.

He carried his overnight bag and his carpentry tools. The plan and the map and the name on the list he kept in his mind.

The second morning, not yet eight o'clock, and he thought he might just get to do some serious dying. It was the sight of the other man that kept him on his feet.

An hour earlier, at breakfast alone and in his track suit that Ronnie had told him the previous night to dress in, Mrs Ferguson had made the introduction. The housekeeper had called him *Mister* Terry. The man was a sadist, a torturer, and a Physical Training

Instructor, a bumptious little bastard with apple-red cheeks and not a hair on the scalp of his head, and a Geordie. He was at least fifteen years older than Bren, and he looked as if he might just enjoy inflicting pain.

Bren sagged against the back of a garden seat. PTI Terry was on the grass beside the bench, rolling on the crisp frost, making a better job of dying. He wouldn't have done this to him if the silly little man hadn't pushed his luck.

He had been allowed to eat three pieces of toast, drink two cups of tea on top of his orange juice. Nobody had told him that he would settle his breakfast down with a four-mile run over rough country.

His lungs heaved. He heard PTI Terry's groan, and the apple red of the man's cheeks had gone to grey white. Bren wasn't one for team games, but he ran twenty, twenty-five miles every week and he worked out with weights every day and often twice a day at weekends. He didn't talk about it in the office so it wasn't on his file. PTI Terry would not have known that Bren was fit, and Bren would not have broken the little bastard if it hadn't been for the exchange after breakfast, clearly and deliberately for him to hear, between PTI Terry and Mister Ronnie.

'Doesn't look much, does he, Mr Ronnie? What I'd call pathetic . . .'

'Young people don't look after themselves these days.'

'I'll loosen him up, take him over the four-mile circuit, then you can have him for the rest of the morning, if there's anything left of him. Your modern young, Mr Ronnie . . . I suppose they think there's always a helicopter warmed on stand-by. I don't suppose you told him what happens when the Provies start chasing him over the hills. Strong young lads, used to the outdoor life, running after our little friend with the old AK ready to zap him if he doesn't keep running.'

Ronnie had grinned, 'I'd like to know what he's made of . . .'

Bren had let PTI Terry set the pace, just sat on his shoulder whenever he tried to turn on the heat, and he'd known when PTI Terry turned for home halfway, that the man was labouring, so he went past him and listened to the wheezing into the back of his neck. Bren had turned and smiled, 'It's time they pensioned you off . . .' He upped the pace, and turned again when the gates of the house were in sight. 'That's what I'd call pathetic, PTI Terry.' He lifted his speed again, all the way up the drive, and let the little man catch him, and then called for press-ups, squat thrusts, knee bends. 'Unless, of course, you would prefer to go and lie down . . .'

Ronnie poked his finger into Bren's chest, 'Very clever, very pretty. Tells me more about you than a dozen sheets of paper.'

'Just that I don't like being taken for a prat.'

PTI Terry was retching behind him.

Ronnie said, 'That's alright, sonny. Parker'll sort you out.'

With a grey mist picture, the image intensifier followed the car up the hill from the bungalow. It was a clear night, bright stars, little moon, the best night for the image intensifier. The words that logged the movement were whispered into the dictaphone.

There was an owl up somewhere, in one of the few trees that had survived the sweep of the winter gales. There was a vixen, coughing a call to a dog fox. The car powered away along the road that already glistened with the first trace of evening frost. The car was gone beyond the range of the camera.

They had an Ordnance Survey map, 1:25,000, and a plan of the fields that had been hand-drawn on a sheet of paper. Mossie had the operational plan. It was for the OC to approve or reject it.

They met in a small farmhouse, one of the few remaining older buildings on the plateau at the top of Altmore mountain. It was the usual way. The front door had been left unlocked, and the television played noisily in the kitchen. The front room was theirs, with a pot of tea and a plate of biscuits left on a tray.

Mossie explained: The police inspector, three years at the Coalisland barracks, eighteen years in the Royal Ulster Constabulary, had taken to hitting golf balls in the field behind his home. He had a dog, a spaniel, that could retrieve game and now was trained to bring him back his golf balls. Most Saturday mornings, early, just after dawn, the police inspector went into the field with his clubs and his balls and his dog and hit his shots for a good half an hour before driving off to play the Dungannon course.

They spoke in low voices. On his close plan Mossie had sketched in where the back-up car would wait. It would be 200 yards from a spinney of silver birches along two hedgerows, past a crumbling cow byre, skirting a final field before reaching a firing position. The shooting range would be 40 yards. Mossie said they would be in the car before the policeman's woman and his kids had gotten out of the house to see what had happened and then back inside to phone or radio through.

That was Mossie's work, to find the targets, co-ordinate the reconnaissance and draw up a bare tactical plan. He alone had worked on the plan. No-one other than the OC would decide whether it should go ahead, and who should be involved. Only the Quartermaster would know what weapons were to be used, where they were currently hidden. It was the cell system that guaranteed their security.

The map was unmarked, that would go back into the glove compartment of the OC's car. He unfastened his belt, unzipped his trousers and let them fall. He dropped his underpants. He stood, white legs in front of the fire, and folded the plan tight and small and then attached it with a strip of elastoplast to the inside of his groin.

The OC pulled up his underpants and his trousers. He was fastening his belt. 'You happy?'

'If they get out fast enough.'

'It's tight?'

'I saw him myself last Saturday, but what I hear is that he's been out like that the past four Saturdays.'

There was the grim smile on the OC's face. 'They did the tout proper, the Castlewellan fecker.'

'Yes.'

'But too good for him, too quick.'

'The Dignan bastard should have been hurt more,' Mossie said.

All the families on the mountain knew the figures. Nine volunteers arrested the year previous, eleven more held by the army and the police that year and the year not yet finished.

The Castlewellan tout had been in South Down Brigade. And there had been a tout eight months back found in East Belfast, dead. And eighteen months back another tout in Derry Brigade, dead . . . There had never been a tout found in East Tyrone. Tout hunts, yes . . . Every last man in the Brigade under suspicion after the Loughgall ambush, women too. There had never been a tout positively identified in East Tyrone.

'Myself,' Mossie said, 'if I ever got my hands on a tout I'd skin the back off him. They'd hear him scream in feckin' London.'

They ran the same route but at a less frantic speed, and PTI Terry cradled a stopwatch in the palm of his hand, and all through the press-ups and knee bends and squat thrusts he stood over Bren and shouted encouragement. It was how it should have been the first morning. At the end of the session there wasn't praise, but there wasn't criticism. Bren could live with that.

Jocelyn had come the previous late afternoon. The first thing he had done after sliding his head round the sitting-room door and announcing his arrival to Ronnie, had been to search out George and demand a good garden spade. Jocelyn had skipped supper and there had been a flashlight beam half the evening out in the garden beyond the vegetable patch. All the time that Ronnie and Bren had been in the sitting room, Ronnie talking and Bren listening, the light had shone down in the vegetable patch. When he had finally come back inside, Jocelyn, with the brushed-back sandy hair, had gone straight to his bath and had not reappeared.

After his hour with PTI Terry, Bren was still panting, still sweating. He was told to pull a set of heavy dungarees over his track suit. He was led to the vegetable patch. The cabbages were doing well, and the sprouts would soon be ready for collecting, and the parsnips were about ready for lifting. Bren knew about vegetables because his parents' entire back garden was given over to vegetables. Mr Jocelyn opened the wooden box that he had carried. Bren saw, fitted into the moulded casing, two service pistols, and when he looked up, looked around him, he saw two man-shaped targets, one thirty yards away, half behind an oak tree, the second beyond the vegetable patch and mostly concealed by the bramble growth up the old stone wall. In front of Bren was a hole, neatly dug, not more than ten inches across, and back against the wall and nearer than the second target were nine filled fertilizer bags. Jocelyn would have had access to his file. Bren had done live firing on a range on the last day of the rural surveillance course. He had done live firing and rural surveillance after unarmed combat, before electronic bugging, after Arabic language, before urban surveillance. All of them on the course, and Bren had caught the mood from the others, had treated live firing as a bit of a joke.

Curtly, Jocelyn talked Bren through the exercise.

The hole was the start. Beyond the hole, Jocelyn knelt and lifted off the turf. The turf had been laid on planks. Below the wood was a trench, six feet by two, and eighteen inches deep, lined with old carpet. That was a hide. He was told that the earth and stones had been dug out, filling nine fertilizer bags; he would have to carry at least nine bags' worth of earth and stone a clear mile from a dug hide, and then spread them where they would never be noticed. He dropped down into the space and Jocelyn replaced the wood strips and eased the turfs back over him. He lay on the side of his rib cage and propped himself on his elbow and the brow of his head peeped through the end hole and above the level of the ground. Jocelyn caught his hair, held his head steady, smeared his face and his hair with the soil of the vegetable patch, then kicked leaves over him. He was asked if he was comfortable and his answer didn't seem to matter. He was told that the minimum he would have to spend in such a position was twenty-four hours, and the maximum was seventy-two hours. He wasn't asked if he thought he could *manage*, just told to keep a sharp look-out and stay invisible. At the end of the first hour, after the numbness had set into his legs, after the ache had started in the shoulder that took his weight, after he had just about decided to piss in the trench, after the two target shapes had merged away into the trunk of the oak and the screen of the brambles . . . Christ, shit . . . a hand in his hair . . . a fist pulling him up from the hole . . . his scalp alive with the pain and not able to force his hands up to protect himself . . .

'Wake up, young man, or you'll wake up dead.'

Bren sagged in disgust. He hadn't had the slightest warning of Jocelyn's approach.

He was told it would be live firing. His eye line was Jocelyn's boots. He looked up and watched as the

68

bullets were taken from Jocelyn's pockets and loaded into the magazines of one of the service pistols. He could have done that, although his hands were now filthy. He was handed the pistol.

'Simulated attack on your hide, where you are, better believe me, vulnerable . . . Without warning, I will run at the hide, you will put down defensive fire on the two static targets, and fast. And you will not forget, my old darling, that these are live rounds. The two static targets represent a lethal enemy. I am not attempting to commit suicide, I am merely trying to create a real situation, so just be slightly careful. Don't mess me. When I start running, you shoot for your life. Simple enough?'

Jocelyn drifted away. The numbness in his legs seemed to bother him less, and the ache in his shoulder was forgotten. The rich musty smell of the earth was around him. He watched a robin take a worm. He heard George barking orders at the dog, hideous brute. He was aware of the occasional traffic on the road beyond the gates. He held the gun tight. He saw Mrs Ferguson come out to the line stretched from the back door to the trunk of a sycamore and hang her washing out. He saw everything that moved. He saw Ronnie come out of the front door with a bucket of water and start to soap down the Sierra. He saw PTI Terry wandering out onto the lawn with a quarter of a loaf and begin to scatter it for the birds and squirrels. He understood. They had all been sent out to distract him, one after the other. Where was the bastard? Had to stretch his eyes to see the two target shapes and behind them was just the grey background of a wall and the darker background of the trees.

Time was slipping by.

Where was the bastard?

OK, good game, game getting boring. How much bloody longer? George throwing a ball for the dog, better keep the fiend well away from the vegetable patch or he'd be one dog short in a hurry. Mrs Ferguson bringing her washing back in. Ronnie hoovering away inside the Sierra. Two squirrels and four starlings competing for PTI Terry's bread. And then, he saw him . . .

He was meant to see him.

The shape in the bulky combat jacket coming through the trees. He hated the bloody man. God rot the bastard. Pistol up, pistol at his eye line, pistol on the moving figure and then the further target. Remembering what he had been told. The moving figure past the target, going wide of it. Shoot the bastard. The hammer of the pistol in his ear. The further target, the moving figure, the nearer target. The whiplash of the pistol like it might take his arm out of the shoulder socket. The nearer target, the moving figure, the further target.

An awful silence around him. His finger was still squeezing the trigger. The ejected cases were beside his forehead.

The dog straining against a leash, George bellowing at him to be quiet.

Mrs Ferguson abandoning her basket and moving smartly towards the kitchen door.

Ronnie gone to ground already.

Jocelyn stood above him, contempt in his eyes. The index finger of his right hand pointed to the hole in the bulging side of his combat tunic.

'You're a right little pillock, you know that? You have one hit on the Target A, not in a stop position. You have three hits on Target B, one of which, give you the benefit of the doubt, might have dropped the man. The nearest you got to a proper hit was this . . .'

Jocelyn's finger jabbed at the neat hole. Three inches right and it would have been a proper hit.

'Glad I got one fucking thing right,' Bren said.

Bren thought that he had actually frightened the man.

Jocelyn said, 'My advice, if there's any real shooting to be done, leave it to Parker.'

He had the only key to the room in the house in Hackney, upstairs and overlooking the back yard. Inside the room, taped to the underside of the mattress were the keys to the Escort. There was a young couple, over from County Cork more than a year, who rented the house and used the front room upstairs and all of the ground floor. The room was Jon Jo's and, when he needed it, the car.

It would have been possible to keep the rifle and the explosives at the Hackney address, but the word in the Organization these days was that firearms and explosives had to be kept in caches. If the couple from County Cork was turned over, then at least the hardware stayed intact.

His principal cache was hidden in the forest area between Crowthorne and Bagshot.

It was the time of greatest risk. The cache itself was brilliant. The top of the dustbin was three inches below ground level, and that was under a splayed and half-capsized holly tree. He'd taken three days to dig it, twice being unlucky with roots when he was far down into the hole. It was a good position, but once he had seen a man walking a dog not fifty yards away and the lid of the dustbin had been open, and he had, Christ, frozen. And in the autumn, when it was still warm, he had had to lie off the cache for an hour because there was a couple, men, screwing within sight of the holly tree. He was most vulnerable there because a hundred policemen could have dug in, within 200 metres of where his dustbin was buried.

He had circled the cache, the first time at a radius of 300 yards. A long way down the rough forestry track, he had seen the back of a bird watcher. The second time he came closer, within 100 yards of the cache. Each time was a risk. The cache on the Welsh coast had been watched for seven weeks by more than eighty policemen, and two good men had been taken, gone down for thirty years. A cache had been found at Pangbourne and more men doing time.

They might shout, they might just shoot, probably they'd shout.

On the ground, a revolver in his ear, handcuffs on his wrists, they probably wouldn't shoot.

Thirty years he was looking at, each time he came to a cache.

Jon Jo scuffed the earth and the leaf mould clear. Between the lid and the dustbin there was a minute piece of black insulating tape. He knew exactly where it should be. That way he would know if the cache had been interfered with. Sometimes if a cache was found they would burrow a homing device into a weapon, or they would disarm it, or they would replace the explosive with a harmless look-alike compound, or they would screw up the detonators. Mostly they would lift, or kill, whoever came to collect the weapons.

In the dustbin, in separate plastic bags sealed at the neck, were two car bombs, a larger bomb for a building, and a Kalashnikov AK47 assault rifle. At the bottom of the dustbin were six loaded magazines for the rifle. Heh, and the dustbin had been filled when he had started out ten weeks before . . . It was like a larder at the end of the week.

He took out the rifle and two magazines.

He replaced the lid, sealed it again with black insulating tape. He pushed back the soil and the dead leaves.

Jon Jo kept watch and listened for a quarter of an hour before he crawled out from under the spread of the holly tree.

The rifle, the stock folded back against the mechanism, was in the pouch pocket of his coat.

Bren came out of the front door. It had been Ronnie's idea. Ronnie had said that it would be no problem for him to get away for five hours. Two hours driving each way, and an hour in the small house in the Filton district of Bristol. Ronnie had said that the backing of a strong family helped a man enduring stress.

So little that he, their son, could say to Art and Sadie Brennard. His father had cancelled his evening out at the horticulture group, and his mother had missed Friday evening Bingo.

He wished to God that he hadn't come.

They had eaten a high tea, scones and cakes, and when it was nearly time for him to take off again, head away out of their lives, he had said that he would be gone some time. That was a sick joke, because it was more than four months since he had last been home. He'd the impression, when they had all sat down, that his mother had expected some momentous announcement, like he'd met a girl. He told them that he was posted to Belfast. His mother, Sadie, had looked as though she might cry. His father, Art, he'd just munched at his food and lowered his head nearer his plate.

The way Bren told it, what he would be doing would be just pretty boring, pushing paper round desks. Of course, nothing about source units or surveillance hides or carrying a personal firearm or playing with men's lives or being looked after and having his hand held by Parker, of course not. He left when he could see that neither of them believed a word he said. His mother kissed him on the doorstep, and his father held his hand and shook it, and the voices of both of them were lost in their throats.

He tried to smile back at them. He waved from his car. Should have told them, shouldn't he, that across in Belfast there was a man called Parker who was reckoned the superstar . . . So patronizing they all were, Wilkins and Ronnie and PTI Terry and Jocelyn. All playing the bloody Parker tune. By the time that he had reached the motorway, joined the great horde of his fellow countrymen who gave not a toss about Northern Ireland and its war, Bren had made himself a very binding promise. He would not be bloody Parker's passenger. He was not going to be any man's bag carrier.

One more night and he would be travelling.

*　　*　　*

Siobhan Nugent stood at her kitchen window and looked out and across at the farmhouse. She was like a widow, that Attracta Donnelly, and widows gathered men to them.

Siobhan Nugent wondered if her Mossie was there, at the widow feckin' Donnelly's. If he was not there then he would be out with the wild boys, bad boys, of the mountain. She knew, certain. All of the wives and the mothers on Altmore knew if their men were involved. Below her bungalow, below the Donnelly farm, were the scattered lights of the homes of the Altmore people. To so many of those homes, before dawn had broken, the priest had come. It was always the priest who was sent to break the news of the shooting dead of another man.

They all ended dead, or locked away.

Perhaps it were better if her Mossie *were* at the widow feckin' Donnelly's.

'Where is he now?'

'Mrs Ferguson's giving him his tea, Mr Wilkins. Then he's just to pack his things upstairs,' Ronnie said.

'I'm going to get his car back to the garage in London,' PTI Terry said.

'She's a soft old thing, that Mrs Ferguson. I suppose because of Six, she's used to seeing heroes packed off overseas. She's a bit sentimental,' Jocelyn said.

Wilkins put down his whisky and walked quietly across the hall to the dining-room door. Bren's back was to him. Mrs Ferguson sat opposite him and was refilling his mug with tea. George sat beside him and was telling some gory tale from his soldiering in Cyprus. The Rottweiler was crouched on its haunches, saliva at its jaws, love in its eyes, and delicately took the half slice of bacon that Bren offered it. Wilkins knew that Mrs Ferguson was a shrew whose services should have been dispensed with when the Ark beached, and that George was obstinate and stupid and hadn't a civil tongue in his head, and the dog was potentially vicious and a liability. The young man had been there for barely four days and he had captivated all three of them.

He walked back into the Library.

'Well, what's he been like?'

Ronnie said, 'He's raw, but he wants to learn. He'll be fine. He's actually rather tough.'

PTI Terry said, 'The Provisionals are in for rather a nasty surprise, if you want my opinion, sir. That's a very fit gentleman. Nice long stint in Ulster should suit very well.'

Jocelyn said, 'He doesn't shoot very straight, and he has no sense of humour. In another three weeks I think I could give you a reasonably competent . . .'

'I haven't got three weeks, Jocelyn. I have got about three minutes.'

Ronnie shrugged, 'Well, it's only a short stay, isn't it?'

Wilkins had had the fax back from Nairobi that morning. Ferdie bloody Penn was fighting his corner. Halfway through the course in Nairobi, expensive effort wasted and there would be a right squawk of anger in the Ministry of the Interior if he was pulled out, job not completed.

'I'm not so sure. Your reports of him are rather

promising. I think we'll have to regard the posting as open-ended, for the time being anyway . . .'

Mrs Ferguson came out onto the front step and stood huddled against the cold as they loaded Wilkins' car with Bren's suitcase and grip.

Ronnie and PTI Terry and Jocelyn wished Bren well, slapped his back, shook his hand. George waved at them as they pulled away. The dog ran the length of the drive barking hoarsely at the car's tyres.

'It's so easy to lose sight of the big picture, Bren. The Provisionals are under enormous pressure at the moment. Arrests are up and their attacks are down. We know that a number of their political end would like to sit at some sort of conference table. What's holding back any substantial advance to political dialogue are the hard men, the military activists. Our most important work of the moment is to penetrate the core of their killers. Destroy them, lock them away, and then peace might just get the tiny chance to breathe. It's a critical time.'

They were late at Heathrow because Ernest Wilkins never drove beyond the speed limit.

'Don't think about the majority. The majority are decent people, excessively friendly, hard working and law abiding. You concentrate on the minority, the one in a hundred or maybe even the one in a thousand, the lethal minority . . .'

Bren grabbed his case and his grip and ran.

Wilkins had missed the chance to wish him God speed.

Chapter Four

The aircraft was continually smacked by Force 8 winds. Bren barely noticed. He sat strapped in his seat, very still, refusing food and declining a drink. His mind was running over and over what Ronnie had told him . . . He was headed for a war in which dinosaur traditions governed and destroyed a gentler and more reasoning age. A pitiless war, unremarkable in the context of what had gone before. It was as always; the gravediggers stayed busy, and every time they paused for breath the war would erupt again to bring new soldiers, new patriots and new innocents to the cemeteries. The war was terrifying to the stranger, not least because it was incomprehensible in its brutality and its apparent irrelevance to the twentieth century. He thought only a native might be able to understand it, slim chance for the stranger drafted in to try to help to put a stop to it.

Bren jolted in his seat as the aircraft banged down onto the Aldergrove runway.

The aircraft taxied. He felt a swift thrill of exhilaration. He was a junior Executive Officer of the Security Service. More than anything he wanted to be worthy of the posting. One step at a time . . . and first step was Parker. Parker, he had been told, would meet him at the airport.

He unclipped the belt. He stood and stretched his cramped knees. He had not the faintest idea when he would next see the inside of an aircraft that was heading back to London. He was breathing hard. He walked down the aisle.

All so normal.

He walked in a cavalcade of grannies and carried babies and collapsed pushchairs and young men who had been to a soccer match in London. The life of any other small airport, anywhere, swam around him. Ordinary and happy and relieved and excited people flowed by him, past the armed policemen and the anti-terrorist posters, the same as in any other small airport. But he was different, because he was a junior Executive Officer of Five and from now on a man's life depended on *him*, and from this moment onwards his own life was on the line. He felt the gush of pleasured excitement, enjoyed it.

She wasn't really a girl, she was more of a woman. It was probably a photograph that she had hidden in her palm. She looked down and then up again at the surge of the passengers. She came forward. She had singled him out. He stopped, put down his suitcase.

'It's Gary, yes?'

'I'm called Bren,' he said brusquely.

'Please yourself.'

'I was told Parker would meet me.'

He thought she laughed at him. She wasn't pretty, certainly wasn't beautiful. The only brightness was in her eyes. He reckoned her accent was money, class.

'I'm Cathy – it's a God awful flight over, right?'

'They said it would be Parker.' He heard the snap in his voice, wondered how he could be such an idiot.

'Did they now?'

'I'm sorry, I didn't mean to be rude.'

She wore trainers and jeans that were threadbare at the knees, and a quilted anorak that was scuffed at the elbows.

'Let's be on the move then.'

'Right . . .' Bren bent to pick up his suitcase. She had beaten him to it. He knew it was heavy. She gave him a withering look. She walked away carrying the suitcase and he followed her.

Her head barely came up to his shoulder. There was a pale blue scarf at her throat. She had small hands and he thought that under the anorak there was only a slight body. She had no make-up, and her cheeks glowed with a weathered colour. Her hair was golden red and cut short.

She led the way out through the doors. When he had run for the flight at Heathrow he had had to change hands on the suitcase because of its weight. She didn't change hands. They threaded their way through the car park.

She unlocked an old Astra. The sides and the wheels were mud-spattered. She tossed his suitcase into the hatch. Presumably the people she collected for Parker wouldn't have been expected to bring with them their bone china. She unlocked the passenger door for him. He laid his grip on the back seat.

She settled in the driver's seat. Bren was belting himself in. She unzipped her anorak and took a radio from an inside pocket. Bren didn't understand a word she said into the microphone. Then she drew a Browning automatic from the tight waist of her jeans. She put the pistol on her seat, between her legs, then shrugged out of her anorak and draped it across her lap to hide the weapon. She drove out of the car park and away from the lights.

He saw her grin in the lights of a passing lorry. 'I'm Parker,' she said. 'And since you are so bloody status-conscious, you can call me ma'am. Otherwise I'm just Cathy.'

The messenger was glad to be gone.

The OC watched young Patsy Riordan run into the darkness and away from the house, and there was the frantic revving of his low-powered motorcycle. He came back inside, slamming the front door behind him. His wife was still in the kitchen, and the baby started to bawl at the hammer of the front door closing, and she did not dare to complain.

He had known by mid-morning that the policeman, hitting his feckin' golf balls, had not been shot. He had been told by lunchtime that his volunteers had made it back to the safety of the mountain. It was not until now, late in the evening, that he had heard the reasons for the failure.

It was the third time in as many months that young Patsy had brought him news of an aborted mission.

The front car, clean, without weapons on board, as was usual, had been a quarter of a mile ahead of the ASU's vehicle. They had seen the first roadblock, and called back on the CB radio. There were two routes to the target. They had tried the second. Again a vehicle checkpoint. They'd quit. The first car had driven the narrow lanes all through the small communities close to the Lough. Well, it could just have been chance. The whole bloody area had been stiff with bastards, not just around the police inspector's home.

Why, that morning, the morning he was to be attacked, had the way not been open to the Chief Inspector's house?

That night, when his wife had gone upstairs to quieten the baby and then to bed, the OC sat in front of the dying fire, and the anger whipped his mind.

The congregation spilled out from the chapel. Ten o'clock Mass was no longer the centrepiece of community life, not as it once had been, though the cars and vans were parked for fully 200 yards, both sides of the road. There were gaps among his flock, the Father had noticed, at the very front and the very back. His sermon had been aimed at those very missing teenagers and young people; he had spoken of a youth in their society that was numbed by television, corrupted by the pursuit of material goals. It was a favourite theme of the Father's. He never spoke of violence. The war, the Provos, the consequences of their actions, were never a part of his Sunday sermons. He was a heavy man with a penetrating voice, but he never used his stature to preach against the war. Had he been challenged on the substance of his sermons, he would have said that his parishioners were intelligent, they could make up their own minds on the morality of the campaign of the Active Service Units. And in the privacy of his bishop's study, he would have said that his work in the mountain parish made for a lonely life, one that would be lonelier still if he denounced the Provisionals. He married the hard men, he baptised their children, and if they were ambushed by the army he buried them in the Republican plot in the cemetery field. He had already told his bishop that it was only his study of French Renaissance painting and the companionship of his books on the subject that kept him his sanity and his faith.

They came out into the frosted sunlight.

They were the businessmen, the wealthy; the unemployed, the poor; they were the farmers and the tradesmen and the skilled workers; they were the volunteers of the Provisional wing of the Irish Republican Army. It would have been the Father's opinion, and his information would have been at least as complete as that of the senior Special Branch officer at Dungannon police station, that on any night he might be called out to inform the family of any of twenty-five men that their loved one had been shot dead on active service. From his view-point, from the pulpit, he could have counted at least fourteen of the twenty-five celebrating Mass with him that Sunday morning.

Mossie had seen Attracta Donnelly with her Kevin and her parents. He would have had to cross the road to speak to her. And then there were others who stopped to talk to her. Mossie waited. His Doloures held his Patrick's hand, keeping him on the pavement. His Francis carried little Mary. His Francis, eight years old and the eldest, that was a boy to be proud of. Siobhan and his mother talked with his mother's long-standing friend, the housekeeper of the Father. His children were well turned out, better dressed than most, good clothes and good shoes. Suddenly behind him a baby, the one that had howled through Mass, screamed in protest. Mossie turned. The OC carried the baby.

'What the feck happened yesterday?'

'We was unlucky.' Mossie ignored the fury of the hissed whisper.

'The place was heavy with them.'

'It's what I heard.'

'. . . There was police and army all over.'

'That's bad.'

'. . . Was they waiting for it . . . ?'

'How would you know?'

'. . . Our boys, they had to cut out . . .'

'Best thing.'

'. . . Had the police, army, information . . . ?'

'I just heard the boys couldn't get through.'

'. . . There was roadblocks all round . . .'

'Best they cut out.'

'. . . I want to know who knew, everyone who knew . . .'

'Wasn't many, couldn't have been.'

'Every last one who knew, because if I've a tout . . .'

The OC's words died behind the bellow of his baby, and he was gone away up the line of parked cars to where his wife waited.

There was a freeze in Mossie's mind, a chill in his gut. He shouted across to Siobhan and his mother. He took little Mary from Francis. He snapped his fingers for Doloures and Patrick to follow him.

He walked towards his old Cortina. Mossie Nugent was tall and spare and with rounded shoulders under a thin neck. He always wore his best suit to Mass.

Heavy, tortoiseshell-rimmed spectacles dominated a pale, gaunt face. His hair was neatly combed and there were flecks of cream paint behind his right ear. He would have admitted that he was a man without friends on Altmore, but that was the way for those who climbed high in the Organization. He had not been spoken to by any of the fellow worshippers, other than the OC. Few came forward to offer small talk to a man known to be deep in the Organization. They hung back around him, they waited for his smile and his greeting before coming forward to shake his hand or slap his back. If he caught a man's eye, if he stared back at it, cold, then that man would flinch. That was the power of the Organization. But he would have claimed that he was liked, and the old people for whom he did unpaid work would have sung his praise, and the young men of the mountain, the Devitt boy and the Brannigan boy and the Riordan boy, would have failed to hide their admiration of him. The younger men, they would have recognized that he had fought the war longer than most, with greater commitment than most. A man who had little to offer in friendship, but who had gained respect for his kindness to the uninvolved, and admiration for his staying power with those who belonged. He was said by the few who knew to be the best, the most thorough, intelligence officer of the East Tyrone Brigade since the twenty-year war had flared again. It was how he would have wished it, that he should be a man alone in the mountain society. His walk was swinging, awkward, the legacy of a fall from a ladder, the damage now past recovery. It was only four years since he had come back to Altmore mountain, and before that he had been on the mainland for six years, in the South for four years, in prison on remand and under sentence for three years. To his own community, where he had been born, reared, schooled, he was something of a stranger.

Mossie was impatient to be gone. He called again to his wife and his mother to hurry themselves.

They were a busy couple. It was what Service life had taught them and retirement had changed nothing.

Sunday was not an exceptional day for them, not a day for rest, it was when they dealt with the week's unanswered letters and other paper work.

Cecily Beck had covered the dining-room table with the receipts from the local branch of the Red Cross, the monthly bills, and would settle them all before tackling the chore that she so enjoyed of writing the weekly letter to her son now flying a jump jet Harrier in Belize.

The village, north of the Buckinghamshire town of Aylesbury, was dominated by its magnificent beech trees, certainly more than a hundred years old, beside the church. Most of the leaves, they annually complained, seemed to fall in their garden, onto their lawns and flower beds. Peter Beck raked leaves, and would not be finished before it was too cold and too dark to stay outside any longer. Then he would work on the speech that he would make next week at the British Legion dinner. It was inevitable that a man who had commanded an infantry battalion would be invited, when he retired to the village, to become the British Legion club's chairman.

He stopped, paused for breath. He watched,

through the window, his wife hunched over the table. He leaned for a moment on the rake. Beyond the privet hedge he could see just the head of a man going along their lane. It was fine weather to be out for a walk. He returned to his raking. He set himself to clear the grass and the rosebeds before he finished for the day.

She had knocked sharply and come into his room before he could reply.

It was late morning. She wore a thin T-shirt that was creased and not fresh that day and it hung half in, half out of her jeans. Bren saw the reddish blotch on the white of her throat and thought she must have scratched an insect bite.

'You sleep alright?'

'Fine.'

'The beds are made for martyrs.'

'I slept well.'

'I don't know what you're going to do with yourself today . . . sorry, I'm not about.'

'There are no meetings?'

'Don't be too keen . . .' Again, what he had seen the previous evening, the bright mocking in her eyes.

'Don't I get to meet anyone?'

'This evening, Hobbes. Not till this evening.'

'I'd like to go into the city, get some sort of feel for the place.'

'There won't be a driver for you. Not on a Sunday.'

She said what time he should be back at the house, and what time she would pick him up. He said that he would find a taxi down the road at the hotel, or maybe, if he wanted to be athletic, then he could walk the whole way.

'Please yourself, don't wander off too far.' The smile was off her face.

Because it had been night when he had arrived he knew only that the house was in the Malone Road. The flat where he had slept was one bedroom, one living room with a kitchen alcove, and a tiny bathroom, on the second floor. She'd gone.

He wore an old anorak and a pair of slacks and good walking shoes. Bren went down the stairs of the house, and there was music playing from one of the first-floor rooms. In the ground-floor hall he passed a man who looked as though he had come out from the cardboard cities of inner London. The man had four days of stubble, hair that was matted, hands that were grimed, clothes that were torn and filthy, and the man ignored him.

Thirty minutes later, Bren stood in the central square of old Belfast.

So ordinary.

The sun was behind the great block of the City Hall. He saw the banner draped high on the building. ULSTER SAYS NO. A Land-rover painted in camouflage green drove past him and a soldier protruding through the roof momentarily covered him with the snub barrel of his rifle. He walked through the circular security gates, clattering the steel bars as he pushed them in front of him. He went down a wide shopping street. They were all the High Street names. Some shops were boarded up, the plywood daubed in graffiti and covered with concert gig advertisements. There were the stores for clothes and furniture and televisions and cosmetics, just as he would have found them anywhere else. He had only seen this street on television, when the fires were burning and the firemen were sprinting forward with their hoses, and shopkeepers were standing on the pavement in shock or in tears. He had never seen the Royal Avenue on television deserted and quiet and ordinary. He turned right, past the shops with the special offers and the travel agents with the cut-price deals and hot-bun cafés that were closed, padlocked, shuttered. Ahead of him were the Law Courts. He saw the young soldiers and their sangar of sandbags. He was behind the public face of the centre and he went along a road where most of the buildings were derelict, and at the doors that were reinforced with nailed planks he saw the rusted nameplates of solicitors and businessmen who had been bombed into new premises.

In Curzon Street, since joining the Irish desk, he had never volunteered an opinion about the war. Last time round, Charlie had said, 'Left to ourselves we could wrap this up in a week, consign them all to the Underground Club.' Archie had said, 'Can't expect to fight and win if you've a hand tied behind your back, must fight fire with fire.' And Mr Wilkins, muttering under his breath as he passed Bren's desk had said, 'Anyone with a solution to Northern Ireland's problems is either demented or merely ill-informed.' He'd have an opinion himself, one day, when he came back. He wanted to learn, to make the opinion worth having. He would walk through the city and taste it, smell it.

Twenty minutes later he found there were high blocks of flats ahead of him, four, five stories, smeared concrete, daubed with slogans, fire-scarred. A cluster of youths on the corner of the first block, smoking, watching, lounging. They wore a uniform: ankle boots laced high, faded and patched jeans, denim jackets with pop group logos hand-scrawled on the shoulders and sleeves, cropped hair. He hesitated. He looked across the wide road at the youths, and the youths stared back across the road at him. The Land-rover came down the street from behind him. It braked, swerved towards the pavement. Two soldiers got out. The soldiers went to the youths. Bren watched. He saw their defiance. They didn't back off, they didn't straighten up, and one of them cleared his throat and spat. He had not seen the second Land-rover pull up behind him.

'You!'

He spun round.

'You . . . Over here . . .'

He saw the crouching soldiers, and a rifle aimed at him. He walked towards the soldier. No sweat, no problem, he was . . .

'Move your arse . . .'

He stood in front of the soldier. There was contempt in the soldier's face.

'Name . . . ?'

'It's alright, I'm . . .'

'Last time, name . . .'

Bren swallowed. He shook his head.

'Your name, arsehole . . .'

Bren looked him in the face, and looked into the barrel of a high-velocity rifle.

'I'm English. I'm a civil servant, and I can't answer your questions.'

'If you're from the Long Haired Brigade, mate, God help us . . .'

Bren reckoned the soldier to be ten years younger

90

than him. The soldier smirked. The Land-rover across the road was loading up, and the youths were left free to smoke and watch and lounge, and the focus of their attention was Bren.

The soldier said, 'This, old cocker, is the unhealthy end of the city. If you've no business here, take my advice, piss off out.'

'Thank you.' Bren turned, started to walk away.

He heard the laughter, and then the thrust of the engine of the second Land-rover. He pushed up the collar of his anorak. He kept walking, all the way back through the city centre, to the Malone Road.

The rest of the afternoon, not much of it because the dusk came quickly to his room, he lay on his bed and waited for Cathy goddamn Parker to collect him.

The target used two lengths of plywood, one in each hand, to scoop up the leaves and put them into the wheelbarrow. The assault rifle, the tubular steel stock folded back, was still in Jon Jo's inner pocket. The magazine was in his outer pocket. He watched from beyond the hedge. The lane behind him was empty. He knew that the target was not regarded as priority. The order was to avoid priority targets who were too well guarded.

The target cursed because the dried leaves spilled from the wheelbarrow onto the lawn again.

He heard the distant call from the cottage.

'Come on, Peter, tea's made. You'll catch your death out there.'

'Just coming, darling,' the target answered. 'One last load.'

The target began to push the wheelbarrow across

the lawn, towards a corner of the garden where a bonfire smoked through the earlier heaps of leaves.

Jon Jo looked back to his right, up the lane, and to his left, down the lane. The lane was empty. Dusk falling, completing a November Sunday afternoon. The car was a full 150 yards away, parked through an open field gate and hidden by a hedge. He was at the upper end of the village and on the high ground above the church and the one main road around which the community had formed centuries before. There was a haze of smoke from the chimneys that blurred the setting sun.

He took the rifle from his pouch pocket . . .

The target had been identified in Dublin. They had good kids who sat in the Trinity Library or the Dublin University reading rooms to browse their way through the English newspapers.

Swift movements, and the metallic snap of the magazine slotting into the underside of the AK47. The target had stopped, rooted . . .

In the Trinity Library every last book, periodical, pamphlet was collected and available to the student. A lieutenant-colonel, recently retired, formerly officer commanding a Light Infantry battalion, had written to *The Times* to protest that a BBC documentary unfairly criticized Security Force operations in Northern Ireland. He had written from experience. His last posting had been to Belfast. The letter and the address had been noted.

The smack of the shoulder stock being wrenched back and locking. The target recognized the sound, turned to run, cannoned into the wheelbarrow, was enmeshed for a long instant in its handles and in the spill of the loose leaves. The rifle was at Jon Jo's shoulder . . .

Lt-Col. Peter Beck, author of the letter, commanding officer of a Light Infantry battalion, had most vigorously, during his last tour, defended the action of his soldiers after they had shot dead two teenagers, a boy aged eighteen and a girl aged sixteen, who had crashed a road-block. He had said then, and had been quoted on the front page of the *Belfast Telegraph*, that the kids were not 'joyriders', but 'car thieves, no more than common criminals who endanger the lives of civilians and soldiers alike'. He'd be a popular hit, because there had been more than a thousand following those kids' coffins to Milltown cemetery.

The target was running into the fog smoke from his bonfire. Jon Jo cocked the rifle. Twenty paces, going on twenty-five. The target stumbled in his fear, was trying to weave, trying to remember everything he had once known as commonplace . . .

Jon Jo squeezed the trigger. An assault rifle on semi-automatic.

There was the battering at his padded shoulder. Over the foresight and V-sight the target was wavering, falling, crawling. He heard nothing. He saw the bullets puff stone shrapnel from the wall of the house, saw them punch into the target.

The rooks fled from the upper branches of the beech trees.

The target was down, deadly still, almost within reach of the back door of the house.

Jon Jo Donnelly ran, up the lane, dismantling the rifle, slowed to a walk at the end of the lane, towards the waiting car.

She went in the ambulance with her husband.

It had been quick and that was luck. The retired surgeon being there had been luckier. He had recognized the blast of a high velocity rifle at the top of the village, and run as best he could towards the source of the sound. The surgeon and the ambulance man worked on the body below them to retain life.

She seemed not to hear the siren. She knew that she had left her front door unlocked and her back door wide open and that there was a pot of tea on the kitchen table. She spoke quietly, and it was as if she did not expect the two men bent over her husband to listen to her.

'He knew he was at risk, but what could we do about it? You can't just expect the government to nanny us with bodyguards. There's scores of people in the country much more in danger than we were, they can't all have an armed policeman sitting by the front door. We talked it through, we took sensible precautions like locking the garage when the car was in there, and then we just had to get on with our lives. That's all you can do, isn't it?'

'Mrs Beck, would you tuck that blanket securely round his feet and hold them still? Thank you.' The gentle growled instruction of a man whose attention was elsewhere.

'He's such a lovely man. It's just not possible to believe that anyone could hate him enough to do this to him . . .'

'Shut up, Cecily, and listen . . .' The faint, bubbled voice from the stretcher.

She leaned forward. They had scissored through

the old pullover and cut his shirt back. There were huge holes in his chest. The voice oozed from the blood mess of his jaw and mouth.

'. . . Big man, above average. Saw him, twice. Afternoon, second time when he aimed. Blue anorak, red shoulder . . .'

'Don't strain.'

'. . . dark hair, short cut, curly. Abnormally pale face. Deep eyes, far down. Hadn't shaved.'

She had left her handbag behind. She had no pen or paper. The ambulance man had a syringe poised. They already had the drips in, blood plasma and saline. She pulled a biro from the slot on the ambulance man's shoulder.

'. . . AK47, sure of that . . .'

The syringe was bedded against her husband's upper arm. He was so horribly white and his breathing was sporadic, forced as if by great effort. He said nothing more.

She wrote down all that he had said on the back of her hand.

At the hospital a nurse caught her, prevented her from going all the way through into the Casualty's X-ray unit. She was sat on a chair. She was brought tea, steaming hot and with sugar, and when a policeman came to her, she was able to dictate from her hand the description of her husband's attacker and the weapon he had used.

Bren locked the door behind him.

Cathy looked up at him. She stood square on the balls of her feet. Her hair was a mess. She blocked his way to the stairs.

95

'We'll just get this over first.'

She had come to his room for him when she had said she would, to the minute.

'What?'

'You were just dreadful this afternoon, and it will not happen again.'

'I beg your pardon?'

'You walk out of here. You traipse round town. Against my advice, you go wandering off out of the city centre and you end up beside Unity Flats. You're not in bloody Bognor you know, this is Belfast. "I am a civil servant, I cannot give you my name and address . . ." How pompous can you get? That soldier was only a boy doing his job, you don't have to speak to him like you're Christ Almighty at a Public School. You come back here and again you take no precautions at all. You go on behaving like that and you're going to be a serious bloody liability.'

It hurt him, but he said it. 'It won't happen again.'

'I had you followed. I wanted to see if you were worth working with. Today's report says you are a disaster.'

'It will not happen again.'

She stared up at him, weighing whether he was worth the effort.

'Come on.'

The Commander shook the sleep from his head.

'That's a hell of a good description.'

The voice on the telephone was calm. 'There's not a great deal, really, but all four specifics, height, hair, eyes and pallor, they're all Donnelly.'

'Is my car moving?'

'Be with you in fifteen minutes.'

'But it's Jon Jo Donnelly?'

'What we've got. It all matches him.'

The Commander put the telephone down. He said the name again. Jon Jo Donnelly . . . and again . . . Jon Jo Donnelly . . . He liked to sleep on a Sunday afternoon, it was the one time in the week when he hoped to crash out of the world of Jon Jo Donnelly. He put on a tie and his suit and he came downstairs to tell his wife to think of something, any bloody excuse to put off the people who were due in an hour for drinks. Sundays were when he made the effort, bloody futile, to keep his work out of his home.

He waited in the hall for his car.

His wife heard what he said, a muttered voice. 'Stretching yourself, Jon Jo, old love, pushing it too hard, too fast. Getting careless, old love, and careless is going to finish you . . .'

The steam had misted over the window. Hot tap on. Jon Jo stripped beside the bath. Last, he peeled from his right shoulder the elastoplast that held the foam rubber padding in position. He felt the water, winced. He looked down into the paper bag, the sort that half a hundred-weight of potatoes were sold in. There was a newspaper in there and fire-lighter cubes. He turned the paper bag: shoes, socks, trousers, underwear, shirt, jersey, anorak . . . where the hell was his woollen cap? Christ, and he hadn't worn his woollen cap. How could he have forgotten to wear his woollen cap? . . . Last into the bag was the shoulder pad to take the battering of the assault rifle against the shoulder when he fired on semi-automatic. Two years back, a good man had been taken, and clean, but he'd a bruise, rainbow-coloured, on his shoulder and the bloody police had called in a medic who'd sworn on oath that the bruise had been four days old, and four days old had matched with a strike. His pale skin was unmarked where the padding had been. He tapped at the bathroom door. He heard the footsteps on the staircase. He passed the paper bag out through the door. He climbed into the bath, and forced himself down into the scalding heat of the water. Jon Jo scrubbed his body and his hair with the soap, every inch of his body, again and again, and again his hair. He removed from his skin and his scalp all trace of the gases that would have blown back from the Kalashnikov when he had fired, the fine film that could be found by a forensic scientist. By the time he pushed himself up out of the bath, had the towel draped round him, he could see the glow of the fire through the misted window. The fire burned in the back yard and destroyed all the clothes he had been wearing. In the morning, before it was light, he would leave the Hackney address and drive to the woodland between Crowthorne and Bagshot. He would bury the assault rifle. He would bring the car back to Paddington station. The young man from Cork or his wife would collect the car. He would take the train again to the Devon coast.

In his room he started to dress, then looked at his watch and switched on the radio beside his bed. The news bulletin had started. '. . . is still undergoing surgery. A hospital spokesman, in the last few minutes, described Colonel Beck's condition as "critical but stable" . . .' He no longer listened. His fist smashed onto the pillow. Fifteen shots, maybe more, how had the bastard lived? His eyes were pressed shut, tight. The frustration swarmed in him.

'You will always find me frank to the point of being brutal, Bren. I think it's right, in this theatre of operations, that every man and woman who works for me knows exactly what I am thinking. It may not be quite the same in London . . .' Hobbes paced in front of the gas fire. He wore carpet slippers and no tie and a primrose cardigan that was unbuttoned. It was still the weekend. The house was in a village beyond Bangor, was less than a hundred yards from the County Down seashore. Bren could hear the waves on the rocks. Cathy had kicked off her shoes and was stretched out on the settee. She'd let Hobbes make the mugs of coffee.

'. . . So you won't mind if I say that I am astonished that they sent you. I asked for specific people and they chickened out on me. You are what I have been sent and I have to make do with you – put another way, Cathy has to learn to live with it. Don't yawn, there's a darling woman. The people I asked for have been brought up to the training standards that I require, and you aren't at that standard . . . Very fast, you have to learn what is required of you. You follow me?'

He had heard, vaguely, Hobbes' name spoken in the office at Curzon Street way back, when he was working to Mid-East Desk, Lebanon. Only odd snippets and as a new boy he had not wanted it thought that he clung to names mentioned in conversations that were not directed at him. Crisis, Iraq, the Atomic Weapons Establishment at Aldermaston. There had been a flurry of occasions when Hobbes' name had been used by older members of the desk, but it had been more than two years back and he had not heard the name since. The man was his boss and Cathy's boss. He had seen from the time that he had been welcomed curtly into the house that she recognized his seniority. They had talked for twenty minutes, seemed that long, before his attention had moved to Bren. They had worked at a large-scale Ordnance Survey and shuffled aerial photographs, and twice he had gone to another room to bring back surveillance pictures of men. She gave his rank deference because each time she made a statement she cocked her head at him and queried with her eyebrows as to whether she had carried him with her argument. When it was their business they were both quiet, close, as if unwilling to waste words, as if their minds were locked together in respect. All different now, and Bren didn't know why she had to play bored and frivolous, and he had to act the big man with a message to communicate.

Bren sat straight. He cradled the coffee in his hands. 'Yes.'

Hobbes said, 'Tomorrow we'll sort out where you're to live, it's best to be off military premises. We'll establish a cover occupation for you, it's usually Department of the Environment. Car, personal weapon, sort all that out in the morning. You've a very great deal to learn in a very short time, that will also start tomorrow . . . About the only thing you've got going for you is that you didn't, I'm told,

100

wriggle when you were propositioned . . .'

'I'm looking forward to the work.'

'Please don't interrupt.'

He was a small man, not yet middle-aged, with a deep voice. There was a chill in that voice. He didn't think this man had ever laughed in his life.

'We'll go over some fundamentals, our ground rules. You work for me, you operate to Cathy. Not one scrap of your information goes to the police or to the military without that I approve it, that Cathy authorizes it. We run our own show here, we have our own Source Unit. The war as fought by the police and the army is a quite separate war, perfectly distant. I am not in the business of short-term results. No medals here for you, Bren, no herograms, no Chief Constable's commendations and no Mentioned in Dispatches. We go our own way, as far as is physically possible and safe . . .'

The coffee mug was cold in his hand. He saw that Cathy stared up at the ceiling, following a fly's flight path.

'That's clear,' Bren said.

'Whether you're up to this job is your business. I'm told from London that you are difficult, awkward, obstinate, that you've got some sort of problem that most obviously manifests itself by the ridiculous name you call yourself by. That's all to the good. I like people to be difficult, obstinate and awkward. If you ever get to be half as obnoxious and bloody-minded as our sweet Miss Parker then you'll do very well.'

There was nothing he could say, and nothing that he was expected to say.

'You'll work with Cathy,' Hobbes said briskly. It was as if the preamble were finished. 'You will do exactly as she tells you, and within a few weeks you will understand the wisdom of that . . . We call this man our "Song Bird". His code name is Song Bird because that is the call-sign he uses each time he rings through to us for a meeting. He has to use that code name. It keeps in his mind, very clearly, that he belongs to us. He's in our cage and he sings for us. He believes, and we have encouraged the belief, that if he stops singing, tries to leave the cage, then we will blow him out to his friends. They would most certainly kill him, and hurt him a little bit in the process. But our aim is to keep Song Bird. To keep the twelve other sources all singing. Quite a little choir we have in the Province, but your exclusive concern until we decide otherwise is to assist Miss Parker in the handling of Song Bird.'

The fear came in tiny shock waves through Bren. He wondered which of them in London had turned down Belfast.

Chapter Five

Cathy worked him pitilessly. Every time she allowed him out of the house he thought of freedom, but he didn't argue, he did as he was told.

He knew when he would slip into the cover of a Department of the Environment civil servant, but it was not immediately. She kept him prisoner in the second-floor flat in the Malone Road.

He was allowed out for exercise each morning. It was four miles to the city centre.

She had gone with him the first morning. All the way back up the hill and the carbon monoxide from the car exhausts catching in his throat, dragging into his lungs, the whole time she was jogging comfortably at his shoulder. Once he had lifted his pace, and made no impression on her at all. They had come back inside the house. Bren felt a little sick, and his legs were stiffening again, but that was because of what PTI Terry had put him through. He had trudged up the stairs, paused once to steady himself against the banister, the first morning. Into his room. He had flopped into the one easy chair.

'Get me a towel,' she'd said.

Bren had come back into the living room of the flat, and she had been standing naked in the centre of the room, her track suit and T-shirt and bra in a heap on the floor by her feet.

'Thanks,' she'd said.

She had dried herself hard. She had pummelled the towel down round her thighs and up round her stomach and across her breasts and under her armpits and across her throat and her neck and her head, and she had tossed the towel back to him and dressed again.

The first morning she had left him with a wad of papers, everything that he needed to know about the Department of the Environment in Northern Ireland.

He had made himself a sandwich at lunchtime, and grilled some sausages for the evening meal.

He knew nothing about Cathy Parker. He had seen the muscles in her body, the biceps and thighs and the tightness of her lower belly. She would know everything about him because she would have seen his file. He had seen the slender dull gold arms of the crucifix that hung low on a chain and rested between her breasts. Everything about him was in the file that would have been sent from Personnel at Curzon Street, his childhood and his education and his earlier work. She had big nipples on shallow breasts, and she had a bruise the size of his palm on her ribs. He knew nothing about her.

And it would be the same on the second morning – the run, the towelling off, and her passing him more papers to read, then leaving him to kill the day with them.

He had never met a woman remotely like Cathy Parker before.

'You didn't find work?'

'No, I got there a day too late. Just missed.'

'But it was the weekend.' The landlady was confused.

'There's friends of mine, they know what's around, they said there was nothing more.'

'You were so hopeful of finding work.'

'That's the way it goes, better luck next time I try . . .'

She thought he had a lovely smile.

'I do hope I'm not interfering, but wouldn't you do better looking for work at home?'

'None there.'

He wore a wedding ring. She had noticed that when he had first come to her door in answer to the advertisement she had placed in the *Herald & Echo*. She thought he must have been married for several years, because since he first chose the ring his hands must have thickened with work and the flesh around the ring now furled over it so that it was tight, too tight to take off if he wanted to wash his hands thoroughly. She was very observant.

'Your wife must miss you dreadfully.'

She saw him start, as if she had nicked the hidden nerve. 'She understands.'

'She sounds a very good woman.'

'She knows what has to be done . . .'

She should not have mentioned the wife, she realized it. She enjoyed so much these brief conversations with her lodger. She was afraid she had spoiled something that was precious to her. She would have rather liked to have told him that she had defended his nationality against the busybody next door, but he had loped away up the stairs.

Later, from the kitchen, she heard him go out again.

The third day of the week. Bren had been ready, waiting in his room and changed, and looking down into the side street that ran to the Malone Road. From the high front window he saw her Astra swing across the traffic flow, causing two motorists to brake and almost collide. He heard the belt of their horns and she seemed to ignore them, didn't slacken her speed until she stopped outside the house.

She looked a wreck when she came through his door.

There was mud on her face and her hands. She wore a boiler suit that was too large for her, navy blue where the material was not obscured by the dirt smears.

'Am I late? Sorry . . .'

Bren said, 'It's only a couple of minutes past eight.'

'Sorry . . .'

She had a duffle bag and she dropped it on the floor. She started to wriggle out of the boiler suit.

'My things are in there,' she pointed down at the duffle bag.

She was kicking off her boots and the mud from them was spread out across the carpet of his room. She was out of the boiler suit, peeling off a sweater and then her jeans.

'Bloody cold old night,' she said.

He had the grip open. First into his hand was the Heckler and Koch rifle, stock folded. Second into his

106

hand were the two magazines taped upside down to each other. Third into his hand was the personal radio. He laid them on the floor.

'Quite a heavy frost,' she said.

He found her track-suit trousers and her T-shirt and her running shoes. He put them on the floor beside her, and then he bent to pick up the mud that she had spread.

'Oh, for Christ's sake,' she mouthed. 'Does it matter . . . ?'

He didn't ask her where she had been, what she had been doing, and he didn't think she would have told him. In a ditch, or in a hole like the one Jocelyn had dug. Out on a hillside, or damp in a bog field. And he had been asleep, slept pretty well through the night. The weapon was old, its paintwork was scratched, but the grease was fresh on it. He looked down at it. He saw where the serial number had been rasped away. The Heckler and Koch was a killing weapon. He felt the winnowing of the fear in his stomach.

'Are you all right?'

'Course I'm all right . . .'

'Honestly, Cathy, wouldn't you rather rest up for an hour?'

'Come on,' she said, and she was going for the door.

They didn't speak when they ran, and they made up the time that she had been late by running faster.

From her car, back at the house, she gave him his file for the day.

She was in his bathroom, and she hadn't closed the door. The first day he had had the file on the Department of the Environment's work in the province. The second day he had had the file on

107

the state of the war throughout the Six Counties of Northern Ireland, designated SECRET.

The file was marked 'East Tyrone Brigade'. It was stamped 'NOT TO BE TAKEN FROM SECURE PREMISES'. It was another SECRET file. He saw there were ninety-three pages, closely typed, and then bound separately inside the outer folder were photographs of men and women and of buildings and of countryside, and there was a large-scale map folded into the back of the file. It was the world he had walked into.

'Would you like some coffee?'

She murmured from the bathroom, 'Be great, lots of sugar.'

He put on the kettle. He was scared, couldn't hide it, couldn't help but admit it. He thought that it was the skill, the smooth talk and soft soap, of people like Mr Wilkins that they could con young men like himself to join up in total ignorance. The file he had read yesterday, he reckoned that back at Curzon Street they didn't know the half of it. The place had terrified him, and all he had done was read. The place had him on a barbed hook. He made the coffee. He knocked gently. No answer. He took it into the bathroom.

She was stretched out in the filled bath, the water lapping at her ears and mouth. She was asleep. She looked so bloody vulnerable.

He poured the coffee down the kitchen sink.

After she had dressed, a long time later, gone, left her mud on the carpet, Bren settled with the file. He studied the digest and the faces and the farmhouses and the countryside of Altmore mountain. The names of the officers of the Brigade were typed out. The man who was OC and the man who was Quartermaster, and Mossie Nugent who was Intelligence Officer. And the young men who were learning the trade, ranked as volunteers. The names of the hopefuls, the couriers and the watchers . . . and the same photograph of Jon Jo Donnelly that he had seen on Mr Wilkins' desk in Curzon Street. He would work until his eyes misted in tiredness. He was again a prisoner in the flat on the second floor and would be until the morning, until she came for him again.

'Is he going to live?'

'The hospital say that he's out of danger, sir.'

'That's a small mercy,' the Prime Minister said.

The Commander said, 'Colonel Beck was pretty alert before he went under anaesthetic. He gave us a good description.'

The pitch of the Prime Minister's voice rose. 'So, exactly where does your investigation stand?'

Ernest Wilkins, who was near the window, felt himself witness to the interrogation, but not a part of it, which pleased him. For the last fifteen years he had been a visitor to Downing Street, and taken his share of flack.

'There are 125,000 policemen who have seen and studied a photograph of Donnelly, taken not two years ago in Gough. Likewise Customs, airports and ports. All the addresses we hold, safe houses, sympathetic pubs and so on, they're all being watched . . .'

'Why don't you publish the photograph?'

'We'd frighten him off, sir. He'd disappear off the face of the earth. Or that recognizable version of him would. We might put a stop to him for a year, but he'd

109

be back, new cover and new method of operating.'

'So. What next?'

'Patient pursuit, sir, that's best. The tedious combing of haunts and possible associates. It has borne fruit before and will again. Every day that passes pushes up the odds against his escaping capture or betrayal. I've told you before, Prime Minister, that he is the one under pressure . . .'

'You will not overlook the pressure my Government is under, Commander, even as I do not underestimate the burden that you personally carry.'

'Thank you, Prime Minister, but Donnelly is the one who is suffering. He would appear to be working alone. Probably living alone. One by one his havens will be shut to him. His weapons are harder and harder of access. His contacts, from what we know, are less and less reliable, that is to say his couriers, his messengers. Some of them are children almost. We have access to one or two of this intake and . . . well, we are due a little luck, sir.'

The Prime Minister stood very close to the Commander. 'I don't believe in the wait-and-the-heavens-will-open approach. I would urge a more positive line on you, Commander. At our last meeting, we envisaged a resolution of the hunt in Altmore mountain. Is that the place?'

The Commander hesitated. 'Indeed, sir.'

The Prime Minister said, 'I would like him to go home, your Mr Donnelly, Commander.'

'Excuse me, Prime Minister.' The tactical intervention was one of the chief accomplishments of Ernest Wilkins. He had been brought up in a hard school. He was a Desk Head. 'That is a most

110

interesting suggestion, Prime Minister. It is an approach to the problem that we have been developing. A little more work and I think . . . Well, leave it with me, Prime Minister.'

There was the slight bow. He acknowledged the Prime Minister's satisfaction. He ignored the Commander's dagger glance.

The meeting was over.

'He is just one man, and making a lavatory of our country.'

'Quite so, sir.' Ernest Wilkins smiled. 'I'll be working on it, be assured, getting Jon Jo Donnelly home . . .'

He had had his supper, washed up his plate, thrown away the empty Irish stew tin and the banana skin. And he had no coffee.

The music came flooding through the floor and the walls.

The pictures, East Tyrone's finest, were laid out on the carpet, all mug-shots, all police station photographs. He had the pictures of each of their homes beside each face that registered the shock of arrest and the defiance and the contempt. He had separated from the rest the face of Jon Jo Donnelly. Not strictly relevant because he was over the water, but the custody mug-shot was different from the others, cocky and controlled . . . He couldn't survive unless he had coffee . . . All day and all evening she had been in his mind. The pearl whiteness of her body in his bath, the hard weight of her Heckler and Koch on his floor. There was the whip of her tongue and the bright laughter of her eyes . . . Now, without looking at the

111

legend on the back of the photographs, he could put a name to most of them, and a ranking to nearly as many, and a history of previous convictions to several of them. There were eighty-two photographs. To match all of the photographs to names and addresses and 'previous', he would be up half the night, but not without bloody coffee . . . All the time that he failed to concentrate on the photographs and the biographies, she was there in his mind, her face, her body, her voice and her eyes . . .

He went down the stairs, carrying his empty coffee jar.

It was Debussy, played loud.

He knocked on the door.

The door jumped open, on a chain. He was swiftly scrutinized. The door shut and then was spread wide.

It was the cardboard city man. 'Yes?'

'Sorry to disturb you, I wondered if you had any coffee . . . ?'

'Coffee, for fuck's sake?'

The man was in a dressing gown. The bed was unmade. Past him, Bren saw the open book on the bed. The Complete Works of William Shakespeare, one of the all-in anthologies with print like a tele- phone directory's. He'd have had a shower since Bren last saw him because the hair on his shoulders and his beard glowed chestnut.

'Just enough for a couple of cups, please.'

'Come on.'

He went inside. It was a flat the size of his own. The man shuffled barefoot into his kitchen. A tin must have fallen from an upper shelf because there was the impact and then the oath.

He was handed the coffee.

He started to unscrew the top. He intended to pour from the man's jar into his own.

'Don't bother yourself, take it. Gin's my poison . . .'

'Are you sure?'

He saw the rifle on the far side of the bed, tilted against the wall. The rifle would have been six inches from the hand of the man when he slept. On the top of the rifle barrel was a bulging night-sight. The smell in the room was of the clothes that were heaped by the open window, as if that might carry away some of their stench. There was a pistol on the table, and a pile of bills and an Inland Revenue envelope . . .

The man must have followed his eyes. 'Those buggers find you anywhere . . . You're Parker's new boy?'

'Yes.'

'She bollocked you out yet?'

'Afraid so.'

The man drawled, 'How do you find her?'

'I don't know anything about her. I suppose I was surprised to find a woman, well, you know, doing this sort of work.'

The man looked into Bren's face. 'Are you good enough to work with her?'

'Why not . . . ?'

'I don't know who you are, squire, and I don't know what you know, but I'll tell you something. There's men here would go through walls for that woman, got me?'

'Yes, I only meant . . .'

'And go through fire . . . Do you know *Henry IV, Part 2*?'

'No.'

'Me neither, so be a good fellow and piss off and let me get into it . . . You're a lucky sod, squire, and I hope you realize it, to work with Cathy Parker.'

Mossie remembered the heavy-type box in *An Phoblacht.*

'. . . No matter how long a person has been working for the enemy if they come forward they will not be harmed. Anyone caught touting will be executed! . . .'

'We'll go through it, one by one . . . Who knew?'

Their cars were parked in a farm gateway off the Ballygawley road. The gateway was on a bend and a steep dip in the road. There was a copse of conifers that masked the gateway from the hillside above. The OC had the farmer, most days, check through the copse with his dogs, so that they could be certain there was not an army observation hide amongst the trees. It was where the OC and Mossie Nugent often met.

'I knew,' Mossie said.

There was the light brittle laugh of the OC. 'You knew because it was your plan. I knew because I authorized your plan. Who else knew?'

'Quartermaster.'

'Knew what he had to provide, only that.'

'Kids who moved the guns.'

'They knew where they had to pick them up and where they had to drop them. That's all they knew.'

'Kids who drove the front car.'

'My wee brother, his girl. I'd go to the grave for them.'

'There's been others, with family in the Organization, they've touted . . .'

114

'Not my brother, Mossie, don't ever feckin' say it's my wee brother. Who else?'

'Those who was going to do the hit.'

'Gerry Brannigan's boy, and the Devitt kid. They were most at risk, tooled up. They were looking at ten years . . . Who else?'

Mossie spoke, so slowly, so quietly. 'I did one recce. The Riordan boy watched there four weeks in a row.'

'He's a little shite.'

'If there's a tout we might as well pack it up. Will you call in people from outside . . . ?'

They were the hard men. They would come from beyond the mountain community. They would be from Derry or Belfast. They would interrogate every man and woman in the Organization. They would watch, perhaps for weeks, maybe for months. The unit would be shut down while they sifted the answers they had been given before they pointed the finger, or called the unit clean. They would interrogate the OC, and the IO, and the OC's wee brother and his brother's girl, and the QM, and Gerry Brannigan's boy and the Devitt kid. The men from outside would have suspicion of every last one of them. Every volunteer in the unit would have a cause for fear if the men from outside came onto the mountain.

The OC shrugged. 'I'm not wanting to.'

Mossie said, 'Best if you don't. Best if you keep it close. The people from outside, they turn every man against his friend.'

There was the hiss of the OC. 'I tell you what I want . . .'

'What's that?'

'I wish to God that Jon Jo was back here.'

They talked another half an hour. They talked of the big one that was being put together in the shed of a farmhouse, proper engineering, with a base plate of steel on the back of a flat-top lorry and a cradle welded to the base plate that would take an oil drum lying on its side and the spigot tube that would be filled with explosive powder and throw the oil drum high enough into the air to get it over the barracks' fence and the oil drum could hold just around four hundredweight of fertilizer mix with a five pound Semtex charge to give it the kick. Done before and getting to be time to do it again. Not ready yet, getting ready. And they talked about a repeat of the brilliant one of three years back, one of the best, when they had taken a slurry cart from a farm and a tractor to pull it and hosed the cart out, and filled it with diesel fuel and oil and driven it out to the Stewartstown barracks and sprayed all over the walls and roof and put enough automatic fire down, and an RPG launcher, to ignite the diesel and oil. Feckin' magic, and Jon Jo Donnelly on the RPG launcher, last one he'd done before going south to rest up and let the heat off his back. Feckin' brilliant, Jon Jo with the RPG missile launcher on his shoulders.

They went their separate ways.

Bren opened the file stamped SECRET and marked SOURCE UNIT. He thought that he had opened Cathy Parker's door, seen behind the façade of the cardboard city man. Top of the file was a background paper, four rather messily typed sheets. Probably typed by a Five man with the errors corrected in biro.

The early morning had been as before. Cathy Parker arriving at eight o'clock, looking as though she had been pulled through a hedge, looking as though she hadn't slept, running with him, giving him a new file and retrieving the one that was NOT TO BE TAKEN FROM SECURE PREMISES. He already treasured the hour, never more, while she ran with him, dried her sweat off in front of him, talked to him. He longed for it all the time that he was shut away with his file and his coffee and his own dismal cooking.

The paper was clinical.

He read of the pressure that could be applied to turn a man to inform against his own. It was set out starkly. Money for a youngster whose girl was pregnant and they had nowhere to live and who could be persuaded to drink in the bars where the men of the Organization met. The menace of a lost livelihood for the taxi driver picked up drunk, who feared for the loss of his licence, and who could report on the men who used his cab and the men he saw on the street corners at night when he was cruising. The threat of imprisonment, for the man who tried to cut away from the old life, who could be sent back into the ASUs with the pedigree of imprisonment to boost his prospect of promotion. The certainty of maiming, the kneecap or the elbow, for the joyrider, who would keep his eyes and his ears open, or know that his name would be quietly fed to a Provo punishment squad.

And this was the war he had been *selected* for? He thought of Mr Wilkins saying that he *knew* Bren had the necessary qualities, was sure of it.

The second paper in the file was entitled, 'Source Unit/Operational Procedures'.

God, and it just wasn't real . . .

A different typewriter, and different handwriting for the corrections. It was standard procedure that all Handlers had a Divisional Mobile Support Unit patrol or an army covert team in the area when they met with their Player . . . At all times, at a meeting, there should be two Handlers, both armed, both in a state of maximum alert, maximum fitness . . . In their relationship with the Player, the Handlers must always seek to dominate . . . The Player must be protected at all times, *unless he killed*. The Player could continue, should be encouraged, to take part in PIRA activities, but not to the point of murder. The Player who killed was not to be tolerated . . . The Player was never to be trusted . . . The Handlers should never place themselves in a situation where the Player could control their safety.

The house was quiet around him. He sat on the carpet, where Cathy stood when she dried herself off, and went deeper into the file. Bren felt the tension grow in him as he turned the pages. 'Source Unit/Equipment'. There was the name and the signature number of the electronic bug that could be secreted in the stock of a weapon that a Player would bring from a weapons cache. There was the miniature camera to be used by the Player to photograph documents he had access to, maps, target plans, personnel evaluations. There was the light beam that was to be put into a cache by the Player and that would be activated when the Quartermaster came to retrieve guns or explosives. There was the bleeper, the size of those carried by a hospital doctor or a Telecom engineer. The bleeper's frequency would be monitored twenty-four hours.

Bren could not imagine why any man or woman would turn informer. Had to be in love with death, no question.

He could not imagine how the handlers had the guts or the simple cruelty to shepherd and corral the poor bastards, but he would learn.

The darkness had gathered inside his room.

He found it at the bottom of the file. Seven sheets, stapled together, marked SONG BIRD. No name, no address, no photograph.

The meeting of the Task Co-ordinating Group was over. The major from the Special Air Service had gone fast, with the Chief Superintendent from Special Branch. The colonel from Army Intelligence was on his way to the senior officers' dining room with the Assistant Chief Constable.

Only the two of them left behind, Hobbes and that bloody dour Ulsterman.

'Did they slap your wrist good and hard?'

Howard Rennie was the great survivor. Hobbes knew the history. A part of the war since the beginning. A sergeant in 1969 when it began, an inspector when the British had first sent over their cowboys to trample on half-decent covert work, a chief inspector when the Provies had been on the verge of extinction through the Supergrass programme where he had been responsible for cajoling the informers into the witness box, to come up with the evidence that convicted the fat cats, until the system had been thrown out by the judges as weak law. Now he was a superintendent in Special Branch. He worked in close liaison with a division of the Royal Ulster Constabulary that went under the title of E4. The Provos, his enemy, knew all about E4. Not many others did.

It was a miracle that Howard Rennie had climbed to superintendent rank, because he had sought no favours on the way up. There was no other man in Northern Ireland that Hobbes would have rather had on his side than the huge wide-shouldered Ulsterman, from whom a civil word was hard, bloody hard, to coax.

'I was sorry you lost your player.'

'Water under the bridge, Howard.'

'Wouldn't have been lost, not if I'd been running him.'

'I don't doubt it.'

There was Rennie's smile, not the smile of a man who was amused. If Rennie had had his way, then Hobbes and his kind would have been on the shuttle flying home. There would have been just one Source Unit, his, the Royal Ulster Constabulary's. No players handled by Five or by army intelligence.

'I suppose you shipped out that Faber? I didn't rate him.'

Hobbes gathered his papers. 'You'll surprise me one day. Yes, we sent him back.'

'And you'll replace him?'

'We already have,' Hobbes said curtly.

'What's your new baby like?'

Hobbes looked into the grey eyes of the police-man. 'Oh, the usual thing, another Englishman who doesn't know his arse from his elbow sent to interfere in the war that the RUC have presided over so successfully that it's been running more than twenty years . . .'

'Fuck you, Hobbes.' There was a clout across Hobbes' back.

The story was part of police headquarters folklore. Rennie, new to E4, and meeting for the first time his opposite number from army intelligence. The military boasting that they were running a hundred players. Rennie, all humble, saying that he only had ten . . . and then very quietly going down the army's list of a hundred, pointing out some who were dead, and several who were in gaol, and one who was in Australia . . . Everybody at police HQ told Hobbes that story, except Rennie.

'Remind me, Howard, where's Jon Jo Donnelly from?'

'He's East Tyrone. Spreading a touch of panic over there, is he? Tweaking the old lion's tail, eh? Up Altmore mountain. A few little bombs, a few hits, it's too sad. Tell them what happens over here every day. His wife's there . . .'

'Hassling her, would that bring him back?'

'Doubt it. More likely make him bomb a bit harder, shoot a bit straighter. They're tough people there, hassle washes off them.'

'Be a start, though . . .'

Rennie was at the door. 'Don't try giving me instructions, Mr Hobbes.'

'Just a request, Howard, and make it good and heavy hassle.'

*   *   *

'Christ Almighty, you're not in bloody insurance . . .'

Her clothes were old and dirty. He had put on well-pressed grey flannels, well-polished shoes, a check shirt with the collar undone and a lambswool sweater that his mother had sent him his last birthday, and his anorak.

'We're only going for a drive, aren't we?'

'. . . "only going for a drive", Jesus! Down there they scent everything that is out of place. They know the faces and the cars that have the right to be there. That I can't help. But I can help that you don't look like you're trying to sell a policy at the weekend. Get those off.' And she was gone.

He could smell the clothes the moment she came back through the door.

There was the mischief smile on her face. 'Get those on.'

'From downstairs?' The trousers were caked in mud.

'Correct.'

'He's not there.' There were still sweat patches under the armpits of the jersey.

'Second-class lock,' she said.

'Don't they have baths down in Tyrone?' The anorak was torn in the sleeve, too large for him, looked to have been rolled in sheep droppings.

She stood back. 'You are so wet behind the ears we could shoot snipe off you. Dear God.' The smile was back on her face and she reached up and ruffled her fingers through his hair, wrecking the parting. It was the only morning that she hadn't called to take him out to run. He didn't think she had slept on any of the other nights. He saw her bite at her lips, as if that were

122

the way she regained her control of herself.

There was a Subaru pick-up outside the house. It was filthy. There were two bales of hay loosely roped down in the back.

'What's this then? Local colour?'

She told him to drive. She unlocked the car and passed him a Browning pistol from the glove compartment and a magazine, told him to put it inside the anorak. She showed him the map and told him where to go.

She was asleep before they were out of Belfast.

Chapter Six

It was the story that the child loved best, the story that had no ending.

'The length and breadth of Ireland, wherever men yearned to be free, they spoke the name of Shane Bearnagh Donnelly. There were few enough priests left living by the English, and they were thrown into filthy prisons and starved, and many were tortured then hanged. There was the walking gallows. A huge man, an Englishman, used to walk Ireland. He wore on his shoulders a harness on which four men at a time could be hanged. But the priests were brave in their faith, and they prayed for the safety of Shane Bearnagh . . .

'For year after year, Shane roamed on Altmore mountain. The men with him were gradually hunted and killed by the English, but Shane they could never capture. More soldiers were sent to Altmore barracks, that's now in the bracken and trees where the road runs on to Pomeroy, where we get the blackberries . . .

'Shane took cattle from the English, and hid them up in the caves on Altmore, and the caves are still called Shane Bearnagh's stables. Shane used to watch the soldiers searching for him from the high ground, and some old people like your Grannie would call that Shane's Chair, and sometimes Shane's Sentry-box. Shane had a wife now, and a fine small boy. His wife gave up her home, and she came to live with her man on the mountain, shared his dangers. He was the greatest patriot that ever came from the mountain, and never forget that he was a Donnelly. He was cheeky with the English dragoons, he played games with them, and all they could do was curse at him from a distance . . .

'The English farmers complained bitterly to the English soldiers: how could one man for so long outwit all their soldiers? So a new officer was sent from England to hunt Shane. His name was Black Jemmy Hamilton. He was the cruellest of all the officers who ever came to Altmore. He tried to terrorize the native Irish into betraying Shane Bearnagh, but they never knew where he was. One of Shane's tricks was to colour the coat of his horse so that they would not recognize him. One day, when Black Jemmy Hamilton was away searching with his horsemen, Shane came down to the unguarded barracks and he was fed by the wives of the English soldiers. He took everything that he wanted. It was as if the wives of the English soldiers were shamed by the way their own men behaved to the down-trodden Irish folk. Hamilton and his soldiers came back from another wasted day on the mountain tired and angry and found that their larders were empty. His fury was terrible. All of the wives were beaten, and Hamilton swore that he would not rest until Shane Bearnagh Donnelly was captured and hanged . . .'

'Did they ever catch him, Ma?'

It was the story that never ended . . . She told him it was time for them to go to feed the cattle.

*   *   *

125

Ernest Wilkins had done it before, and he would do it again.

The afternoons of a weekend were a good time to reach the Prime Minister's aide. The Principal Private Secretary could always ensure that a brief message reached his man.

He had travelled into London from his home.

'. . . The Prime Minister made a quite excellent suggestion at our last meeting. I would like him to know that it is already being acted upon. We are starting rather a vigorous programme this evening. You'll make quite certain that this is reported to him? I am very grateful . . .'

All the way into London at a weekend, into the near-deserted Curzon Street building, to make one secure telephone call. It was the way he had advanced to Desk Head. Within ten minutes of entering the building he was leaving it.

It was a cold, grey day, with a mist hanging in the valley. There was a fleck of sleet in the air. They looked down from the crest of Altmore mountain.

Bren no longer smelt his own clothes, nor could he smell Cathy. Bitterly cold in the cardboard city man's anorak, no gloves in the pockets. He could see the villages and on down to the Ballygawley road, and at the edge of his vision, before the cloud took over, were the towers and the smokier haze of Dungannon. It was a journey's end, it was where he had been volunteered to work. Beneath them the bracken and heather ran down a long way to the farmland below: the gold brown of the dead bracken and the dull dark green of the heather. There was no sign of life in the upper part of the mountainside. There were trees that were bent and stunted. His gaze shifted to lower down. The farms on the high ground were the smallest, the houses and the fields on a seemingly smaller scale. Bren knew nothing of agriculture, but it didn't take a trained eye to recognize that this was mean land. He saw a man walking with a dog along the edge of a field. He saw a car speeding along a narrow lane. Cathy passed him a pair of binoculars, the sort an ornithologist would have in his pocket on a weekend hike. His vision roved further down the slope, larger farms, larger houses, larger fields. He found a village, then another with a tall steeple, with a graveyard behind the church, and he could see the black marble of the stones and the colour flicker of flowers.

She slipped her arm round his waist. He felt the warmth of her. She scratched with her finger at his hip, as if she were teasing him, like tickling under a cat's chin. 'Don't panic,' she said. 'It's only in case we're watched.'

He had the Browning automatic pistol in his belt, and she had the Heckler and Koch in her hand, hidden under her anorak. 'It's just like home,' he said.

'Is that right?' She was grinning at him. Her head was against his shoulder.

'Stupid, but I can't feel the threat.'

'Concentrate and listen.'

She talked, and the binoculars were hard against his eyes. 'The village, the top one . . . There was a UDR man used to do a milk round, didn't think that anyone knew he did soldiering at night. One day he had the 'flu, lucky for him, because that was the day they were going to kill him. Another man did the round. He died in the street near the shop. See the bar? The shop's beside the bar. Everything was fine, though. They apologized for murdering the wrong man . . . Go to the top end of the village, where the bend is. That's where the SAS man crashed his car. They had a guy pounding him with an AK sticking out through the sun-roof of their motor, real Wild West stuff. It was very sharp thinking to get his car into a ditch, gave him cover and two free hands. He did really well, he closed them down with his pistol, scared them off, hit at least one of them. We know he hit one of them because there was a stake-out, an ambush, nine months later and one of them who was killed then had scars in his gut . . . Got the little road, running across us, north to south? Got the bridge? They had a come-on bomb under there, eight dustbin loads of fertilizer mix. They got the army up there and set off the secondary bomb, the killer, took a whole group of squaddies right out . . . Go back to the village, far side of the road, near the bar, the flagpole and the heap of rock, that's the memorial to a hunger-striker, dead before they called it off . . . The village down the hill, tiny place, get the church and the cemetery at the back. The big Celtic cross, that is the Republican plot, there's half a dozen of their best in there . . . Go on down the road, away from the village, that's where they killed three police, culvert bomb, you can't see the new tarmac from here . . . The guys who do the heavy stuff over in Europe, they're from here, and on the mainland too. Forget Belfast, this is where the aggravation is. Time we were off. Put the binoculars away. Been out here too long. Just hold on to me for a moment. Try and look as though you were enjoying it. Lie back and think of England, Bren.'

The heat of her body had found him. He felt a spreading fear, a growing excitement. Bren gazed down the mountain slope over her shoulder. He saw the smoke from the chimneys of the lonely and dotted farmhouses. He heard, so faintly, the shout of the man walking his dog, and the dog was two fields away and springing in pursuit of something too small for Bren to see. It was where Jon Jo Donnelly was from, the home of the man whose photograph he had seen briefly on Mr Wilkins' desk. He wondered how a man from here, the raw countryside, could survive in any city.

'Are they watching us?'

'Might be, might not be . . . the third or fourth time, if we were recognized again, if the vehicle became a habit, then we would be. Does that frighten you?'

'There's nothing to see to be frightened of.'

'When you do see something it's probably too late. Come on, you smell revolting.'

Her arm was away from his waist. He stood his ground. 'Where is he?'

'Who?'

'Where's Song Bird?'

'Down there, somewhere.'

She had reached him, spread the fear in him. 'In God's name, how does he stand it?'

'I don't know and I don't care. It's only important to me that he keeps singing.'

She snatched at his sleeve. She dragged him away.

129

He let her into the Subaru. 'Is this where you come when you're out at night?'

'Come on,' she said. 'Let's get a cup of tea.'

Bren drove.

In the village, on the corner by the bar, near the hunger striker's memorial, a group of youths watched them go by. Past a small and well-built school with a tarmacadam playground, and a gaelic pitch. Prosperous bungalows on the edges of the villages. And Cathy was alert beside him. He had seen nothing that was different, out of the ordinary. She showed him where a police reservist driving a lorry had been ambushed and shot dead. He turned onto the Dungannon road and she nodded to the low wall, told him they had hidden behind it when they had waited to shoot and kill a police inspector.

She directed him through Dungannon. They crawled in the traffic jam up Irish Street and turned at the big school building, and again at the second church.

Small town anywhere. Crowded pavements loaded. Bright shop lights. People bent with their shopping bags.

She told him where to turn.

Nothing ordinary about the army fortress.

Tall iron sheeting as far as he could see, and high above the iron screens were the watchtowers. The sentries had the car number and Cathy flashed a card. The spiked chain across the road into the barracks was dragged back and they were waved through.

There was a sudden tiredness on her face.

She told him where to park. She led him to the open

sand weapons pit, cleared her weapon, waited for him to do the same.

The colonel wrapped his big arms round Cathy and kissed her forehead as if she were his favoured cousin. The adjutant had brought the tea and his eyes had lingered on Cathy, as if she was God, and had left reluctantly. Bren was introduced, perfunctorily, the decent thing and nothing more, and gestured to sit down by the wall furthest from the electric fire.

'You poor old love, how are you?'

Cathy was flopped in an armchair, legs spread, knees wide. 'Tell you what, that bloody mountain is arse-bendingly cold at night.'

'Hoped you'd call by . . .'

'Been showing my new man the countryside.'

'And the other fellow . . . ?'

'Gone home. The player who was head-jobbed was his. Asking for trouble if he'd stayed. Looking very pretty up there this afternoon . . .'

Bren thought she was fighting to keep her eyes open. The colonel sat on the carpet in front of the fire and refilled Cathy's mug and stirred in the sugar.

'How's your mother?'

'Haven't heard, not in the last couple of weeks. She's not riding any more. I suppose she's petrified.'

'Yes, well . . . Your father managing?'

'It's getting him down. I've told him to put in a manager. He'd get a top man there. But he won't hear of it. You know the trouble, I know it. He still thinks that one day I'm going to jack this lot in and take over.'

'One day.'

'Never the right day, is it? Can you imagine walking away from here?'

'Not ever out of my mind. I dream of dear old Scotland. No newspapers, lousy television reception, walking and fishing and stalking. You should come up in August.'

Cathy smiled sadly, 'I'd love to.'

'How are they when you go home?'

'They look at me, big spaniel eyes, pleading. You know Rupert, 'course you do, Rupert did the damage. After his prostate last year he went down there to rest up, and spilled the beans. Stupid prat, told them what I did. Still . . .'

'You could do worse.'

Cathy snorted. 'Certainly, be a regular at the Bath and West, trot all round the west country with the Charolais bull trying like buggery to win Best of Breed again? It would kill me . . . You can chase your grouse round Cromarty and do the John MacNab thing. I could do that for about, well, once, and then I'm bored rigid . . .'

'Their loss, our gain.'

'For Christ's sake, don't go soft.'

'OK, OK . . . when are you back down?'

'Be using the hide . . .' She jerked a thumb behind her. 'Get the new boy familiarized. Meet the player and so on.'

The colonel pushed himself to his feet.

'We're doing the Donnelly place tonight . . .'

Her eyes glinted, she seemed to throw off the relaxation. 'Oh? Why?'

'Orders from on high.'

'She's done nothing, Attracta.'

'Orders.'

'Why doesn't anyone at Curzon Street *ever* ask me why we are loathed in this goddamn corner. God, I could tell them. She just happens to be married to the man.'

'And away a long time. So it's harassing women and kids that I'm now paid for.'

'There are some right pillocks we have to work for, Johnny . . .'

The colonel said, 'I had him in here once. A patrol had lifted him on Charlie One. He was here for an hour before the branch came to run him down to Gough. I rather liked him. It was his attitude that tickled me. I mean, he despised me, he probably had a little plan for me, he'd have been very happy to see me blown away, yet . . . He seemed to regard himself as my equal. Two officers, two armies. As if . . . well, if we'd met in a bar somewhere a thousand miles away, we'd have had a good chat, beefed over our mutual tactics, broken a bottle open. What I thought at the time, he'd have made a very good company sergeant major in a good regiment. He wasn't frightened of me, and I don't mind saying it, I'm glad he's someone else's headache.'

'Great mug of tea. Thanks. Come along, Brennard, I need to be driven home to kip.'

She walked to the door. Bren followed. For a short moment the colonel's arm was round her shoulder, ushering her to the door.

Outside the door, she turned back to him. It was the great winning smile.

'You know what they say about you?'

'Who? Curzon Street?'

133

'No. The kids up on Altmore. We picked it up on one of the bugs. They say, "What's the last thing that'll go through Colonel Johnny's mind?" It's their crack.'

'What's the last thing that'll go through my mind?'

'They say it's an AK bullet. Bye, sunshine.'

'Cow.'

'Thought you'd get it.'

She didn't look back. There was just her muffled laugh into the anorak collar that she held tight across her face. The colonel, Johnny, caught Bren's jacket as he made to follow her.

'Look after that lady. Don't ever think of taking a liberty with her safety. If anything you did, or didn't do, endangered her, then I'd break your back.'

The Officer Commanding East Tyrone Brigade knew, so did his Intelligence Officer. But, by that Saturday afternoon, the word of danger had shimmered down the mountain and through the bungalows and farm-steads and Housing Executive homes. Word travelled fast, whispered mouth to straining ear, of new risks to the men who had sworn the oath. Every man and woman on Altmore would have been able to recite the Constitution of *Oglaigh na hEireann*, would have known General Order 5, Part 5 . . . 'No Volunteer should succumb to approaches or overtures, black-mail or bribery attempts . . . Volunteers found guilty of treason face the death penalty.'

There were few amongst the bungalows and farm-steads and Housing Executive homes who could have denied involvement, strong or tenuous, with the Organization. There were sons, nephews, cousins, the children of neighbours, who were dead or imprisoned or 'away' or active. It was the life of the mountain, in the twenty-second year of the present war, that no man and no woman knew whom they could trust. Fear ruled. See nothing, hear nothing, know nothing, was the order of survival. The men took comfort in the village bars, their women more often sought the help of valium and librium. But drink and sedatives gave only noisy or drugged solace. Willing or dragged screaming, the community was involved. There was a family on Altmore . . . the son shot dead by the covert Special Forces, father interned in the fifties, grandfather active in the twenties and thirties, great-grandfather shooting until the barrel of his rifle was red-hot in Dublin in 1916, great-great-grandfather a part of the closed group seeking Home Rule a full century before the young man was buried under the grey cloud and the gold green slopes of the mountain. Where was escape? Escape was not possible.

Behind closed doors and closed windows and closed minds, the community of Altmore braced itself against the menace of an informer.

The OC had begun, and she told him that it was about feckin' time, to put the new units into his wife's kitchen.

She watched him. She was beside him on the kitchen linoleum and she marked by pencil the places for his power-drill to make room for the screws, and she passed the doors and frames from the packaging to his hand. She knew the anxiety that bit at him, and that brought him cold and violent to her bed. She knew that he commanded the Brigade, and she knew also that the man before him was shot in an army ambush and finished with a bullet to the forehead; she had seen the pallor of the face in the coffin and the small, neatly cosmeticized hole. And the man before that was now in his twelfth year in the Kesh with more, many more, years to endure; she knew that each Sunday morning that man's wife and his child took the bus from Dungannon to the prison to make small talk with the caged bird.

She made the marks and passed the materials.

She could do nothing.

His daughter knew when the strain was at him. The Quartermaster had come in through the door, with the mud on his feet. Straight to the cupboard beside the fireplace, straight for the whiskey.

Her mother was in Dungannon, down on the bus for the weekend shop. Her mother had to go by bus because her father had been away with the car. The girl went outside and took the keys from the ignition and switched off the sidelights, and locked the car. He was pouring again when she came back into the sitting room.

She was seventeen. She did waitressing in a hotel in Dungannon. If her father were arrested again, charged again, sent to gaol again, then she might lose her job. The job was her lifeline, vital to her. Her father had been in the Kesh for four years. Between the ages of eight and twelve she had seen him only on those weekends when her mother had pushed and forced, and once punched her, onto the prison visitors' bus. They were brilliant kids that she met working at the hotel, and the management sent her home to the mountain by taxi at night. She could not know he was the brigade's Quartermaster, but she knew that he was again involved.

He had no work, her mother had no work. She was the oldest of four, and the only breadwinner of the family. She gave £30 each week to her mother . . . If she lost her job . . .

The glass shook from the tremble of his hand. He challenged her to criticize him. She couldn't know whether he had been out to move weapons, whether it had been reconnaissance, whether it had been on a hit. He was home. He felt safe in his home. The strain was from being out and abroad on the Organization's business. She did not know whether it was the fear of being shot or the fear of being lifted that drove him to take drink as soon as he returned to that safety.

The whole of the village knew that it had been a bad summer and a worse autumn for the 'boys'.

Mrs Devitt bottled up inside her the shock of discovering her boy's involvement. No-one of her family had ever before been in the clutches, as she would have put it, of the Organization. Coming back on the bus from Dungannon, early in an afternoon, after doing dinner-lady duty at St Patrick's Academy, she had found him in the bath. A steaming hot bath, on a Tuesday afternoon, and the boiler going like oil was free. There had been pictures of the bomb debris on the Ulster telly's news, a haberdashery store in Cookstown. She hadn't told her own mother, nor her sister, and they had never had a secret between them, nor Vinny's father, nor even the priest.

He lay on his bed. A Saturday afternoon, and he

was a fine big fellow, and there might have been work for him on one of the farms if he cared to shift his backside and look for it. She tidied around the bed. Her son stared at the ceiling. He had nothing more to say to her now. Men came at night, called for him. She knew some of them, didn't know most of them. He was paler than he had been before. She would not have known what to say to him, she never asked him.

The last Saturday she had heard him go out, before it was light. She had heard the squeal of her front door, while her husband snored his Friday-night drink away. Since the last Saturday he had been tighter than before, as though the pressure was increasing. Each Sunday she took flowers to her brother's grave, a coronary attack, and she passed the Republican plot where the men were buried. Clear fine photographs of all of them, in their best suits, sealed into the stone.

Her Vinny had a best suit, and there was on the front-room mantelpiece a clear fine photograph of him at his cousin's wedding, with a white carnation on his lapel.

She had an armful of his shirts and socks. His face was a heartbreak to her.

Gerry Brannigan's wife was what they called on the mountain 'a holy decent woman'. Gerry Brannigan was what they called in Dungannon police barracks 'the armchair Republican'. She had tried to keep their youngest out of the Organization, he had given the boy the chat and the talk that had pushed him forward.

Gerry Brannigan would have liked to have been admitted to the secrecy of the Provisionals' army, but had been rejected because he took drink. His three elder sons were away in England, on the building, his daughter was in Glasgow working as secretary to a solicitor's business. For three years Gerry Brannigan had basked in a sort of pride because his youngest son was involved. The boy's mother wanted him to 'break the stick', as they said on Altmore, cut his links, but he paid her no heed.

They kept fowls in the back garden. There was a chicken coop they had made themselves, knocked up out of spare wood, and a good fence round it to keep the fox out. They were both there, Gerry and his wife, hunting for eggs in the last light of a Saturday afternoon, so that there would be scrambled egg for Sunday morning breakfast after early Mass. He saw his wife look up. She was a good woman, neat and tidy and careful with their money. He saw the sadness on her face. He followed the line of her eye. There was the face of their boy at the kitchen window. He looked haunted. He had encouraged the boy, taught him the songs and told him the folklore. And now that he saw the face of the boy, Gerry Brannigan cringed. He could see the pressure building on his awkward, snapping, bloody-minded youngest son. He felt a great guilt; Gerry Brannigan felt the danger that was alive on Altmore.

The priest called for Patsy Riordan.

He came each Saturday in the winter, when the boy was usually in the lean-to garage. When Patsy was cleaning the plugs or polishing the chrome of

139

his motorcycle, the priest stood at the door and talked to his mother, and he could hear their voices.

The priest came each Saturday to ask whether the next afternoon, Patsy would rejoin the gaelic team, Under 19s. He would talk to Patsy's mother, get her encouragement and then he would go to the garage, and with his best smile he would tell the boy that there was still the need for a good defender in his team, and that the position was held open for the boy. The priest saw the way that young Patsy gazed back at him, as if he wanted to catch the line that was thrown to him, as if he was just helpless. The boy had great potential, with commitment and fitness it was the priest's belief that the boy could play for the County Tyrone team, Under-19s. This Saturday, like last Saturday, and Saturdays before, the boy just shook his head, mumbled words that were indistinct, turned his shoulders away from the priest and hunched over his motorcycle. In the priest's eyes, young Patsy was just a silly boy.

Perhaps if he had sat down on the oil-stained floor of the garage, spent an hour, two hours, talking with the boy then the priest might have melted his hostility, but he had the sick to visit and his team to collect.

The priest knew that it was said there was an informer on Altmore . . . He could only wonder how long it would be before the troops and the police swooped on the Riordans' house and took the silly boy away.

She had lost an earring.

It was not an expensive earring, but it was gold and

it held a single pearl that was real, and her mother had given it to her. The earring was important to Siobhan Nugent.

He was down at Attracta Donnelly's, where he always was at the weekend, where he said he was painting and wallpapering. She could not remember when she had last had the earring. Ridiculous, but it was two full days since she could last remember noting the earring. She was irritable as she searched for it, because it would have been noted in the shop that she had come out with only one earring, gossiped over and not pointed out to her. And his mother hadn't told her, but then she saw nothing. His mother was out for the afternoon, otherwise she would have been fussing in Siobhan's way, and criticizing her for her carelessness. She stripped the bed. She flapped the sheets and nothing fell clear. After she had remade the bed she went into the small bathroom and turned out the wicker basket that held the family's dirty clothes. Francis helped her, Doloures and Patrick and Mary watched the television across the hall. Back to the bedroom. She started on all of the clothes, dresses and coats that she had worn in the last two days.

There was a raised false floor to the wardrobe.

'Could have gone down here, Ma.'

There was a crack at the edge of the false floor. It was the type of wardrobe that had to be assembled from a kit, and those kits were never properly satisfactory. Her Francis found it. A clever wee boy her Francis. She looked down. She saw his fingers drop into the crack, the gap. The false floor moved as the boy tugged it up.

Her Francis held up what he had found under the false floor of the wardrobe.

'What's this, Ma?'

He never talked to her about the part he played in the Organization. She thought it was minor. She knew he had been in prison before they had met, long before they were married, because his mother had told her. His mother told her most things about her husband, she could wheedle answers to her queries from the old goat. His mother thought that it was Siobhan's fault that Mossie, her golden boy, was diving ever more inside himself, as if the weight of Altmore's granite increasingly pressured the spirit from him. His mother thought it was Siobhan's fault that rare laughter, occasional fun, was now drained from her darling.

He was way down at the 'widow' Donnelly's . . .

Little Francis passed her the Building Society account book.

The scream was silent in her throat. She turned the pages.

'And there's this, Ma.'

Little Francis passed her the plain steel box, the size of a cigarette packet, with a red plastic button recessed into the face.

Jon Jo walked the headland. It was where he came when he could no longer abide to remain inside the small room in his landlady's house.

Hard, impossibly hard, to believe what he read in the papers, that the target was alive and was already classified as 'stable'.

On the headland he was closest to his Attracta and to his Kevin.

Dusk on the headland, grey light merging grey cloud with grey sea.

It was good to look out over the seascape. He thought that it brought them together. They were across the water from him, away to the west. He watched the gulls wheeling, the cormorants diving, the guillemots perching on the sprayed rocks.

He would have wanted his hand to hold Kevin's, and his arm to be round Attracta. He would have tried to give them his love. He wanted for them to be here too.

His enemies, policemen and soldiers in their thousands, those who had studied the file, would not have short-changed his intelligence. He assumed that long ago they had access to the school records at St Patrick's Academy that would have designated him as bright, good potential. There had been a question of University, something the Headmaster had once told his mother. Not to be, he had been diverted.

Jon Jo knew that to come to the headland and to gaze over the sea and to think of his Attracta and his Kevin was just indulgence ... He was a creature of the mountain, born and reared there. But then so too was his brother. The mountain was not his brother's war. He had chosen to be the man who would move the rock up the mountain, to push forward the progress of the war. He believed in a future for his people, and the future was to be earned by the war, by sacrifices too. He came to the cliff edge to dream of his loved ones, and to think of the future. In the peace and beauty and relative safety of the headland he could begin to come to terms with the truth that in other places, in the greater loneliness of the big city, was close to overwhelming him: that only at the very end of the war would he be at peace with Attracta on the mountain.

How long . . . ?

Christ, how long . . . ?

He turned, he wiped the wet smear on his face. He would spend the evening with his plans, maps, that were under the floorboard of his room. It was never done, it was never finished. Not till the bastards had packed up, gone with their foreign soldiers and their prisons, would it be done and finished.

'What did he mean . . . ?'

They were almost back in to Belfast.

'. . . Your Colonel Johnny, what did he mean . . . ?'

The oncoming lights were into his eyes. She had shifted in her seat, shown him she had woken.

'. . . What did he mean by "being paid to harass women and kids"?'

'Does it matter?'

He had thought of it all the way back from Dungannon. He had waited for her to wake. 'It just seemed a pretty peculiar thing to say.'

'He's a good man,' Cathy said.

'Which means . . . ?'

'It means, lucky bugger, that he has still retained a stroke of decency in his pig-sty. It means that he can see a difference between a bad boy and a bad boy's family. He's still a human being.'

'Keep going.' The sleep was out of her voice. Her face was close to his. On his face was the warm whisper of her breath. 'Everybody who comes over here, they all think it won't touch them, but it does. It touches everyone except good old Colonel Johnny, and at the end of the day he too does what he's told to do . . .'

Bren asked, 'Does it touch you?'

'Don't be tiresome, Bren.'

He drove on. He came down the Malone Road.

Cathy said, 'Tomorrow evening you'll meet Song Bird.'

The boy didn't cry and Attracta didn't scream at them.

They held Mossie upstairs, in Kevin's bedroom, with his dust sheets and his paint pots. He sat on the floor beside the ladder and all the time he was watched by the barrel of a rifle. From his own home Mossie had seen the two previous times that the army and police had come to the Donnelly farm.

He thought this was different. It was like it was cold. They seemed to him to be just clinical. No swearing, no fast talk. Like they were programmed. His Siobhan would have raised the roof, his kids would have been bawling and little Francis might have been trying to kick the skin off a soldier's shins.

Did the beggars have no charity?

Like it was just a job, like what they were breaking was not the home of a woman and a child.

Mossie sat on the floor and he asked the soldier if he could smoke, and each movement that he made, taking out the packet, taking out the cigarette, striking the match, putting the match into the ashtray, putting away the cigarette packet, was followed by the rifle barrel.

The noise of the breaking of the house would have

145

been easier to stomach if he could have heard their protests, Attracta's and Kevin's, or their swearing, the soldiers' and the policemen's. Only the sounds of splintering furniture and the screech of lifting floorboards.

After they had gone, with their guns and the jemmy and the sledgehammer, after the shattering thunder of the helicopter powering away from the field beside the cattle shed, Mossie helped Attracta to clear the damage. They collected everything that was broken from the front room and the kitchen and the dining room and she threw them out through the back door into the rain. Small tables, chairs, the television with the back off it, the electric fire with the front off it, plates from the kitchen, the vinyl roll from the floor of the dining room that had been torn to get at the floorboards, all of it out into the rain. Mossie brought a blanket down from upstairs, from where it had been pitched out of the airing cupboard, shook off the feathers from a ripped bed bolster, and used it to cover over the cuts in the upholstery of the settee. The boy was on his knees, sweeping glass into a dustpan. She hadn't spoken, nothing, and the kid hadn't cried. Mossie would have gone to his grave for the both of them. She had the framed photograph in her hand. She carefully picked the shards from the frame, and put it back onto the mantelpiece. He watched. Her lips brushed the torn soft-focus face of her man. He saw the pride on her face and the way that her son came to her and hugged her. Only the idiot Brits would have believed they could break her.

She said that she would make tea for him, but he had no more business in the house.

He would never be loved, not as Jon Jo was loved by Attracta Donnelly. He thought she leaned on him more now than before. She seemed always to have another small job he could do about her house. But Jon Jo was never spoken of. She was sharp, she could put the numbers together and come to the answer. Jon Jo was the hunted man. They never let up in the hunt for a killer. He would be hunted for ever. Siobhan called her the 'widow Donnelly'. Siobhan had it right. Attracta and the face in the photograph had nothing ahead of them.

He made his excuses.

He hadn't his key in the door before Siobhan had it open.

She had him by the collar and she marched him through to her bedroom.

He saw the wild anger in her face.

'You bastard, what's you at?'

Chapter Seven

She saw him flinch from her.

Siobhan Nugent held the Building Society book out in front of her face, in front of his eyes.

'What's this?' Her hand trembled in her anger.

It was only a spitted whisper because the children were in the sitting room across the hall. There was a moment when she thought he might try to snatch it away and then she saw that he was afraid.

'I can't . . .'

'You feckin' well will.'

'Don't ask me.'

'What's this? It's £500 a month, first of every month. It's interest paid every year. Two years and more . . .'

'Don't ask me.'

'It's money we don't dream about. It's more than fourteen thousand feckin' pounds. When did we have fourteen thousand feckin' pounds? When did we have £500 paid in each month, clockwork?'

'Siobhan, don't ask me.'

'Correction, not "we"; when did Moss Aloysius Nugent have fourteen thousand pounds and more?'

'It's not for talking of.'

'I want to know, I've the right to know. I darn the heels of your socks. I turn the collars of your shirts so's you can go on wearing them. I buy cheap. Damn you, I've worried myself sick about money, and there's fourteen thousand feckin' pounds . . . Who's paying it?'

'You don't need to know.'

'Why's they paying it?'

It was the twelfth year of their marriage. Her own mother, rest her soul, had told her she could have done better. A new life, a good life, in England, six years of it, and then he had insisted that they come back to bloody Ireland. Nearly six more years of living cramped in his mother's bungalow, because they had no money for a place of their own, and the Housing Executive list stretched away above them because they had been away and lost places on the ladder.

'I want to know, damn you.' She stood her full height. She felt her lips against her teeth.

'Best you don't ever know.'

'Is that your last word?'

'You can't be told. You'll not be helped by knowing, believe me.'

She heard the pitch of her own voice rising. 'What do I believe? I find a Building Society book that has been kept a secret from me, fourteen thousand feckin' pounds. What should I believe . . . ?'

There was the click of the front door. There was his mother's voice, and the babble of the kids and the loud laughter from the television. She saw his face lighten, as if his rescue had come. His hand reached out and he took the Building Society book from her. His face seemed to say that he was safe, that he had seen her off, that she would not raise her voice now that his mother was back. He slid the Building Society book down into the hip pocket of his trousers. Her hand was in the pocket of her trousers. Her fingers were round the shape of the box. His mother called out, to let them know she was back, that she was putting on the kettle. He went to go past her. She stood in front of the closed door of the bedroom. His hand was on her shoulder and she felt the gentle pressure as he eased her sideways.

'And what's this?'

She held it in front of his face.

They were very close, almost touching.

She held in front of him the small steel box that was the size of a cigarette packet.

'What's this, then?'

The blood colour running from his face. 'Give it me.'

Her thumb rested over the red button that was recessed into the box. 'Tell me, what is this?'

'Don't, for the love of Christ, please, feck you, don't . . .'

There was his mother's voice again, penetrating into the room, telling them that their tea would be ready in a minute.

She felt her power.

'What happens if I press this . . . ?' Her thumb lay across the red button.

'Don't . . .'

'Is it a bomb switch . . . ?'

He shook his head. It was as if his voice had died, and him never short for words.

'Is it a warning bell . . . ?'

She saw the fear in his eyes.

'Do they come running? Who'll come? The slob that you bloody jump for? The Devitt boy? The half-wit Riordan kid? The little Brannigan bastard . . . ?'

Again the shake of his head. The smoothness of the red button was under her thumb. He would have known that he could not wrench it from her, not before she had pressed the button.

'Who comes running when little Mossie presses the button . . . ?'

His mother was outside the door. Siobhan leaned against it. His mother said that the tea was poured. The door was pushed against her back. Siobhan's weight took the pressure. She called, the loving daughter-in-law, wheedling voice, that they would be out in a moment. She heard the footsteps shuffle away.

'Who comes running?'

'Please, Siobhan, you can't know.'

'Or I press the feckin' thing . . .'

'Don't!'

'I press it.'

She held the steel box right in front of his face, where it would have filled his eyes. He was breathing hard. His face was white.

'You don't know . . .'

'I press it.'

He crumpled against her, pushing her against the door. The steel box was driven into his cheek. She had destroyed him. She did not know how, nor did she know why. Her arms slipped round his neck. She held the box against the frayed collar of his shirt.

His voice was in her ear, in her hair.

151

'It's the army that comes running, or the police. I'm theirs, I *belong* to them . . .'

For a long time she held him, fearful for herself, fearful for him. His breathing had slowed and steadied.

'You're a tout?' she said, still not believing it. 'You tout for the Brits?'

'Since way back.' She wondered if, before, he had ever been near to telling her.

She had no more anger, only fear.

'Jesus, Mossie, you get killed for touting.'

Siobhan gave him back the steel box. She put it into his hand and closed his fingers round it. She had seen the helicopter land in the field that evening between her home and the home of Attracta Donnelly. She had seen the soldiers bent low under the flailing rotors, running to the farmhouse. The box was her husband's link to those soldiers. There was a woman in the village, and her son not more than ten years older than her Francis and the boy had been shot dead by the army. And she knew the woman and made small talk with her after Mass or in the queue at the Dungannon supermarket cash desks. There was another woman in the village, her husband had been killed by his own bomb, detonated by the electronic sweep of the army. She knew the woman, and thought she was lovely and brave, and talked with her at the school gate before Doloures and Patrick came out.

Her arms slid from his neck.

'The book's your give-away. You take a risk with the book.'

Mossie said, 'We goes to Belfast four times a year, right? We all go, you and me and the kids; that's

152

known, you tell everyone that'll listen that we go to Belfast four times a year for the big shop, and I get my new brushes ... Everyone knows ... And I leaves you, because you and the kids don't want to buy paint brushes, right? I buy the brushes and I get the entries marked up into the book ...'

'You's bloody stupid, Mossie, keeping the book here.'

'I need it.'

'That's idiot talk, Mossie. Why's the book not in a bank safe, why's it not in Belfast?'

'It's all I have. It's the future. The bleeper box, that's feckin' present. It's a future that matters. Yours, mine, the little ones'.'

'You carried it all with you, you poor love.'

'I thought you'd hate me, if you knew.'

'God, why?'

'For turning, for being turned.'

She blazed her eyes at him. 'You think I'm a Provo? You think they matter to me? Do you know nothing of me?'

'I didn't think you'd want it told you that your man was a tout.'

'If we're going out tonight, we'd better be changing,' she said.

Through all those days and months and years of marriage, he had lived in fear with his secret. He was still slumped against the door ... Just madness, but she could have giggled. For all she had known she might have been living with a child-molester or an adulterer or a rapist. Could have been worse, her husband was only a traitor against his community. She giggled because she remembered the story of

153

Ann Flaherty, gone with Maeve who was her friend, to see her boy sent down for eight years at the court in Belfast for possession of explosives and kidnapping. Eight years, and not past his nineteenth birthday, and Ann Flaherty coming out of the court-house and dabbing her eyes, and her friend Maeve who had travelled up on the bus from Dungannon with her had said, 'Don't be upsetting yourself, dear, could have been worse, could have got eight-een months for thieving . . .' The whole of Altmore knew what Ann Flaherty had been told by her friend Maeve. She should have cried, and her eyes were dry.

His mother minded the kids.

They sat in the shadow of the bar, sheltered from the music and the laughter. He wore his suit, and Siobhan wore her best frock. She shared her Mossie's secret. Sometimes, during the long evening, she put out her hand and gently touched his rough hands. He drank pints of Guinness, fast. She toyed with gins and bitter lemon, slowly.

Men sidled through the noise of the band, came to bend close to her Mossie's ear, ignored her and whispered to him, and moved away.

The secret was now hers, and the weight of it pinioned her. If it were known then Siobhan would be without a husband and Francis and Doloures and Patrick and Mary would be without a father.

The drink going faster and the music louder and the laughter talk fiercer. It was where they were born and where they belonged.

Her secret was that her Mossie was a traitor.

154

She leaned forward. Her lips were against his ear. The noise was a wall around them.

'We don't need their money.'

'They'll never let me go.'

'Tell them you want out.'

'You tell the bitch.'

'Is it just a woman who has you on the end of her string?'

'I tried once . . .'

'What happened?'

'It's not the place to talk . . . What happened? The bitch, she doesn't let go . . .'

The band played. It was the 'Mountains of Pomeroy', it was the song of Altmore mountain. It was the celebration of a highwayman from far back, who had no teeth. Shane Bearnagh Donnelly's song . . . She tugged his hand and pulled him to his feet and took him to the floor that was clear of tables for dancing.

> 'Fear not, fear not, sweetheart,' he cried,
> 'Fear not the foe for me,
> No chain shall fall, whate'er betide,
> On the arm that would be free!
> Oh, leave your cruel kin and come
> When the lark is in the sky;
> And it's with my gun I'll guard you,
> On the Mountains of Pomeroy.'

She sang as she danced. She sang so that he would hear her voice.

> 'An outlawed man in a land forlorn,
> He scorned to turn and fly,

155

But kept the cause of freedom safe
Up on the mountain high.'

She dragged it from him. She must live with his secret. In her arms she felt his fear and his weakness. The secret pounded in the mind of Siobhan Nugent. She thought that she knew every man and woman and youth and girl in the bar. She had been brought up with them, she had lived with them for every year of her life excepting the six that she had spent with Mossie across the water. She knew the tightness of the society that was her home. And her Mossie was a tout . . .

It was not anything that he said, but it was the look of the man. It was the middle of the Sunday afternoon, and they were alone in an underground carriage on the Circle line. It was where they could talk and know that they were not overheard, and where they had the best chance of seeing if there was a tail on either of them. The courier didn't think that the big man had slept, not for two nights at least. He was haggard and unshaven and bowed at the shoulders. It was the first time that the Limerick boy had been in England. He was shocked from the time that he had first seen the big man, shambling down the platform towards him. He had travelled by train through the night from the ferry. His only fear, before, had been when he had to pass the Special Branch officers at Holyhead. And he had walked straight past them and gone to the waiting train. It was the appearance of the man that unnerved the courier. It was like the man was hunted, like the pressure had weighed on him. He had not, of course, been told the man's name, only where he should meet him.

When the courier had arrived at Euston mainline railway station, he had telephoned to Dublin from a pay phone. He had been told what else he should tell the man when he met him. He put off for as long as possible what he had been told to tell the man.

The courier handed him four envelopes. The courier watched the man, dirty hands shaking, open the envelopes and skim with red-rimmed eyes from the first a wad of bank notes, in the second a newly-made birth certificate, in the third a long list of names and addresses and from the last a handwritten letter.

It was what he had been sent to do. Later the courier would stay overnight with his married sister in Wandsworth to solidify his cover, and then travel back to the ferry.

The courier gulped, breathed deep.

'What I was told to tell you . . . was that your home was done again last night, searched by the army. Your woman's alright, and your boy's alright, they said, but there was powerful damage to your home. They said you wasn't to call home.'

He was too young to say that he was sorry for what had happened. He watched the anger in the man's eyes, burning through the tiredness. And then they were coming into a station and the man stood and said, 'Thanks for the letters. Safe journey home, son.'

And then the big man was gone, lost on the platform as the train carried the courier on.

Howard Rennie thought that Cathy must have been shopping around.

157

She'd have preferred her escorts from what he called the Hereford Gun Club, if she could have had them. Must have been turned down or she wouldn't have come to him.

She was frank enough with him, what he'd have expected of her. He was right. Special Air Service had a full programme of stake out and surveillance, couldn't deliver . . . Sunday afternoon they were standing on the doorstep of Rennie's home, his wife was inside buttering the bread for the tea. He was in his carpet slippers and the out-of-shape cardigan, and his pipe nestled in the palm of his hand. He towered over the girl. He'd fix the back-up, of course he would, but only because it was for her. A hell of a way for her to be spending her Sunday. She'd have traipsed round the Hereford crowd, and then she'd have been up to Lisburn to the Headquarters and tried to get a car load or two of the 'Dets' – the army's mob, those Detached to Special Duties – and they would have found a dozen more excuses. Nobody liked Five. Five was a pain in the arse in the Province. Five was the intruder who didn't share, too bloody high and mighty. Hobbes was Five, and Hobbes typified them. But if Cathy asked Rennie, then she'd get her back-up.

She looked bloody awful. She needed a bath and needed a rest and needed half a day in a hairdresser's chair. The pair of them stood on his front doorstep.

There wasn't any point in asking her in to take tea with his wife and daughters. He asked her anyway and she said no, for both of them. Of course she shouldn't have come to his home. She'd just said she was arriving and rung off, and he'd taken his pistol out of the drawer in the living room, slipped it under his coat and walked to the top of the cul-de-sac, and back and quartered the road. She wouldn't come into the hall, hadn't been inside the house since Christmas morning, and then for half an hour and one glass of sherry. She'd declined a place at the lunch table. He didn't know where she had eaten her Christmas lunch.

She was folding the map. It was a great smile she had with her.

When it was dark he'd be in front of his television, probably asleep and perhaps snoring, his wife would be knitting, and Cathy Parker would be out in the bloody jungle, off to meet her tout. His daughters might have stayed in and they might have gone to friends, and Cathy Parker would be chatting up that lump of pig shit they called Song Bird.

'You need a damn good holiday, get the hell out. Go on, get away for a bit. Give yourself a break.'

'Oh yes, Mr Rennie, and where?'

'Anywhere a long way away. Anywhere you can forget all about us.'

'Never seems the right time,' she said.

He played the older man. 'You can't win it on your own . . .'

She'd told him a bit ago, she didn't hold back from him, what it had been like when she had last gone home, and her mother had had a few of the local *better* families round for sherry. Cathy had told him it had been just a super-scale disaster. He doubted she talked with many others, not the way she talked with him, confidences. She'd told him about Sunday morning drinks in the English countryside across the water. All quiet, parked in the corner and watching every new fool and his wife come in and wondering why they had to shout so loud and laugh so much. She had stood away from the window and facing the door, her training. Her mother had dragged her to meet the guests. How was she? Where was she working? Going alright for her, was it? Nothing she could answer . . . and nothing said by her mother and father after the guests had gone, just their unhappiness and anxiety paraded in front of her.

'Leave it to you buggers and we'll never win,' she said.

He laughed with her and closed the door. In the drawer in the hall was the secure phone. He arranged for two back-up cars.

He didn't really think that this was women's work, but then he was only an old-fashioned copper. He settled himself at the end of his table and ate his tea.

She had followed him round the bungalow. All he had told her was that he was going to be out in the evening. She followed him round like she knew he was going to see the handler. He could have counted the words she had said to him that day on the fingers of one hand, and his mother had never stopped her bleating, and Francis had kicked Doloures on the knee, as if to show that he was affected by the strain between his father and mother.

If he went into the bedroom then she followed him. If he went into the sitting room to sit down in his chair then she was hovering behind him. If he went out into the back garden to fill the basket with wood for the fire then she was waiting halfway down the path for him.

160

It was as if she didn't believe him, was waiting for him to say that it hadn't been real, just a feckin' nightmare.

Mossie had just gone into the bedroom to change his shoes, put on a clean shirt, when the doorbell rang. He heard the voices, and his name called.

Patsy Riordan was in the doorway.

The boy was always used for messages.

It was how it would end, he knew that . . . It would end with a call to a meeting . . . It was what they always did . . . They called the tout to a meeting, and they kicked him inside and they had the hood over his head, the tout's head, and the twine round his wrists, the tout's wrists, and the beating would start . . . That was how it would end.

'Yeah, no problem, tell him I'll be right down.'

A few minutes later he was gone out into the night and Siobhan had followed him right to the car.

Her father was down with his drill to get the shelves back on the walls. Her mother, with a needle and strong thread, worked to repair the ripped fabric of the chairs. Melvin had been and gone, satisfied himself that the wiring in the roof had not been damaged. Mrs Rea, from the far end of the village, had brought new plates and new mugs, her own spares. Gerry Brannigan had hammered the floorboards down hard where they had been lifted, and muttered all the time that, so help him, the 'boys' would make the bastards pay for this. Help poured through her door, comfort was Attracta's company, and the priest after Mass had held her hand longer than usual and then put the same hand on Kevin's shoulder and called him a fine young fellow, and smiled on mother and son.

Now Attracta laughed.

It was the first time she had laughed, smiled even, since the soldiers had been.

The whole of Altmore laughed with old Sean Hegarty.

Two plastic hip joints, and a waddling walk, Hegarty had breezed into the farmhouse half hidden by the television set he carried. Up in his barn over the crest of the mountain Hegarty stored enough appliances to fit out half of a new housing estate.

'Is the cooker working, missus, did the feckers break the cooker?'

'Cooker's fine, Sean.'

''Cos I've cookers when you need one.'

'Not this time, Sean.'

If she'd wanted a tumble drier, she had only to ask. If the refrigerator was damaged, she had only to say. Hegarty would have it. She laughed out loud.

Hegarty was the most popular man on the mountain, no doubts. He could bring down from his barn the oldest and dirtiest cooker, and if he was asked he had the skills to make it spark like it was a death trap. Not last year, would have been the year before, Hegarty had carried around his pride and joy, his very worst cooker. Fourteen families had taken in the cooker in the one twelve-month, and then gone down to the Department of Social Security in Dungannon, and demanded the Inspector come out, and had received the grant for a new cooker. The Inspector had caught on after seeing the cooker only twice, but he didn't want his car torched so he signed the grant papers. The original cooker back in place, Hegarty back up the mountain with his filthy dirty cooker; money for the bar and the horses or for a deposit on a new car.

It was said that Hegarty was the best-read man on the mountain, and not a day of college education in him, and that when he could be bothered, he went down to the priest's house and beat the man at chess.

She made tea for all those who were in the house and helping her. Jon Jo's name was never spoken. It was Attracta's surprise that kind Mossie Nugent had not been back that day.

As the darkness fell across the mountain she waved them all away from her door. Her parents, and Mrs Rea and Gerry Brannigan, and Sean Hegarty. Hegarty tweaked her cheek with his sharp fingers.

'There'll be an answer for this, Missus, there'll be a debt paid.' She kissed the rough stubble of his cheek.

Attracta shut the door, she leaned back against it, her eyes were closed. Kevin was beside her, not touching her and not crying. Kevin had never cried since his father had gone away. She yearned for Jon Jo's return . . . God forgive her, and she yearned for the body of a soldier, dead, torn, bleeding, brought to her door as payment.

They were in the shed at the back of the Riordan house, where Jimmy Riordan kept his caged canaries.

The OC paced as he talked, and twice when he faced away Nugent had stolen a glance down at the watch on his wrist, because time was running out.

The OC talked fast.

'. . . If there's a tout here then they'll think we'll lie

163

down. They'll think we'll go to ground. It's the best time to hit them, you with me, Mossie? There's a 50-calibre coming up from Monaghan. Look at the map, see, we can get inside the house and we're right across from the barracks. The big house in the barrracks is where they're at for lunch. And the beauty of it is, the house is right in the middle of the estate, what's they going to fire back at? You and me knows, no other beggar. No-one else has the picture, Mossie. The lads who do the shooting, the drivers, they won't have the target and the routes out until my say so. You'll be in charge of the house, Mossie. Just you and me, Mossie, we're the only ones who'll know. Tight as a duck's arse, that's how it'll be. You with me? . . .' The door opened.

Patsy Riordan came in. He smiled. He held two mugs of tea. He put the mugs on the bench where his father kept the canary seed. He let himself out.

There was the OC's savage glance at the closing door. 'How long was that little bastard there . . . ?'

Fifteen minutes later and Mossie was away, driving fast because he was late.

There were two unmarked cars assigned, three men to each car. They were parked up now. There was a disused quarry near McCready's Corner off the Armagh road. The radios of both cars were tuned to the frequency that had been given them. They knew the drill. One car was north of the quarry in the direction of Blackwater town, the second car was off the winding lanes to Ballytroddan, to the west. The policemen, heavy in their anoraks and waterproofs, smoked in the cars. No talk. To have talked might

164

have meant missing the call on the radio frequency. They *thought* the quarry was secure. They had driven past it twice, each of them, and they had cruised the lanes and seen nothing that was suspicious. It was part of the work of the E4 section of the RUC that they should provide back-up for handlers out in the night to meet a player. The engines turned over quietly. It would have taken the one car four minutes to reach the quarry if the handlers' panic button had gone, it would have taken the second car forty seconds longer. Tense, quiet, waiting.

Bren had heard the car a long way off, coming at speed.

The bastard had not shown. Because Bren was frightened then Song Bird was the bastard. He hated to be afraid, had done all his life.

Bren had pulled the Browning from his pocket, checked the safety. A black and cold night, rain in the air, and Cathy's hand had fallen on his wrist and she had muttered that it was Song Bird's car, she knew it was Song Bird's car because she could hear the distributor problem and the missing of the engine. The car had swept into the quarry, too fast, and skidded to a halt, and for a moment he and Cathy had been lit by the headlamps. He'd cringed and she'd cursed when the light beam had found them. The lights had died, the engine had been cut.

She had gone forward, Bren had been left beside their own car. He was conscious of the tautness of his arm that held the Browning.

She was ten, twelve, paces from him. Bren could see the outline of their bodies. The man seemed to dwarf

Cathy. Bren's arm was rigid at his side, the Browning was clamped in his hand. He couldn't hear what was said. The wind swirled down from the dead bracken above the quarry.

'Come here, come on.'

Her sharp command.

He went forward.

He was blinded by her torch light. The beam was straight into his face. He held the pistol behind his back. Then the darkness again, and he blinked to find his vision.

'That's him, got the face? That's Gary. Gary, this is Song Bird.'

Bren couldn't shake hands, if that had been the proper thing to do, because he had a Browning pistol in his hand.

Cathy said quietly, 'You want me and I'm not on the line then you'll get Gary.'

'If you say so.'

'It's what I say . . . What's the bloody fidgeting about? You need to piss, then get on with it.'

The soft Irish of the country voice. 'I want an answer, I want to know how long.'

Cathy said gently, 'As long as I say, Song Bird, that's how long.'

'It's my neck . . .'

Cathy whispered, 'Fuck me about, and I promise it'll be your neck.'

'What I told Siobhan, you're a hard bitch.'

Cathy chuckled, 'Always had a way with words, didn't you, Mossie?'

'What I told Siobhan . . .'

'Shut up, Mossie . . .' She had turned to Bren. 'He's

166

been crying on his Missus' shoulder. Good thing or bad thing? Take time to tell. She'll have told him to quit . . .'

'Don't you understand anything, *Miss*?'

Cathy had her hand up in front of his face. Bren watched. The snap was in her voice. She would count the points off on her fingers. 'One, you've nowhere to go without my say so, if you quit and run then they'll find you, nut you. Two, you're damn well paid, and you will continue to be well paid, and you're set up for the future when I agree you can split. Three, you mess me and you're into Crumlin Road court, and PIRA intelligence officers tend to be looking at twelve years minimum. Four, you've missed the amnesty and don't forget it, you go and ask for your own crowd's protection and tell them you're sorry, you wouldn't last a week, and when you're pushing up daisies the lovely Siobhan and your kids will be ostracized with a traitor's stain. Five . . .' Her finger yanked at her thumb, '. . . Five, you know I'll look after you, Mossie, you know with me you're safe.'

He was sheepish, she'd clattered the fight out of him. 'So what do I do?'

'What I've told you to do, just that. And you wear the bloody clothes I've told you to wear.'

Bren listened. He understood only a little of what was said. They talked names and places, sharp questions from Cathy, rambling answers from Song Bird. He could make little of it. The names were Attracta Donnelly and Vinny Devitt, and Patsy Riordan with mugs of tea, and the Brannigan kid. There was OC and QM. Talk of a hide being dug that would hold a flame-thrower if they could get it up

167

from the south . . . She dominated Song Bird. She could make him laugh and she could make him cower. Song Bird was Cathy's marionette . . .

She had him in the palm of her hand. At the end, the bastard thanked her.

He was gone, his car coughing away into the darkness.

Two miles down the road, when she told him to, Bren used the radio to pull off the back-up cars.

Bren said, 'You were pretty hard on him.'

She turned her head away, as if she didn't want to hear him. 'Just trying to keep him alive.'

Chapter Eight

He watched the major ease back into his chair. The map of the operation plan that he had drawn was left on the easel. The Assistant Under-Secretary knew all their names, bar the one. Hobbes, scratching the side of his face. The Assistant Chief Constable, making his notes. The colonel of Army Intelligence, paring his nails. Howard Rennie, gazing out of the window. The young woman was the only outsider, and she stared throughout at the ceiling.

The Assistant Under-Secretary of the Northern Ireland Office tilted his head to see the map better through his bifocal spectacles.

The Special Air Service always drew good plans. There was the Killyman Road where it ran out of Dungannon towards Maghery. Below the road was drawn the web of streets of the housing estate. Above the road was the shaded line marking the perimeter fence, and the square block in red was the old house round which the barracks had been built. It was a good map and it had been a concise briefing.

The question before the Task Co-ordinating Group was whether to sanction the plan. The final approval rested with the Assistant Under-Secretary.

The young woman had made no contribution to the meeting, and twice had to conceal her yawns. Rennie had started to excavate the bowl of his pipe and used his coffee saucer for the debris. The major sat patiently, his arms folded. The Assistant Chief Constable and the colonel, wily and experienced men, were content to wait on the Assistant Under-Secretary.

He shuffled his papers. All their eyes were on him now.

'Isn't there another way . . . ?' His voice was high-pitched, sibilant.

They gave him no help. It was only the fourth time that he had sat in on Task Co-ordinating Group. They seemed to mock him, the Assistant Chief Constable and the colonel, as if he were merely squeamish. The major met his questioning glance and didn't respond, as if *his* job was completed. Every time there was an ambush shooting his Secretary of State was forced onto the defensive. Rennie, billowing smoke from his new-filled pipe, screened himself. A community worker had told him recently that Special Air Service ambushes were the best recruiting sergeant the Provisionals had. The man from Five, Hobbes, looked back at him, through him, as if no possible alternative existed to the action that was proposed.

There was this young woman sitting behind the man from Five.

'. . . There is always an alternative way, surely?' The Assistant Under-Secretary fixed on her. She was yawning again. He thought she yawned because she was tired, not because she was bored. She was appallingly dressed. A skirt that was too short, a hideous mauve blouse, a cardigan that was too large, and a handbag in which he could comfortably have hidden his briefcase. He had not been introduced at the start of the meeting. Clearly not a secretary because she had no paper, no pencil, just a rather lovely smile that went with the yawn. Like his own niece, who'd back-packed round Australia, who couldn't abide . . .

She looked at her watch, said decisively, 'No, there isn't.'

'I beg your pardon . . .'

She said brusquely, 'There is no other way.'

What he had wanted was for the debate to start. Debate he could influence. He turned away from her. 'I think we might explore alternatives. We are looking, after all, at a situation in which lives are . . .'

'Listen . . .'

He turned sharply to face her.

'*Please*, don't interrupt me . . .'

'I said for you to listen.'

He saw that her eyes were a very pale shade of blue. He thought her hair to be truly golden. She had a clear voice, not loud and not hectoring. He felt afraid of her.

She said, 'I'm what's called a handler, I handle an informer. Are you with me? My informer is always at risk, and my greatest priority is to protect that man. There is going to be a heavy-calibre machine-gun attack tomorrow on the Dungannon barracks. My informer is going to be a part of that attack. His boss – that's the Officer Commanding East Tyrone brigade – knows the exact time, and the place. My informer also knows the time and the place. There is a strong suspicion in the East Tyrone Brigade of an informer in their ranks . . . therefore the OC will not brief the remaining members of the active service unit until the last moment. To protect himself my informer must go through with the attack.

'So explore your alternatives to our proposal . . . We can do nothing. We can allow PIRA to take over the home of a 71-year-old woman and blast the daylights out of the camp, and have them laugh themselves sick at our lack of preparedness. Or we can set up road-blocks round the town. That will cause them to abort, hold another inquest, check who knew, identify and eliminate my informer. Or we can watch them into the house, surround it, lay siege to it, starve them out and arrest them all, in which case my informer goes to prison where he is of little use to me . . . Or, we can let matters run their course, as outlined to you. I cannot agree to anything that jeopardizes my informer.'

The Assistant Under-Secretary looked round the table for support, and found none. He saw the fresh skin of the young woman's face, and the eyes that showed no doubt. He assumed she used so large a handbag the better to conceal a firearm. He believed he saw a young woman of quite terrifying certainty, and that he was watched by every one of the men round the table for his weakness and for his strength.

He said, 'You want my blessing for the killing of three, or four, young men . . .'

No emotion, no drama. 'I want a guarantee that my informer will not be put at risk, which is to say identified as such, tortured for all he knows, and shot. Any alternative you choose will do just that. Cost him his life and the security services a priceless asset.'

His voice was a whisper. He saw Rennie, the big policeman whom he thought to be an honest man, lean forward and cup his ear. He felt quite sick. 'I never thought to have such hateful power. So be it.'

Rennie carried the tray with the coffees that he had poured.

He passed the cup and saucer, and the sugar.

Hobbes said, 'I thought that went rather well . . . Thank you, Howard . . . Very well, in fact. Such a change when we're not at each other's throats.'

Rennie said, smiling wickedly, 'Don't delude yourself. You got a soft ride because the common enemy was in attendance. If the big man from Stormont hadn't been there I'd have had you on the floor squealing for mercy. There's no love on our side for your cowboy operations, Mr Hobbes. Best you remember it. It's just that an idiot like the Stormont fellow closes ranks . . . and Cathy did well . . .'

'I told her she shouldn't come dressed as a navvy. Impertinent young woman.'

'She's your jewel, perhaps the best reason we have for tolerating you.'

'What do you think is the prospect', Hobbes asked with studied politeness, 'of your being able to raise, for example, a biscuit?'

The Assistant Under-Secretary reported back to his Secretary of State. The Secretary of State expected to be told when a major stake-out was in place.

'She was quite extraordinary, really. Only a slip of a thing. Verbally, she picked me up, shook me, then put me gently back in my chair. I'll try to think of it as

173

part of my learning process. When I was at Trade and Industry, if any young woman, any woman at all, dammit, had spoken to me like that then she'd have been looking for a new career later the very same day. She talked me through her world of informers. It has been in my mind all the way back here that some poor devil out there, in that cruel wilderness, is the pawn of that young woman. His life must be one long terror . . . She certainly terrified me and I'm on the same side, at least I think I was. I'm not proud of myself, but I acquiesced . . .'

It was the third time that Jon Jo Donnelly had read the letter.

There was no signature, only the typewritten legend, the name of a man who had gone to the gallows in a British gaol more than fifty years before. The first time he had merely read it, hardly taking it in. The second time he had boiled with anger, checked himself with difficulty from tearing and burning the pages. The third time he felt only overwhelming lone-liness. The people below, the young couple from Cork, were watching their television. It was out of the question that he should go downstairs and talk with them, look for their companionship.

He was alone. It was the new way, men operating alone, the control of risk.

They had no feckin' right, not from Dublin, to write that first page, that first part.

'. . . We have to demand that greater care is taken on all operations carried out in our name. Very large resources are allocated for the operations inside the British mainland, necessitating cut-backs in funds for the many commitments that burden us. The families of men imprisoned in the twenty-six counties and the six counties suffer considerable privations, and it is essential that those families believe that money allocated to the Organization's overseas active service units is not wasted money.

'We regard the South London attack as a disaster. The deaths of two small girls have caused us to face widespread criticism at home, and given our enemy a capital propaganda coup. Such errors cannot be condoned. We understand the difficulties of operating on the mainland but require much greater care in pressing home the attack on the nominated target.

'Sadly we have been given further occasion for complaint. The shooting of Beck was unsatisfactory. Each time that we fail to execute a member of the Crown forces we provide the enemy with the opportunity to ridicule us. We expect greater resolution in the carrying out of attacks. The Crown forces oppressing our people in the six counties are ruthless in the murder of volunteers. We should be no less determined when we strike back at them . . .'

The men in Dublin had no greater worry, Jon Jo thought, than whether or not they had lost a police tail. They risked nothing. They never carried firearms. They never had to scrub, fast, the explosives traces from their bodies. They had their women waiting for them. They had the bar on the corner. No man in Dublin was as alone as he was.

'. . . As to targets: every target must have a national profile. The execution of an army recruiting officer is forgotten by the British public within hours. The British are a complacent and apolitical

175

race, if they are not shocked they are not interested.

'Brighton they will not forget. Downing Street will be remembered for years to come. Future targets will be selected on the basis of their capacity to damage the enemy's security system . . . Railway stations, airports, and defence installations are to be given priority . . . We are investigating the further supply of mortars and of RPG7s. Progress has been made in the use of lasers to detonate pre-placed explosives . . . The graves of many martyrs cry etcetera, etcetera.'

It was just cow shit. Some of the targets on the list were downright suicide. Did they want him dead? Is that what they wanted? Him in a box and the big crowd walking behind to the church on Altmore? More feckin' use to them dead, was he?

Did they want to write a song about him, was that it?

> 'The radio said
> There was another shot dead
> And he died with a gun in his hand,
> But it didn't say why
> Billy Reid had to die . . .
> He died to free Ireland.'

Billy Reid, volunteer, shot dead 15th May 1971, and there was a Billy Reid Commemoration each year, and a Billy Reid Memorial Band. There would be a Jon Jo Donnelly flute and pipe band, for Jon Jo Donnelly dead.

Just not possible, most of what the list called for. Secret Intelligence Service, Century House. Security

Service, Curzon Street. Ministry of Defence, main building. Just not possible for Jon Jo. Director General, GCHQ, Cheltenham. Chief of the General Staff. Oh, yes, certainly. Should be able to manage that. Shouldn't be more than a twenty-four-hour guard twelve deep for one of those. Commissioner of the Metropolitan Police. Head of the Civil Service. Possible for an arsehole sitting in Dublin and writing cow shit . . .

Alone in his room in the house in northeast London, the unlovely, uncomforting room. Attracta was in his mind, and his boy.

He stood up, turned out the light and opened the curtain. He saw her, and he thought she was white-faced and too proud to weep as the home they had made together was wrecked. He saw that she held little Kevin against her body. It was what he had brought upon her. The smashing of her home.

Jon Jo worked at the list, to find what was possible.

It was Bren's second day in the office. The office was an offshoot of the Department of the Environment. He had been allocated a room on the second floor at the back of a new building that was called Progress House. Room 2/63/B was protected by a Chubb lock in addition to a Yale lock. Hobbes had introduced him to a manager, explained that Mr Brennard was the new representative of Audit and Cash Flow Control from London. Any file he wished to see, it would be provided. The manager was plainly anxious to have nothing to do with him. He gave him one swift look, hostility and nervousness mingled, and closed the door on him. For the second day, Bren had studied the new Downpatrick sewage scheme and the proposed extension of the dual carriageway out of Strabane, and the proposed revision of the salary structure for clerical workers at the Department's main office.

His room was a model of Civil Service Spartan. His table, his chair, and two more chairs under the venetian blind which was drawn down over the window. There was a map of Northern Ireland all over one wall, a calendar beside the door, above a hip-high wall safe. On a shelf behind his chair were three telephones, one black, one green, and one white. Song Bird's line, the switchboard's line, and the third one, which was purring at him.

'Yes?'

'Me, out the main door, turn left, 150 yards or so, same side, a bus stop. I'll pick you up in twenty minutes, the Astra.'

Bren took the Browning pistol from the safe and tucked it into the back of his waist. He took his anorak from the hook on the door.

He sat again in his chair. Every five minutes he checked his watch. It was what he wanted, more than anything he knew, to be with Cathy Parker.

Twenty minutes after her call, to the minute, she drew up at the bus stop. He smiled his surprise at her. She looked terrific.

He shouted, 'Where's my red coat?' It had been on the hook beside the front door the night before, it was not there now.

His mother was close to him, getting the older children ready for school. She eyed him. Must have been needling her, sensing there was crisis between the two of them and not knowing the cause of it.

Siobhan called, 'It's dirty.'

'I wants it.'

'It's for the wash.'

'Shit, woman, I want my red coat.'

He saw Francis, his satchel over his shoulders, back away from him, and Doloures watched him with a coldness because she was her mother's child and schooled to despise obscenity.

Siobhan came out of the kitchen. She carried a crumpled red anorak, and there were dirt stains on it and paint smears.

'There's your coat, if it's important to you to look like a tinker . . .'

'It is.'

It was past the time he was usually gone when he was going to work, so she would have known that he was ducking out, and he'd said that he wasn't taking the kids to school. She threw him the coat to catch.

Siobhan flounced past him and threw on her own winter coat, and she picked up little Mary and pushed Francis and Doloures and Patrick out through the door, slammed it after her. His mother went into the kitchen. He leaned against the wall in the hallway and the emotion boiled in him. He heard Siobhan's car starting up, reluctantly, outside. He didn't know whether he would see the kids again, and he hadn't said goodbye to them.

Fear and helplessness welled in him. He was trapped by the bitch. He could remember the first time . . .

They had been four years in England. Francis was born, and Doloures. Patrick was started. A good little

179

business going, a fresh start, and more on the black than shown to the Revenue. A painter/decorator business in Acocks Green in Birmingham. Doing his own thing and also called in by the big builders, plenty of work and the past buried. Coming back late, drink taken, and waved down by the feckin' coppers. Blood test, urine test, three times over. He had a bank loan on the van and a mortgage on their brick-built home, two bedrooms and a back garden and perfect. He could work out what had happened. They'd a Paddy in the cells, and they'd pumped his name into the computer. Booked him on Drunk in Charge, then held him on the Prevention of Terrorism. All spilled out by the computer. 1974, five years, possession of a Luger pistol and Thompson sub-machine gun, Belfast Crown Court. 1979, three years, conspiracy to cause explosions, Dublin Special Criminal Court. Less than frank, they'd said, with the building society. Less than honest, they'd told him, with the bank. Big trouble . . . He was looking at a driving ban, the calling in of his mortgage, the winding up of his loan, plus an exclusion order. She'd come to the cell, the third day. Very quiet, just business, none of the swagger and bully of the detectives. She'd worn a navy suit. She'd had a typed-up exclusion order and the drunk-in-charge paperwork in her hand. She had stood in front of him, torn them both up, and gone to the lavatory and flushed them away. He could remember it still, the way that he had feckin' dribbled his thanks to her. He'd eat from the bitch's hand, then, now. They had walked out of the police station and left behind the detectives and the desk sergeant, and she'd looked at the lot of them as if they were beneath her contempt.

In a café down the road, over two cups of tea that she paid for, she had told him she would be in touch, said she'd see him. A small smile on her face, like she'd know where to find him.

Vinny drove.

Jacko from Pomeroy was in the passenger seat, and Malachy from Coalisland was in the back with Mossie.

Vinny thought it downright daft to wear a bright red coat, the sort that couldn't help but be noticed. But he was only Vinny Devitt, the driver, and Mossie Nugent was the big cat . . . Not for Vinny to ask why.

They went up the mountain first, to the derelict barn that was screened by a conifer plantation. No talking in the car, the talking would be when it was over, time then for the laughter and the cheering and the unzipped excitement.

At the barn they collected the gun from the OC and the Quartermaster. It was for Jacko, and Malachy would feed the belt. Easy enough for Vinny to see that Jacko and Malachy knew the weapon, bloody great heavy thing . . . It was the first that Vinny knew of the plan, and Jacko and Malachy. They were talked through it by the OC.

There was an old bedspread in the barn, pink flowers on yellow, and they wrapped the 50-calibre in it and carried it back to the car.

All of them quiet in the car when Vinny drove back onto the road that ran down the mountain from Altmore.

*   *   *

One of them had a beard that covered his throat. One of them had long greased hair onto his shoulders. One of them looked to be from the Pacific islands, perhaps Fijian. One of them was the cardboard city man. They all knew Cathy.

Bren watched from the colonel's office. It was her world and not his. There was no tension in the room. The colonel had gone because it was not his world either. The plan was on the colonel's desk with the coffee cups and the plate of biscuits and the ashtray that was already filled.

She hadn't talked about it in the car, just told him to drive to Dungannon, said what time they were expected, allowed him to get on with the job of reaching the barracks on her schedule.

They were planning a killing. That was their world and Cathy was a part of it. The world was Cathy and the calm light of her eyes, and it was four men wearing bulky black overalls and woollen caps that were folded up and could be pulled down for balaclavas.

No fuss and no hurry. Time to pour more coffee.

Bren knew they had been in the Colonel's office for hours because the room was fogged with cigarette smoke. On the floor, discarded amongst the big olive green backpacks, was the all-in anthology of the Complete Works of William Shakespeare, open now at Act Two, Scene Two, *King Lear*.

Bren saw that she was not interrupted. She was part of their territory, as if by right . . . Bren wondered if it were just because she was a woman, or how it was that she had earned the respect of those hard men. Hard? Of course they were bloody hard. They were going out killing with no more fuss than Bren managed when he was off down to Mr Manjrekar's corner store with his weekend shopping list. He wondered whether Mr Wilkins had the least notion of what was planned that morning, and whether Hobbes sat beside a telephone and waited for news.

He just wanted to be a part of her world, and share the light and warmth of her as did these four men.

Cathy said, '. . . He's wearing the red coat, that's what we agreed. He'd bloody well better be wearing it. He's a dozy slob, but I think he took it on board. So just don't spoil my day, there's good darlings, just don't forget that it's a red coat, and if, God help us, they turn up in Pink Panther suits, my man is heavy, he's big, he's late thirties, going bald at the back, and he limps. And we don't shoot limping grouse, do we? Not out of season, anyway, eh, David?'

Nothing flamboyant, not theatrical. None of the leadership crap, and nothing that was an excuse for feminine softness. She was amongst her own.

Cathy said quietly, 'Good luck.'

The semi-detached and whitewashed houses climbed the hill to the west of the Killyman Road. The barracks on the far hill, across the road, across the rough ground, behind the steel perimeter fence, dominated the estate. Smoke from living-room fires pushed from the chimneys. A child played in the road in front of his house with a tricycle. A doctor hurried back to his car. A baby, tightly blanketed in its pram, bawled with healthy lungs. A woman put down her heavy shopping bag, reached for her house keys. A young man walked to the newsagents for cigarettes, went slowly because he had time to kill and no work to go to. The estate ignored the soldiers who looked down at them from the watchtowers of the barracks, didn't speak to the soldiers when they patrolled through the back streets.

Mrs Byrne hung out her washing and didn't think much of the chances of it drying.

It was the Donnelly woman at the door.

Siobhan forced the smile, and she took the eggs. She said that it was so kind of her to think of them for fresh eggs again, they tasted so much better, didn't they, than the eggs from the shops. She enquired, caringly, whether the house was repaired. She told her that her Mossie had been busy, so busy, that was why he hadn't been round to help her with the house repairs.

Siobhan didn't ask her inside. She took the eggs on the doorstep. She was alone in the house and it was the way she wanted it. Grandma was gone walking Mary in the pushchair. Too great a confusion for Siobhan Nugent to invite her neighbour in for a cup of tea and a gossip about whose daughter was pregnant, whose son had found work, whose father was taken sick, whose uncle had gone bankrupt . . . Too great a confusion because of her husband . . . She closed the door.

She went back inside. Too great a confusion for her. Her Mossie a tout, and her Mossie was gone today without explanation. After she had come back from the school, Siobhan had listened to every news bulletin on the BBC . . . coming close to one o'clock. One day it was going to be on the radio . . .

*   *   *

There were two in the ditch on the east side of the Killyman Road, where the brambles grew across the banks, hiding them. There were two in the car parked between two blocks of garages at the top of the estate.

All the men could see the front door of Mrs Byrne's house, in the first row of houses that faced the barracks.

No chat, no cigarettes.

They were readied, the guns were armed.

Mossie Nugent's mother's cousin lived in the second line of houses. It was the sort of estate that he thought Siobhan might have wanted to live on, if they had not been so far down the Housing Executive list, if they had not had to live with his mother.

Vinny Devitt was driving . . . They had come the long way, down to Edendork, then back towards Dungannon on the country road that would bring them to Killyman Road about opposite the road into the estate. Jacko not able to stop talking, yapping louder and faster the closer they came to the estate. Malachy breathing harder, like he'd a blockage. Vinny missing two gear changes, as if he were first time on a driving test. Mossie shared the back seat with Jacko and the 50-calibre that was wrapped in the old bedspread, pink flowers on yellow . . . Devitt, driving like the little arsehole he was, turning into the estate.

Pretty quiet 'cos it was lunchtime. Lunchtime in the officers' mess across the Killyman Road and up the hill.

Mossie pulled the snub-barrelled pistol from his pocket, held it against his chest. His hands sweated inside the thin rubber gloves.

185

'You right, Malachy? Vinny?'

Jacko quiet. Malachy heaving breath. Vinny Devitt pulling on the brake.

A dozen paces from the car to Mrs Byrne's front door. Number 17. Mossie felt his flesh shiver inside the quilting of the anorak. He climbed out. He walked, stiff-legged, from the car to the door of Mrs Byrne's. On the pavement, outside her door by the young cherry tree, he looked right and he looked left, and he saw no one. It was lunchtime. He held the pistol hidden inside the anorak. He looked behind him. Three white faces in the car staring back at him . . . Shit, and there was a car coming down the road, maybe 100 yards away, should be in and out of sight by the time it got level. Remembering what the bitch had said to him. Didn't know when, didn't know from where. Trying to remember each last word the bitch had said to him . . . He rang the bell. Christ, and he wanted to piss. They had both doors part open behind him, ready to come running when he bullocked inside, and he could see Jacko's legs half out and the jutted tip of the old bedspread, pink flowers on yellow. Wait till the car is past, you daft buggers . . . Taking her time, Mrs goddamn Byrne. He tucked the pistol further into his anorak and turned his back on the road. He'd bundle her back in. His job, to watch Mrs goddamn Byrne, while Devitt stayed in the car, while Jacko and Malachy put the 50-calibre up in the front bedroom.

'Who's wanting me?'

He spun. She was a tiny woman, nothing to her, at the side of the house, holding a big plastic basket of washing.

It was because he had turned, because he faced up

the road and into the estate, that he saw two men jump from the car stopped on the road.

The frozen moment . . .

Mossie looked up the road. Two men spilling from a car, black overalls, black balaclavas, black short-barrel rifles. Jacko, his back to the men, bent under the weight of the old bedspread, and Malachy halfway round the car to help him. Mrs Byrne piping, 'What's you wanting . . . ?'

He turned again. There were two more men, dark dressed, coming up the road, threatening, into the estate, armed.

The first shots.

Nugent wheeling, spinning.

The windscreen in front of Devitt frosted, then holed, then disintegrated. Vinny Devitt's head, gone.

He was holding the pistol out in front of his chest, and the tiny woman heaved the washing basket at him. There was a shirt snagged on his shoulders and a pair of knickers falling from the red material of his anorak. He threw the pistol at Mrs Byrne and ran.

Jacko was on his back, and writhing, and the bedspread that was half across him and the weight of the heavy machine gun pinioned him. He never saw Malachy.

A shot clattered into the masonry above him. He ran past the front of the next house. Another shot. He half tripped on low wire dividing two front gardens, stumbled, regained his balance. The whine of a ricochet going off the pavement and by him. He turned into the path between the houses. His ears were deafened. His eyes were misted. He charged through a dug vegetable garden, slithering. No more

187

shots, not since he had found the cover of the houses. He launched himself at the garden's back fence, battered his way through it. There was open waste ground ahead of him.

Mossie ran as fast as his damaged hip allowed.

He ran for his life and the red anorak billowed from his body.

Bren saw it all from the watchtower.

He was back from the firing slit, behind the sentry. Cathy was beside him, reaching onto her toes for the height she needed and peering through binoculars.

Bren could hear the shots.

It was a tableau in front of him. It was a grandstand view. He felt as though he had been hammered with a fist into the pit of his stomach. There was just the bile taste in his mouth.

He looked straight through the broken windscreen of the car and he could see the slumped head of the driver. He looked past the offside of the car and he could see the young fellow, jeans and denim jacket, lying still on his stomach. He looked past the nearside of the car and he could see the thrashing arms of the third man. He looked past the car and he could see the two soldiers walking easily down the slope of the hill, their weapons at their shoulders. No haste, no urgency. And there were two more soldiers jogging up the road to meet them, one circling, still jogging, backwards, to cover behind them. But there was no movement, it seemed, anywhere in the estate, not even a door slammed. One of the soldiers bent over the man on the ground at the nearside of the car, then lifted the cloth beside the man, lifted it away from a heavy machine gun by the look of it. The soldier crouched once more over the man. Bren heard the shot.

The helicopter was already in the air, coming low over the watchtower, deafening the peace.

Bren yelled, 'Are you satisfied . . . ?'

Cathy didn't raise her voice. 'It was to protect the source.'

'Is any source worth that, bloody tell me?'

She lowered the binoculars. She looked him square in the eyes. 'The source is worth everything.'

The helicopter perched in the grassy patch beside the Killyman Road. The four soldiers loped towards its open door. The bodies they left behind them.

The fight had gone from him. He swayed on his feet. He felt her hand at his elbow. Cathy steadied him.

'How far will you go to protect the source?'

'As far as it takes,' Cathy said.

Chapter Nine

Through the wall behind the bed-head he heard his mother's coughing. Her chest was worse this winter. At the foot of the bed he heard their little Mary shifting in her sleep.

He lay on his back. He stared up into the blackness. The best years of their lives, his and Siobhan's, had been before the bitch had her nails in him. They were good years in Birmingham. In the same bed, shipped back with all their furniture, he had told his Siobhan that it was necessary for them to return to Ireland. She had cried and submitted. He thought that she had come back with him because she had no other choice. She was hard against him, his arm slipped gently around her shoulder.

'You's alright . . . ?' He had thought she was asleep.

'Course I'm bloody alright.'

'You's alive . . .'

He was alive because he was the bitch's toy thing. And Vinny Devitt, who wasn't, was in the mortuary of the South Tyrone (General) Hospital, with Jacko and Malachy.

'Why didn't they shoot you?'

190

'I'm precious, because I'm precious to the bitch.'

'Did you's think they'd shoot you?'

'I was wearing the red coat.'

'You weren't shot because they'd told you what to wear?'

'Why I had to have the red coat.'

'You's important to them?'

'It's what the bitch says.'

'Will you get more money?'

'I gets one hundred and twenty-five pounds a week. I gets five hundred pounds a month. I gets six thousand pounds a year. That's what I get . . .'

'How long does you get the money?'

'Till I'm no more use to the bitch, till the trap's closed.'

'How long's that?'

'For feck's sake, I don't know . . .'

'You'll be waking Mary. Why was they killed today?'

His mother hacked her cough again. He could hear the fire dying in the sitting room, the last spit of damp wood.

'To protect me.'

'Three men . . . ?'

'To keep me alive.'

'Keep you alive?'

'So I survive, that's what three men died for, so I live to tout another day.'

'Is you frightened, Mossie . . . ?'

Always the fear was with him. The fear crept with him to the bed. The fear stalked him when he pasted wallpaper and painted. The fear bit at him when he went to the meetings with his OC, and when he went to meetings with his handlers. The fear was with him when he kicked the plastic football on the back grass patch for Francis, and when he dressed Doloures, and when he cuddled Patrick, and when he cut little Mary's food for her. He was never without the fear.

'I don't know how to leave it, the fear . . .'

'Leave it behind you?'

'I don't know how to.'

'Is you more frightened of your own people, or of them?'

'No difference, both bleeding me, and no going back.'

'When could you have gone back?'

'Doesn't matter, too long ago . . .'

Yeah, great, Mossie Nugent could have told the redhead to go feck herself . . . Could have had his driving ban, and his mortgage recalled and his bank loan revoked, could have been put on the ferry boat with his exclusion order. No vehicle and couldn't work, bank loan revoked and debt, mortgage called in and bankruptcy, exclusion order served and home to the north where every man knew that the names of those served with the Prevention of Terrorism Act exclusion order were slipped to the Proddie bastard murder squads. He'd thought of that scene, over and over. He had thought he was going to get a beating and he'd found himself thanking the bitch. Oh yeah, that was too long ago.

He had gone home, had told Siobhan it was a mistake, all sorted. Three months later, going down the shop for fags, hadn't recognized her at first, old jeans and scruffy anorak. All she needed was that he drink at a certain pub, that he watch a certain man.

Regular meetings, and then the suggestion that he should sell up, take his family home . . . too late then to go back. Returned to Altmore mountain, bumping into her in Irish Street, and the note passed with her scribbled telephone number, and the money . . . too late then to go back.

'Would you like me to make you a pot of tea?'

'It'd be good.'

'I's with you, Mossie. It'll be easier now.'

He held her tight, crushed her against him. For six years he had lived that lie.

His voice was quiet in her hair. 'Last year I tried to break with her. Lasted three months. I cut the meetings. When I was down in Portadown last year, working on the new council place, she caught up with me. I never saw her, but she watched me. Letters were left for me, no beggar ever seemed to remember seeing them left, but they had my name on them. There was a photograph, Joey Fenton who was shot for touting, that was first. Next month, after I'd broken the second meeting, there was a bullet. Third month, after I'd broken the third meeting, she sent me the note, her writing, addressed to the OC, it named me as a tout . . . If they thought you knew, they'd kill you too . . .'

He felt her lips brush his forehead. She said she'd go and make the tea.

He had never been so cold. The damp seeped through the sides of the hide and puddled on the flooring of plastic. The cold numbed his feet, it ached in his buttocks and his shoulders shook with it. The only part of his face that was exposed, between the woollen

193

cap pulled down over his forehead and the scarf wrapped across his mouth and throat, was raw with cold. It was as if she tested him. They had come to the hide as the dusk settled. They had hugged the hedgerows and crawled in the gorse, light enough for him always to be able to see Cathy as she had led the way. He was ice cold and he did not complain. His teeth chattered, a distraction beside the suppressed hum of the electronics.

He felt the dig of her elbow in his ribs. She pulled his head round and she fed him a stick of chewing gum. There was her chuckle, very quiet, beside him. His teeth pounded on the chewing gum and the chatter was gone.

The light at the back of the bungalow came on.

The white brilliance flared the television screen.

There was barely room for the two of them in the hide. Bren's body below, and Cathy's half on top of him. Her leg was over his thigh.

So much that he wanted to know about her . . .

'Bren . . .' Her voice was abrupt.

'Yes.'

'I ate too many sausages.'

'Yes.'

'You silly bugger, I want to crap.'

'Fine by me, Miss Parker.'

He had seen her the day before, treated as equal by the men of the Special Air Service, taken as a friend by the man who could kill and then eat a plate of sausages and beans and chips with her before they made their dry statements to the sympathetic detectives and the supercilious bastards of the army's Special Investigations Branch . . . He had been with

194

her the day before, in the watchtower, and seen that she had never flinched through a shooting that left three men dead . . . and the head shot off the one whose legs were still jumping.

She wriggled away from him.

She was crouched half over his legs, bent double.

She cursed and he thought that her fingers were too chilled to work the buttons of her trousers.

She swore again as she tried to unfold the tinfoil.

Bren stared ahead of him. He saw the light go out in the kitchen of the bungalow. The only street lights were away to the left, the village lights. The mountain was black-cloaked. The darkness was around him.

She wriggled, struggled, in the confined space.

She would have closed the tinfoil over, sealed it.

She would have pulled her trousers back to her waist, fastened them.

She lay beside him, and her leg crooked over his and he could feel the sweet heat of her breath on the nape of his neck.

'Sorry about that,' she said.

They left half an hour before the first smear of the dawn, and she took her wrapped tinfoil with her. She didn't tell him that he had passed any test. He thought she would have told him if he had failed.

Late, always late, the story of his whole damned life.

The big Mustang, left-hand drive, swung off the Killyman Road and into the estate. He was late, very late, a whole twenty-four hours late, but that was because he had been on *assignment* up on the north coast all through the last day and it was now two

195

weeks since the radio in the Mustang had been screw-drivered out in the Belfast centre car park and he had heard not a damn thing of the business before the late night news.

With a pounding heart he saw the woman with the bucket advancing on the pavement.

And he would have been there at dawn, first light, if the overnight rain hadn't seeped into the electricals under the bonnet, and certainly would have been there by mid-morning if the garage, scoundrels there, had accepted his cheque for petrol.

Eighteen stone and dieting, trying to, he pitched his legs out. 'Hold it, Madam. Give me time.'

She stopped. She was a tiny woman, and she carried a plastic bucket in one hand and a kitchen mop in the other.

'Hold your good work, Madam, two minutes will satisfy.'

She stared at him.

'The blood, Madam, give me two minutes for the blood.'

He had the driver's seat tipped forward. The harness had snagged the seatbelt. He swore, he pulled the harness out.

'Have to have the blood, Madam, can't have a killing story without the blood.'

He used two cameras, and that was the beauty of the harness. The harness was a frame across his chest, supported over his shoulders. A camera to the right of the frame and a camera to the left, and a mutual micro-phone held between them that recorded sound for both. The sound, as was pointed out with increasing frequency by his clients, was often little more than the

196

billow of his breathing when he exerted himself.

She watched. Silly little woman, didn't have to stare.

'Who's news is you's?'

He tugged at the hair on his lower chin, where the whitened sideburns curved towards his upper lip. It was his familiar gesture. There were children emerging from gardens and houses, horrible-looking urchins.

'Peregrine Forster is the name, Madam, camera correspondent of the NHK network of Japan and the Globo channel of Brazil, known to the trade as "Perry", well known . . . Now, if you would be so kind as to stand back from the blood . . .'

It was a rich English accent, cultivated over six years as a Flying Officer in the Royal Air Force, first with Accounts and then transferred to Kitchens. Always had trouble getting the cable leads into the right sockets under pressure, being watched. The urchins were gathering, sharks coming from the deep at the scent of cattle offal; he had done time in Singapore and knew about sharks, more about sharks than cameras.

'Is they interested, in those places . . . ?'

To lie or not to lie, always better to lie . . . 'Interested? Tonight they'll be holding open the lead position in their newscasts . . . But there has to be blood.'

His head tilted to the left. His left eye closed on the viewfinder of the NHK network of Japan. The blood was all but dried onto the pavement and into the gutter. There was one good dribble that he could follow. His head tilted to the right and his right eye locked to the viewfinder of the Globo channel of Brazil. The pictures would be air freighted to London and would be lucky, damn lucky, to get further. Pity there weren't any flowers. Pity all his cash had gone on the petrol and he couldn't run to a couple of tear-jerking bouquets. The children were all around him.

'Very quiet, please, and stay back from the blood . . .'

He filmed. Patch of blood, Madam with bucket and mop, dribble of blood, wide-eyed and dirty faces of children.

Very professional. Peregrine Forster, late of selling insurance and more late of greetings cards and very late of the Royal Air Force, had based himself in Northern Ireland three years back . . . it was a living.

He stood back. Again the cameras were switched on. The pulse lights flashed in his right eye and his left eye. He ran forward. He came ahead at a good trot. He jerked to a halt and he peered from one viewfinder to another, into the patch of blood and the blood dribble.

The small woman called out. 'Mister, you's filmin' things that aren't happenin' . . .'

'Reconstruction, Madam, gives added poignancy to tragedy.'

He started to heave the harness from his shoulders. He laid the cameras back onto the rear seat of the Mustang. The little blighters were all round him, giggling.

'Shouldn't you be showing more respect, Mister?'

'Casualties of war, Madam, yesterday's grief and today's statistics . . . Bugger off, you little bastards . . .'

The kids fled. He heard the life of their laughter as they went. It was only when he sat back into the

Mustang that he appreciated the fuckers had let out the air in his rear right tyre. By the time he had jacked up the car, and changed the wheel, and jacked down the car, the woman had gone, and the pavement and the gutter had been scrubbed clean.

Not a blood stain to be seen.

Well, Perry Forster would have said, perhaps as he filled in so expertly his expenses sheets, 'We all have to earn a crust, and the tools of my trade are old blood on the pavement.'

It was the last funeral of the day, Vinny Devitt's. Mossie went. He was far back in the procession of men and women and children who walked from the Devitt house to the church. A piper led them.

Mossie had stayed away from the funerals of Jacko and Malachy. Both of their families had told the Provisionals, given it to them straight and then slammed the family front door on them, that they wanted no part in a stunt. No tricolour flag, no black beret, no black gloves on either coffin.

Devitt's was a funeral with full honours. There had been shots fired in the night by masked men close to the Devitt home. In the middle of the afternoon, when the rain clouds masked the crest of the mountain, the piper led the procession the mile to the church. A narrow lane was the route. The piper's lament was blotted out by the drone of the helicopter above, and there was a phalanx of police in front of the piper walking sober-faced beside the procession so that the Altmore people were hemmed in by the men in their visored helmets, who carried the riot sticks.

It was a good turn-out.

199

The man from Belfast Sinn Fein, over the open grave, spoke of a hero and of the certainty of ultimate victory.

Twice Mossie met the eyes of the OC inside the church and across the grave, cold and bitter. What Mossie had heard, Gerry Brannigan's boy had gone, run for the safety of the Republic, gone after saying that East Tyrone Brigade was as secure as a feckin' sieve.

He thought the tout hunt would start as the last shovel of dirt covered the coffin, and he had been guaranteed that he was protected.

It was the aftermath of a killing, not the planning of it.

The Assistant Under-Secretary stayed away from the Task Co-ordinating Group. The colonel, Army Intelligence, took the chair, his right by rota.

First business from the major, a cache on the Limavady road out of Londonderry that had been watched for twelve days now without result – how much longer could manpower be deployed? A report by the Assistant Chief Constable on a police approach to a North Antrim volunteer – early days but promising. An inquest, led by Rennie, into the appearance of an Andersonstown 'bad boy' at a Sinn Fein news conference where the little bastard had squealed that he had been approached, offered money, and gone straight to his solicitor and then the Provos – damage limitation, and the lesson was that the handlers had moved too fast. A query from the colonel, the increasing quantity of 'traces' on a south County Down man, presumably rising in the Organization – questioning whether it would be a suitable time to pull him into Gough Barracks, Armagh, and let the Southern Region crime squad fellows have him for seven days and three sessions a day. Agreed.

Last item before coffee, and Hobbes broke his silence.

'Dungannon, I thought, was good.'

The major said, 'It was first-class information, made it pretty straightforward.'

The colonel said, 'A good example of what can be achieved when we all pull together.'

The Assistant Chief Constable said, 'Invaluable source, your Song Bird, would there were more like him, but I'd say we got away with it by the skin of our teeth. Parading their weapon was critical. But I'm getting it on the grapevine that one of the team got clean away.'

The major said softly, 'A householder was right behind the target. It was very responsible fire control . . .'

Rennie spluttered on his pipe.

Hobbes smiled. 'Yes, Howard.'

The smoke clouded Howard Rennie. He let them wait. He coughed from the depth of his throat. 'If the safety of Song Bird, whose identity Mr Hobbes is unwilling to share, has been preserved then the shooting was justified. If the risk to Song Bird has been increased, then the operation was a disaster. Time, gentlemen, will tell us whether self-satisfaction is in order.'

Hobbes bit at his lip. 'Thank you, Howard, I'll minute that.'

* * *

201

He put the milk bottle down onto Mrs Byrne's kitchen table. The petrol was amber in the clear bottle. He put the box of matches beside the bottle.

The OC said, 'It's a nice kitchen, missus.'

She told him what she had seen.

She talked because of the threat to her kitchen of scattered petrol and a thrown match. And she talked to the OC because her nephew's wife's brother was on remand in the Crumlin Road gaol, and because her neighbour's cousin had been under psychiatric treatment for two years in Belfast after four days in the Castlereagh holding centre. And she talked because she had seen three young men cut down by the soldiers, no warning shout, no chance to surrender, not even a priest allowed near them for an hour. She talked.

'You're sure on that, missus . . . ?'

'Jesus was looking for him. He went by Mrs Hylton's door, half fell on her fence, then by Mrs Smyth's door, then he went down the side of Mrs Smyth's, I don't know how they missed him, God is my witness, one of them was not ten feet from him. I thought he was dead, all fast I was praying for him. Bright coat he had but it was like they didn't see him. Definite, he had Jesus watching for him, and he'd a bad leg and he didn't run that quick. It was just butchery, what was done to the rest of them . . .'

There was a washing basket, filled, beside her kitchen door. Mrs Byrne rummaged in the bottom of it, and there was her grin that was a little bit of mischief, and she handed the OC the short-barrelled pistol that had been thrown at her.

'And they didn't see that either, the soldiers . . .'

He apologized to her, and meant it, and he took away with him his matches and the milk bottle that was filled with petrol.

The OC went back to his home, to write letters for hand delivery, to send a message for a meeting.

There was the stinging blow of the fist against Mossie's cheek.

The OC snarled in his face, 'There's three men dead.'

'You've no call to be accusing me.' Tears welling in his eyes.

'They let you run.'

'Who told you?'

'I was told.'

'Who?'

'The woman, she sees it all.'

'You's taking her word, not my word?'

'She says they let you run.'

'Is you blaming me for running?'

'Why'd they let you run?'

'To prove myself, what do I have to do? Have to get myself feckin' stiffed?' Mossie yelled back at him.

'She says . . .'

'Been sneaking round her, have you? Shame, that's what you should have.'

'What she says was . . .'

'And you wouldn't feckin' know what happened, 'cause you weren't there, 'cause you're never there, too feckin' important to be . . .'

The OC had him by the throat. The OC was smaller than Mossie and reaching up to snatch at the flesh under his chin.

The barb sunk home. The hatred, and the hesitancy. 'OCs is never operational, every bastard knows that.'

'I went, I was there, I was lucky.'

The anger in Mossie was fear. Good act, played well, because the fear was real. The hands came away from his throat. He didn't know whether he was believed. If he was not believed . . .

The OC said, grim, 'There was three men shot dead. There was one who ran. The one who ran can't go fast. The one who ran was right in view of the soldiers, past two houses. You tell me, Mossie, because you was there, you tell me why one, only one was able to run from the soldiers. Tell me, Mossie . . .'

Better when they were shouting, face to face, easier eyeball to eyeball. He'd had five years to prepare himself to answer the accusation. Five years of churning the question in his mind. Was he a tout? Five years to prepare the answer, and never knowing when the question would come. He had just run, panicked, hadn't even seen the bastard soldier, only heard the crack of the bullet against the wall, then the ricochet whine. The question was with him . . .

'I don't know.'

'You're staying here. You'll stay while I'm gone. You think of running, and you think where you'll go. You run now and that's my answer.'

Mossie stood his full height . . . fight, to fight was the best, fighting for his life.

'You're not fit to lead, you're rubbish. If Jon Jo Donnelly was here . . . You're not fit to be in Jon Jo's shoes.'

He saw the loathing in the OC's eyes. 'My question, why'd they let you get clear? Just you, why? You run and I've my answer, and Jon Jo isn't here.'

Mossie was left in the barn. There was nowhere to run to and there never had been.

The OC came back to the barn in the middle of the afternoon, driving his tractor with the trailer bumping behind. The tractor, open-topped and without four-wheel drive, had been in his family since before he was born. He had driven it first when he was too small to sit on the seat and reach the wheel and the pedals. There were hay bales on the trailer. Standing behind him, gripping his shoulders, was a man who had come from Lurgan in answer to a summons. The OC was elaborate and careful because he assumed, always, that he was watched. He assumed always, too, that his enemy had him under surveillance from cameras and from the soldiers of the Close Observation Platoons and from the police of the E4 section. He had not met the man from Security before, never had cause. The man wore heavy-framed clear-glass spectacles to disguise his face. If they were under surveillance, it would not be thought unusual, shifting bales of hay.

They splashed through the puddle in the doorway, below the broken guttering. Mossie sat facing the doorway, knees against his chest, arms around his knees.

The OC and the man from Lurgan dumped down the bales of hay they had carried inside.

'So, you's Mossie Nugent . . .'

The man from Lurgan had a voice from far down in his throat.

'I am.'

The OC watched. Mossie pushed himself up against the wall behind him. It was not for the OC to speak. He had called in the security section. He would stand aside while they trampled through the Brigade. He lit a cigarette. It was a sort of humiliation that he felt because until a tout was found, until the Brigade was sanitized, he had handed away his control of the war.

'I'm from the security, Mossie, I'm from the security because I've a nose for rats. What I say, Mossie, is that rats are best shot. We had a rat last month and we shot him. To me, touts is rats.'

He had thought Mossie Nugent great, a fine and careful intelligence officer. He didn't know the working of South Down Brigade or the Mid Ulster Brigade, but he had once been on a hit with the Derry Brigade and he'd thought the intelligence officer of Derry Brigade was just shit, all talk. Good times he'd had with Mossie. Couldn't fault him. He saw that Mossie looked the man from Lurgan straight back in the eyes.

Mossie said, 'I'm not a tout.'

'Did I say you was, Mossie? Did you hear me accuse you?'

'I hear you talking of touts. I's no tout.'

'My position is laid down by Army Council orders. I'll quote it for you, so there's no misunderstandings. "We wish to reiterate our stated position on informers. No matter how long a person has been working for the enemy, if they come forward, they will not be harmed. Anyone caught touting will be executed." Be difficult not to understand that, eh, Mossie? I'm going to ask you the question . . .'

'Go feck yourselves, the both of you. I've had all I

206

need of this joke. Away and play somewhere's else.'

'Just listen to my question, Mossie. You may want time to think on it, because it's just the one chance, Mossie. It's like the Army Council says, a tout comes forward, a tout won't be harmed. But the Army Council says also, a tout lies and is then found out, that tout's dead. I give a man the one chance to come forward . . .'

'I'll remember you, you bastard, don't think I won't.'

The OC watched. He thought the man from Lurgan terrifying, and he saw the way that Mossie's eyes never left the face of the man.

'Haven't asked the question yet, Mossie,' the voice ground softly on, 'because I'm being fair with you. Can't say I'm not fair. The chance is never offered again, that's why you might be wanting to think on your answer. I told you, Mossie, I've a nose for rats.'

Mossie said nothing, only stared at the man. Tense, his fists white-knuckled. Ready to spring.

The OC felt the shiver of his body. Frightening to him, the tap drip of the man from Lurgan's voice. He had known Mossie since he could remember. He had been at the small kids' school when Mossie had first gone to prison.

The voice beside him was chilled, quiet. 'One and only one chance . . . Mossie, is you a tout?'

'Go feck yourself.'

'Is you a tout?'

'No, I'm not a tout. I'm the Intelligence Officer of this Brigade . . .'

The voice beside him hardened. 'You was the only one who knew.'

207

'Not true.'

'Your OC knew, and you knew.'

'Not true.'

'Who else knew?'

Mossie's finger stabbed at him. 'Ask him.'

The OC flinched.

The man from Lurgan turned slowly, precisely for a big man, towards him. 'You told me it was just him and yourself. Who else knew?'

The OC blurted, 'No-one else knew.'

He saw the finger again pointing at him. 'You lie. What did you say yourself? You said, "How long was the little bastard there?" When the Riordan kid brought the tea. I've given my life to the Organization. I's done time for the cause. Before you look to me you should go talk with the little bastard . . .'

The man from Lurgan spat, 'You didn't tell me.'

He said, weak, 'I hadn't remembered . . .'

Mossie, shrill, 'Go look at Patsy Riordan. Go look at anyone else he's forgotten.'

They let Mossie go, let him walk back to his home. The OC talked with the man from Lurgan about the kid who was not the full shilling, who was just used to run messages. On their lips was the name and the history of the kiddie who could have been good on the gaelic team, Under-19s. Patsy Riordan.

'I had no choice.'

There was wonderment in her voice. 'You gave them his name?'

'I gave them his name or I was gone.'

He had shouted at the little ones to drive them from the room. He had slammed the door on his mother.

Mossie sat on the bed and cupped in his hands was the whiskey bottle. He felt the shake in his body. Siobhan stood above him. He drank from the neck of the bottle.

'She's a grand woman, Mrs Riordan . . .'

'Gone. They don't finish till they've it out of you. You can't stand against them. Don't you understand, it's torture, it's beatings . . . I had to.'

'He's just a simple, stupid boy . . .'

'I was dead.'

'He's never done you no harm . . .'

Slowly, trying to control the splutter of his voice, he explained to her what must be done.

He told her the way he thought it would be. He had bought himself time, that was all. He was still the suspect and he would be watched. There was a chance, possible, that the security could tap into a phone. He would not dare to use the telephone at home, nor could he dare to drive to Dungannon and use a public telephone. He would be followed.

'Should you be using the bleeper thing?'

'You needs to slip away, natural, not in a bloody helicopter so's the whole mountain knows.' It would be the living death. It would be five years, ten years, twenty years, of living with minders and with fear at his shoulder. To press the bleeper was the last resort.

'What do you want me to do?'

He breathed deep. He involved her.

'You go down the town. You take the kids, like it's just visiting . . .'

He wrote the number on the inside of his cigarette packet and slid the tinfoil wrapping back over the number.

'. . . You ring this number. You ring it for as long as it takes. Might be a man, might be a woman. They may make you ring them twice. You have to tell them it's for Song Bird, that it's a meeting you need, no feckin' about, right now. They'll tell you where. You go where they tell you. Tell them what happened to me, and tell them I named Patsy Riordan.'

'What'll happen to Patsy Riordan?'

'Not my worry.'

He slumped on the bed. He lay in the darkness and he smelled the whiskey on his shirt front. He heard Siobhan rounding up the kids, telling his mother that she was taking them out, going visiting.

Not Mossie's worry, what happened to Patsy Riordan.

She was seen to drive away. She was identified when she turned from the lane onto the road from Aghnagar to the village. It was seen that the children were with her. The men resumed their watch on the bungalow. There were no curtains drawn. They saw Mossie Nugent moving inside the bungalow, silhouetted against the lights.

The men of the security section gathering on Altmore came from Lurgan and Armagh city, from south County Down and from north County Antrim, from the villages of west Tyrone and east Derry. They came because they were called to a tout hunt.

Across the mountain they also watched the Riordan home, saw a man go out to feed his caged birds, saw a youngster in a garage working at the engine of a motorcycle.

* * *

He lifted the green telephone. He had let the bell ring for a full half-minute. He had been by the door, his coat on, his briefcase in his hand, when the bell had started.

Hesitant, 'Yes, can I help you?'

A woman's voice. 'Hello there, I was wondering . . .'

Brisk. 'I think you have the wrong number.'

'It's for Song Bird.'

Christ . . . snatching for a pen from his inside pocket, for paper. 'Yes?'

'I'm Siobhan Nugent, his wife. He told me to ring you . . .'

The telephone was Bren's link with the jungle. He heard the desperation of the woman. He tried to be gentle. He heard the choke in her voice. She was to ring back. He went through the procedure. In exactly ten minutes she should telephone again.

Frantic now. Ringing the number for Cathy, waking her by the sound of it, being given a meeting place, being told when she would collect him, given the numbers to call for back-up. Asking for Rennie at Lisnasharragh barracks, couldn't be reached. Asking for a major at Lisburn HQ, told there were no personnel available. Asking for an Assistant Chief Constable at RUC's Knock Road, hearing the dry chuckle, telling him it was panic time, giving him the co-ordinates, being told there would be Divisional Mobile Support Unit presence in the area, and the radio code they could be reached on, grovelling thanks to the Assistant Chief Constable. Picking up the green telephone on the first ring.

211

It was the fear that she communicated to him, it was her fear that was still with him all the time until Cathy came for him.

She thought the young woman was wonderful, the one that Mossie called the bitch. So calm, and such a lovely face . . .

'There is absolutely nothing for you to fret over. I'll take care of everything. Just trust me, Siobhan . . .'

There was a young man behind her and when she turned away then he went to her car and opened the door for her, like a gentleman. The faces of her children were pressed against the back window.

'Super children, Siobhan, you must be very proud of them. No worries now, I'll see you're safe, that's a promise . . .'

Chapter Ten

Bren watched.

Hobbes blanched.

Cathy explained.

'It's what has to be done. There isn't another alternative . . .'

They were in Hobbes' house, they had driven to that privileged community on the north County Down coast. They were in the kitchen at the back of the house and through the picture window were the small lights of coastal freighters in the Belfast Lough. The sink was piled high with the plates and cooking dishes that would stay there until the 'daily' came in the next morning. The table was littered with used glasses from the dinner table and finished bottles and emptied ice boxes. The smell in the kitchen was that of vindaloo sauce. Hobbes' guests were still in the dining room, and Bren could hear their laughter. Bren thought that Cathy cared not a damn that she had disturbed Hobbes' dinner party.

'It'll take the flak off him. It'll give him a breathing space. He was thinking on his feet, really well. If he hadn't been sharp then he was for the hood and the bullet. It's just that he's too good to lose . . .'

It was where they all lived, the best and the brightest of the British administration seconded to Northern Ireland, in the big houses in the little lanes that led down to the beaches and rock shores of the Lough. It was the area of the cruising RUC cars and the security cameras and the multiple alarm systems. It was the territory of the Assistant Under-Secretaries and the Senior Principal Executive Officers, and it was reckoned to be beyond the reach of the arm of the Provisional Irish Republican Army. Where there were good golf courses and good squash complexes and good restaurants, and good expenses to pick up the tabs. The drink was in them, the first and the finest, and their chatter and joking bayed from the dining room into the kitchen that was harsh lit by the neon strip.

'I think he's stronger now that Siobhan's alongside. If we can steer him through these next few days, if we can deflect them, then we've saved him. It's that important. I want to let it run, Mr Hobbes.'

Bren watched.

Hobbes cleared the dregs at the bottom of each bottle on the kitchen table, poured them into a used glass, drank fast and the red wine dribbled from the side of his mouth.

Cathy stood solidly in the centre of the kitchen, arms folded across her chest, stared at him, dared him to refuse her.

He was rocking on his heels. Bren thought him in shock. It was Hobbes' decision. Bren thought he had the right to be in shock. The decision wouldn't wait on a carefully drafted paper, nor a committee, nor could the decision hang in the air for a week's reflection. There was none of the arrogance he had seen in Hobbes before. Hobbes was pale, breathing too fast, drinking too quickly. He thought Cathy had been brilliant, and he thanked God, which for him was not often, that he was just the bystander. He thought Cathy had been brilliant because she had simply, clearly, laid out the facts and then driven them home, a hammer on a nail head. There had been no panic, less emotion. The facts were so simple. It was Mossie Nugent's life, Song Bird's life . . . it was Patsy Riordan's death, a nothing kid's death. There was no escape for Hobbes. She played for life and she played for death. Bren did not know where she found the strength.

Hobbes said, 'You give me no choice.'

Cathy said, 'Thank you.'

Hobbes said, 'I feel like I want to throw up.'

Cathy said, 'Please yourself, Mr Hobbes.'

Hobbes said, 'It's just a fucking awful job.'

Cathy said, 'And hand wringing won't make it a better job.'

Hobbes swayed as he led them into the hall. Once he grasped the bottom of the banister rail. They passed the open dining-room door. The laughter and the conversation cut. Bren saw the eyes peering at them through the doorway. The men wore suits, the women were dressed well. He thought that some of them round the dinner table would have known, in general terms, what was Hobbes' work, and they would have been curious. They would have allowed their imagination to let rip at the reason for the young man and the young woman, casual and scruffed, who

215

had taken their host from the table and into the kitchen. It was a real war, that sort of crap, that intruded into a private dinner party, Bren thought it was that sort of shit. Hobbes let them stand in the hall, and he went into the living room that was well furnished by government procurement standards, and he pushed a small chest aside, near the fireplace, and exposed the wall safe. He took a key from his pocket and unlocked the safe and took out a thin envelope, passed it to Cathy. He relocked the safe and heaved the chest back, flush to the wall again.

He had no more to say.

Hobbes showed them to the door.

They walked off down the drive under the brightness of the security lights.

Cathy chuckled, 'He's going to be a ball of fire the rest of the evening, the life and soul of the party.'

Bren stopped at the car. It had welled in him. 'What you do, don't you care?'

'Christ's sake, it's not a big decision. It's not strategic. It doesn't have to go to Curzon Street or up to Cabinet. It's just day to day . . . listen, young man, you are just a little cog, so am I. East Tyrone, Song Bird, just one operation running here, and over each hill there's another. What we do doesn't *win* the war, maybe it stops us losing it a little. Learn, young man, that you're not the centre of the universe . . . That curry he'd done, smelt revolting.'

There was just the wind in the roof and the singing at the telephone wire and the beat of the rain on the windows.

Her head was in the crook of his arm.

216

She whispered in his ear.

He lay rigid on his back and it was as if there was a coldness over his body.

'She was just wonderful. She was great. There's no side to her. She said that I wasn't to be worrying, that I was to leave everything to her. Funny word she used, she said that I wasn't to "fret". "I'll take care of everything," that's what she said. She said that I was to trust her. She's a lovely way with words, that one. She said the children looked so good . . .'

'What's she going to do?'

'Just said that you'd be safe, that was her promise.'

'Did you give out to her?'

'I did not.' Siobhan whispered, 'I trust her.'

She heard the bitter wheeze of his voice. 'She hooked you, like she hooked me, the bitch.'

To Rennie it was a madness. Anyone else, anyone who was not Cathy Parker, would have had short shrift from his tongue. He was on his doorstep and the wind blew leaves into the hallway behind him, and the rain spattered the legs of his pyjamas below his dressing gown. The bell had woken his wife, disturbed his daughters, and he had taken his pistol down the staircase with him and held it ready to shoot before he had identified her through his spyhole. She looked half drowned. The young fellow was behind her but with his shoulders turned away as if he guarded her back. It was a madness to come banging on doors when the clock in his hall showed past midnight. No-one else, only Cathy . . . He'd have had the skin off the back of any of his own men who had come and kept a finger on the bell until his whole family was shaken from

217

sleep. He didn't argue. He wanted them gone. He agreed. A long time ago, before her nerve had gone, his wife had bred dogs for showing. Such a long time ago, before the present phase of the war had started, before he had gone into Special Branch, before it had become unsafe for him to walk alone in the fields and woodlands close to where they lived with their labradors. It would have been insane now, just as it had been for twenty years. It was the price he paid, that the dogs were gone. It was the price his wife had paid, ever since their home had been invaded by a scumbag with an automatic rifle. There was a phrase from those days, such a long time ago, when he walked the labradors and his wife took them to shows. The jet-black bitch, dead now, had been called by a vet their *alpha female*. The top bitch who could quieten a flood of puppies with a growl . . . He thought Cathy was the *alpha female*. He listened to her, and he saw the way that the young fellow watched her back, the one with the idiot name. She was top bitch and the way he looked at her, it was obvious that the silly bastard was soft on her.

Rennie said, 'I will make the calls, I will go back to bed, I will try to get to sleep, and I will see you tomorrow. Now, please, piss off . . .'

If he had been the young fellow's age then he might have been soft himself on the *alpha female*, bloody nuisance woman.

He was still up when the message was received on the secure teleprinter line.

He was often up, prowling the barracks far into the morning's small hours.

When he had first come to the province, two decades earlier, as a young lieutenant, then it had been the day of military rule. Now, in his eighth tour of duty, the accent had shifted. It was the time now of police primacy. The message on the battalion teleprinter was not a request but a requirement that he provide back-up for an operation the following morning. His third and fourth tours had seen the change of emphasis and he could remember the resentment that all soldiers had felt then. By now, it was accepted.

Colonel Johnny spent much of the night drifting between his Operations Room and his office and the Mess where there was coffee on tap. So much of his operational work was carried out under the cover of darkness. More patrols, more roadblocks, more surveillance teams at night than during the day. He lived in a twilight world of dozed sleep and cat-napped rest. Because the tasking for the morning was a requirement and not a request, he immediately set about the orders. He noted the name of the suspect and where he was to be arrested. He studied the police plan. He was to provide protection. Even in daylight there was the need for great vigilance. Colonel Johnny had learned that of Altmore, always to take every possible care. Two sections to be in position before dawn. The first section that would be to the north of the pick-up block would have the heavy machine gun, the second section on the lower ground to the south would have the 66-mm anti-tank missile launcher. He had the Night Duty Officer bring him the photographs of the crossroads where the arrest would be made. He was always thorough. Colonel

Johnny could not tolerate the military funerals that were the mark of commanders who were not thorough.

When the two sections had gone, tramped out of the barracks into the darkness laden with their weaponry and their signals equipment, he could wonder why an operation was to be mounted at such short notice to lift a kid who hardly figured on his Intelligence Officer's files. But within ten minutes of his two sections disappearing from the barracks' lights he was asleep in his office, splayed out on the sofa dreaming of deer to be stalked, grouse to be driven, peace.

'I'm dead,' she said.

Bren thought that he ought to have offered to drive. There was little traffic on the road, but he turned to look at her face when the next car approached them. She was pale as marble in the lights of the oncoming car.

'Where are we?'

'Near to my place . . .'

'I'll get a taxi.'

She stifled her yawn. 'Taxis take for ever this time of night.'

'Then I'll . . .'

'Bed down at mine,' Cathy said.

The next car rushing towards them, and he looked at her again. She was expressionless, impassive. And the light was gone fast from her face. He shifted in his seat, awkward. She drove fast. There were no police roadblocks, no military checkpoints. He wondered if it had been like this for his predecessor, the man who had been compromised and withdrawn. She had the heating on in the car and the all-night radio station was playing quietly. It was Jim Reeves on the radio and that was about right for Ulster in its time warp. Wondering all the time that she drove, wondering whether she was just lonely, wondering whether he would just be a fix or a different hypodermic. She turned off a side road. She headed through the opened gates and pulled up outside a two-storey block of modern flats. She leaned across him and her elbow brushed his knee and she took her personal radio from the glove compartment and tucked the pistol from under her thighs into her jeans. Bren fumbled the door handle before he could get the lever in his fingers. He hurried round the back of the car and opened her door for her. When she was out of the car and locking her door then it was so obvious that she was vulnerable. So small, so huddled in the vastness of her anorak. He walked into the building a pace behind her. The gold of her hair was in front of him. He thought she was so precious and he was afraid to touch her. It was a smart block, well decorated. Up a flight of stairs. Her door had a spyhole that was too low for him, right for her height. He didn't know when he should touch her. Two locks, two keys. The lights flooded on in front of her after she opened the heavy door. She walked inside and Bren followed her.

'It's not bad . . .'

She pointed to the wide, three-seat sofa.

'. . . I'll get you a pillow and a blanket.'

Cathy was away across the room and a door closed behind her. He sat on the sofa. He could have laughed and he could have wept. She wasn't lonely, didn't need a fix from him. She was just too tired to drive all the way down the bloody Malone Road and drop him off. His head was in his hands. He might have kissed the back of her head while she was opening the door . . . He might have slipped his arms round her in the moment before she had switched on the lights. What would she have done, if he had touched her? Probably she'd have kicked his kneecaps off.

Bren sat on the sofa and took off his shoes, and he slipped off his anorak and dragged off his sweater.

He reached into the pocket of his anorak and took out his Browning pistol and detached the magazine from the stock and cleared the breech. He waited, good little patient boy, for *Miss* Parker to bring him his pillow and blanket.

She came out through the internal door with a pillow and a tartan blanket.

She wore a blue towelling dressing gown.

'You alright . . . ?'

'I'm fine . . .'

'Sorry, did you want something to eat?'

'No.'

'Sorry again, did you want the bathroom?'

'After you.'

And he hated himself because it was just bloody, bloody, obvious that she was tired. He stood. She put the pillow in place. She bent to arrange the blanket for him. She made it into a sleeve. She was bent over the sofa and the dressing gown gaped and he could see the white bulge of her breasts and he thought she was naked under the dressing gown. She might have only slapped his face, if he had touched her, she might have softened into his arms. No way of knowing . . .

'Thank you,' Bren said.

222

There was an envelope in her hand, the one that Hobbes had taken from his wall safe.

'Let me know what you think of that,' Cathy said.

Before her door closed behind her, she had shown him the bathroom and told him where in the kitchen he could find a drink.

He forced himself to read what was in the envelope. Should have kissed the back of her head . . . The paper was from Ernest Wilkins. The paper was headed DONNELLY J. The paper was the minute of a meeting in London and called for input from Belfast. Should have been kissing the tiredness from her . . . but in his mind was the view of a farmhouse, seen from the ground with the magnification of binoculars, seen from the height of Altmore mountain.

He was woken by the street-cleaning wagon. Still dark in his room except for the slash of orange light between the curtains from the high sodium lamps on the pavement. Jon Jo had not been asleep more than two hours. It was always difficult for him to sleep at the London house. The bastard was that the sleep was broken and had been so long in coming. After the street-cleaning wagon had gone, moved on, he lay on his back and stared at the ceiling light. When he could not sleep, when he was in London, then his thoughts of the country and the mountain that was his were at their keenest. Little Kevin and Attracta should have been in his picture. But they swam around him. They wore their work-day suits, they carried rolled umbrellas and bags of tools and attaché cases. They were decked out in their school uniforms, they gripped their lunch boxes, and their satchels were

223

slung from their shoulders. They were all round him in the brightness of their frocks for the shop floor and their severer skirts and coats for the office. They were the school children, they were the girls and the men and women heading into the capital city. He could see clearly the railway station that was around them. He could not see their faces. They were the faces of the enemy, and they were hidden from him. He saw what they wore and what they carried and they were always beside the rubbish bin at the end of the ticket windows. Each man was beside the rubbish bin, each child, each girl or woman. They were his enemy . . . He was in London because those in Dublin believed he could hate the men and the children and the girls and the women who swam past the red rubbish bin. Holy God, a flash of light, a rumble of thunder . . . a torrent of shrapnel and glass splinters . . . a screaming, crying, calling . . . Holy God . . . He lay on his back, there was the sound of the night street in his ears, there were the shapes without faces of the men and the children and the girls and the women in his eyes.

He had never wondered it before, whether he could hate enough.

The foxes fled from the dawn and sought the safety of their dens.

The owls took shelter in the wind-racked barns.

The crows flew high to find what carrion was left abandoned in the fields by predators for whom the dawn had come too soon.

In cover, under the groundsheets camouflaged by quickly pulled bracken, down in the ditches that skirted the sodden fields, two sections of

224

troops watched the ground behind them for danger and a crossroads ahead of them for the arrival of a young man who would be waiting for a lift into Dungannon.

In three cars, and in a van, were the men who had not slept through the gone night, and they hacked their cigarettes' muck from their throats, and swore at the cold, and watched the bungalow and the house as they had been told, and talked quietly of their homes in Lurgan town and Armagh city and south County Down and north County Antrim and west Tyrone and east Derry.

It was the man who brought the milk who told the priest. Pius Blaney told the priest that there were strangers in cars and a van on the mountain lanes. Pius Blaney told the priest, as he checked his bill and paid it in cash, that there were strangers, not soldiers and not police, out on Altmore. He took the change that was pecked from Pius Blaney's old leather purse, he pocketed the receipt, he closed the door on Pius Blaney. It was what he had expected, that there would be a tout hunt through his parish, that strangers would come in to ferret out a victim. The priest knew of no help that he could find. He could have walked or driven to the home of the OC or the Quartermaster or the Intelligence Officer. He knew them all, and knew also that his capacity to intervene was negligible. They would all be beyond argument, beyond faith, all except the one who was doomed to die for informing. In the fair isle, in Ireland, it had never been different. He could pray, and his prayers would be uttered in the certainty that a tout's life would not be saved.

Mossie drove away from the bungalow.

In the back of his car were his ladders and tins and dust sheets and brushes.

He did not see it at first. He was halfway to Dungannon before he could be certain that the car twenty yards behind him was tailing him. He had pulled into a lay-by where the council workers stored grit for the frosts, and the car had not come past him.

He was uncomfortable in his seat. The bleeper was strapped with tape to the inside of his thigh.

A cold sweat on him as he drove, each time he looked into his mirror and saw the tailing car. He was afraid, of course he was afraid, but always with the fear was the coursing excitement. He could live with the fear, he could not live without the excitement. The excitement was his fuel . . . Mossie Nugent was the big man. Mossie Nugent was *important*. The bitch, she needed him . . . The car followed him down into Dungannon town.

Beyond her land, climbing the slope, were the Mahoneys' fields. They were the old couple that Attracta hardly saw. They ran sheep and a few beef cattle. They went once a week to the shop. Their lives were for themselves. Their kids were gone, married and working on the mainland. The Mahoneys were a part of the land, but they had cut themselves off from the community. The bracken was creeping back onto their land and the gorse clumps were thicker.

She walked up the lane with an apple pie and a loaf

of soda bread that she had baked for herself and little Kevin.

The Mahoneys would have known that her Jon Jo was away with the Organization, and they had to have seen the military helicopters that had brought the troops and police to her home. She didn't know whether they would welcome her in, the wife of a Provo fighter, or whether they would slam the door in her face.

She walked up the lane to ask the Mahoneys if it were possible that she could graze her bullocks on their upper fields for perhaps a month. She had not enough fodder to last her through the winter. Little enough grass in their fields, but enough for a month.

Attracta would not have needed to ask the favour of the Mahoneys if Jon Jo had been home, if the leaking barn roof had been repaired, if she had not lost a quarter of her winter fodder, rotted under the leak, if she had not been sharp enough to believe that her Jon Jo would never now come home.

When he had his own place, whenever, when he was allowed to move out of the bedsitter in the Malone Road, then there would be flowering bulbs in pots, herbs growing on the kitchen windowsill. There would be bookcases, piles of newspapers, pictures on the wall. One wall all cork for his 'memory board': all the Marilyn pictures and especially the poster of La Monroe swathed in towels on a winter beach that he had seen in the shop behind Royal Avenue, and a thousand postcards of Old Masters, a mosaic of himself. His weights, maybe. A cat – he was certainly going to need company. When he had his own place he would engrave his mark on it. His rooms would be *him*. Just in case he got lost in this God-forsaken job and needed to remind himself who he had been. This room said nothing of her . . . if it hadn't been for Mr Wilkins' memorandum and the questions that it posed then the frustration of knowing so little about her might just have had him searching every last inch of the flat for clues. Mr Wilkins preserved his sanity.

The geography made it so obvious. A farmhouse on a hillside, and further down the whitewashed bungalow.

A farmhouse belonging to a PIRA activist and close to it was a bungalow that was the home of a PIRA activist turned informer. He didn't need a 2.1 in Modern History to sink that one in a corner pocket.

Bren folded the tartan rug. Her bedroom door was still closed. Song Bird was the solution. Mr Wilkins had to be a very great simpleton not to have cottoned on. Hobbes . . . well, *presumably* he had put it together. A little academic problem, nothing more, taking the heat off Mossie Nugent.

A little brain teaser, how to divert the pressure to Patsy Riordan.

Christ . . .

Nothing that Bren had done in London had prepared him for it. He had pushed paper. He had worked on the surveillance teams for the Arab desk and for the Irish desk. He had never played God. Never been detailed for that one. But he was heading that way, racing up the ladder, volunteering for Belfast because that way lay the bright prospect of Senior Executive Officer rank. He wondered how he would have explained to his mother and father what his real world was. He might not know much about Cathy Parker, but by heaven he knew that she was strong enough for the real world . . .

Christ . . .

He tapped on her door. No answer. More firmly. Still no answer. He thought that if he opened it, then he might just get his head blown away.

'Cathy,' he said. No answer. He opened the door.

The light from the window was on her. It was another anonymous room. One bed, one wardrobe, one chest of drawers, one chair, clothes on the floor. The bed was a mattress on the floor. She had tossed the sheet and the blankets off her body. She held the pillow in her arms. Her breasts were against the pillow, the white of her arms was around the pillow. Total calm on her face. He wanted to kneel beside the mattress and kiss the face of the woman who slept with the peace of a child. Her pistol was beside the bed on the carpet, within easy reach if she had loosed her hold on the pillow.

He left a note for her, a page torn from his notebook, on the folded tartan rug.

He was the outsider and the thought was seldom far from Detective Sergeant Joseph Browne's mind, and each time he drove towards Altmore the thought was closer. It was the same country as his home. He was from County Derry, what DC McDonald would have called County Londonderry. The farmers on Altmore were the same kind as his family. On Altmore the people loathed the RUC.

He drove up through Donaghmore and away past

229

the old Celtic cross, the symbol of his culture.

There was a mountain behind his parents' land with the bracken and the gorse and the heather and the windbent trees. Being on Altmore twisted the wound. It was more than four years since he had last spoken to his father. To his mother he was a cross of agony because he could no longer come home in safety, and their meetings could only be in Belfast. To his brothers he was a traitor.

DS Joseph Browne was the rarity in the force because he had been reared at home and educated at school as a Roman Catholic. His point of contact with the man beside him, eight years older, was the job. When they were together, when they were a car team or an interrogation pair, then the work was the only factor that linked them.

He believed himself, as the token Catholic in the Dungannon RUC station Special Branch unit, to be widely resented by the Protestants and Presbyterians with whom he served. He assumed it was thought that his promotion owed as much to his religion as to his competence.

The car was armour-plated in the hope that its doors and windows could withstand an attack from high-velocity weapons, and the chassis was reinforced to protect the crew from culvert bombs. They wore their own clothes, he and DC McDonald, and he had a pistol in his anorak pocket and DC McDonald nursed a loaded Sterling under a raincoat across his knees. They had been told at what time they should reach the pick-up point. They had been shown the exact place on the map. They had been shown the photograph of the youth they were to lift. The number-plates were fresh on the day before, but that was small comfort because the way the armour weighted down the car on its tyres said more than a new set of number-plates.

It was what he had wanted to do.

Bloody-minded, opinionated, stubborn, he knew himself to be all of those when he had told his family that he was accepted into the RUC, and his father had left the room, and his mother had cried, and his brothers had thrown their abuse at him.

He had made a frightened misery of their lives, and that he had not intended.

He slowed the car. It was a feck-awful place to be hanging about. They were at the crossroads, where the lanes running between the high hedges met. The relief sighed in DC McDonald's teeth. The youth had appeared, had walked round the corner, ambling without a care, his work tools in the bag on his shoulder. He had been told the area around the cross-roads was stiff with army; if they were there he couldn't see them. He reversed hard into a side lane, and then as the youth came past them he pulled out again facing the way that he had come.

'Patsy Riordan?'

'Who wants to know?'

DC McDonald flashed his card and there was the barrel of the Sterling to reinforce it.

'It's RUC.'

The fear glowing. DS Browne saw it.

'So?'

'So get in,' McDonald growled.

Joseph Mullins was a detective sergeant and on the force to show there was no discrimination against Catholics in the Royal Ulster Constabulary.

'No problem, lad, just get in,' he said quietly.

He heard the door close behind him. He pulled away. He glanced up at his mirror . . .

Down the lane, behind them, a car was stopped.

Chapter Eleven

It was the story that the small boy loved best, the story that had no ending.

'. . . *All the time they were moving more troops onto the mountain to hunt Shane Bearnagh. There were men brought from Charlemont with their families to the Altmore barracks, worse even than the dragoons, they were called the 34th Foot. There was no good Irishman that was safe from the English soldiers and the gallowglasses, those were the paid men that came with them. If a man helped Shane, fed him, gave shelter to his wife and his little one, then the roof was burned over that man's head, and his crops were ploughed in, and his cattle were taken. But for all the suffering there was no resentment, not amongst the decent folk, for what Shane stood for. He embodied the freedom that his people yearned for. The poor people stayed loyal to Shane Bearnagh.*

'*More troops came, more cavalry. They did everything they could to terrorize the people into telling them where they could find the patriot. Every day that passed made life more dangerous for Shane. Of course, he could have left. There were many Catholics who had gone abroad into exile and safety, but that was not the way of Shane Bearnagh.*

'One day Shane was out walking with his wife, as pretty and fair as any woman on the mountain, and his boy who was a fine wee fellow, and the soldiers on their horses saw them. He told his wife and his son to hide and he ran off across open ground so that the soldiers would follow him. He saved his wife and his son and drew away the dragoons. In his ears he could hear the thunder of their horses' hooves and he could hear them yelling their excitement as if he were a fox they chased. He led them on, across moorland, through forests and all the time they were gaining on him. When they were close to him, when the breath was panting in his lungs, when the leading soldiers were little more than a sabre's cut from him, Shane reached a gorge. A hundred feet below him the mountain river tumbled on sharp rocks. The sides of the gorge were too steep for him to scramble down. Shane jumped. Jesus was with him, and the Mother of Mary. He jumped the gorge, and the gorge was too wide for the horses of the dragoons to follow, but Shane Bearnagh had jumped it. He was gone into the trees leaving them to curse their anger. If you know where to look, if you go to the gorge, there is said to be the place where you can see, set in a stone, the footprint of Shane Bearnagh's boot, where he leaped from to clear the gorge . . .'

'Did they ever catch him, Ma?'

It was the story without a finish.

'It's time you was asleep, Kevin.'

Rennie's voice was low, as if the suspicion of being overheard was always with him, even in the heart of a Special Branch section in the core of Lisnasharragh barracks. Bren sat against the back wall, listened. Cathy Parker was in front of Rennie's desk, straight-backed on a hard chair, sometimes giving him her

234

attention and sometimes staring vaguely out of the one window. Rennie was talking softly but urgently.

Patsy Riordan had been taken into police custody. First to Dungannon police barracks and then to an interview room at the regional holding centre in Gough barracks, Armagh. He would be held overnight, and interrogated.

Attached by a tangle of wires to Rennie's desk telephone was a small tape recorder. Next to the desk was a black and white television set and a radio, both on a wheeled table beside which was a computer console. There were two filing cabinets, each with a padlocked bar running top to bottom that prevented their being opened.

The following morning he would be taken back to Dungannon, and released.

'That's it . . .' Rennie reached into a desk drawer for his pipe.

'Thank you.'

'Coffee?'

'No, thanks.'

'Perhaps your colleague would like coffee?'

'He wouldn't, no.'

The pipe was filled, lit. 'Heh, come off your high horse, Cathy.'

'We don't want coffee, thank you.'

Rennie leaned further forward, waving away the pipe smoke. No longer the policeman of Special Branch, no longer trying to play the cold man who didn't know emotion. Trying now to play the friend. 'Cathy, you know what you're at? You know what you're into . . . ?'

'I don't need telling.'

'You know what'll happen?'

'I'm not a fool.'

Sharp, staccato. 'Heh, Cathy, it's a big boys' game out there.'

'Don't patronize me.'

'That's speeches, Cathy, that's not you.'

There was the flush on her face, Bren saw it. She seemed so small to him, and he could see that her eyes blazed back at the big detective, and her chin jutted defiance at him.

More matches, more tobacco smoke.

'I've done what I was asked.'

'And I'm grateful.'

'I'm not asking for bloody thanks. I want paying in kind.'

'What's that mean?'

'I want Song Bird.'

She snorted. 'Go jump . . .'

Rennie slammed his fist on the desk and said so softly Bren hardly heard him, 'I want Song Bird's name and I want partial control.'

She shoved her notepad into her handbag. The bag was formidable, heavy leather, she handled it like a weapon. She pushed herself up out of the chair.

'No way, no bloody way.'

'You owe it me . . .'

Bren watched.

She turned to him, 'Come on.'

Rennie hissed, 'You stay where you bloody are. Parker, you are the biggest pain up my arse. Don't play the arrogant English *Miss* with me . . .'

She smiled. Bren saw the slow spread of the grin

236

across her face, like she loved the hard-edged policeman. 'And don't you go getting yourself a coronary, Howard.'

'I want him.'

'Well, get it into that thick Ulster skull that you shan't have him.'

'I'll go to Hobbes . . .'

'Wasting your time.'

'I'll cut you off.'

Her laugh was a tinkle. 'Then I'll do without you.'

Rennie was up out of his chair. He was pacing the room, his clenched right fist pounding the palm of his left hand for emphasis. 'You can't go on as if you're the only person fighting this war . . . You have to share the pressure . . . Go on like this, Cathy, playing the bloody queen and all of us dancing for you, and you won't have a friend left, not a bloody squaddie and not a copper, you'll be *alone* . . . we're not all dirt, Cathy, we're not every one of us idiots. And you don't have the God-given right to walk into our backyard and piss all over us. If you're alone, Cathy, then you're finished . . .'

She stood. 'So be it.'

Rennie came to her, put his hands on her shoulders. 'Understand me, you *can't* do it alone.'

'You're shouting, Howard.'

He shook her, as if to exorcize the exasperation. 'Did you sleep last night?'

She moved his hands off her shoulders. 'Why not?'

'Damn you, because of the Riordan boy . . .'

She went to the door. She gestured for Bren to follow. 'I'll be in touch, Howard, and thanks for the help.'

*   *   *

They had held him for twenty-four hours. He had been brought to them three times for interrogation. To DS Browne and DC McDonald it was just routine. Most of the Provo names in the area were brought in at least once a year, sometimes twice. DS Browne would have said that Patsy Riordan, courier, look-out, errand boy, had done well. Doing well was buttoning the lip and looking at the ceiling and refusing to answer any questions beyond name and address. They were taught how to do it, and taught well. It was very rare that you would get a Provo to incriminate himself during questioning.

DS Browne and DC McDonald had been given no operational reason as to why the boy should have been singled out for questioning.

Twenty-four hours after they had picked him up they set him down in the Market Square of Dungannon. Joseph Browne liked his fishing. He liked particularly to go after good-sized pike. When he had hooked them, played them, netted them and weighed them, then he slid them back carefully into the water. They seemed to take a moment to sense their surroundings, then dived for the cover of the reed beds. He thought of the pike when they let Patsy Riordan out of the car.

A moment's hesitation, then the kid was running for Irish Street, gone from sight.

At the end of the day she heard his key in the door.

Mrs Riordan asked her boy where he had been.

Patsy told his mother that he had been lifted.

She asked him why.

238

He told her that if she wanted to know why, then she should ask the bastard police.

Was he in trouble . . . ?

He could handle it . . .

She told him that men had called for him.

Who had called for him?

She felt the bad taste in her mouth. She disliked to talk of them. They were strangers to her. They had come twice to the door of her house as if they had the right to come. Even early in the morning.

'I didn't know who they were. They weren't from here. We was at tea when they came yesterday, and they came again this morning and woke us, and the man said they'd be back again for you's this evening. Who was they?'

'I don't know who they was.'

'Why's they want you?'

'You worries too much, Ma, you worries when there's nothing to worry for.'

He walked out on her. He left his bag of tools in the hall. She watched him walk off to the garage. Later she heard the whining of the engine of his motorcycle.

She was in the kitchen and turning the sausages when there was the sound of a car braking. She was about to shake the chips in the fat when there was the noise of doors slamming. The table was laid. Her man was in the bathroom and washing off the dirt of the farm where he helped two afternoons a week, work-shy and thought it was full employment. She went into the hall. There was a car parked outside the front gate and its exhaust spewed fumes into the evening. She could see the shape of the driver's head but not his features. There was a man who walked away up

239

the drive-way from the garage and her Patsy was following behind him, and there was a third man who walked behind Patsy and close to him. The light was falling. It was difficult for her to see the faces of the men. The man who walked behind Patsy, his hand was on her son's elbow. She wanted to shout out, yell the warning to him, and the shout and the yell were dead in her throat. She couldn't see Patsy's face, just his hunched back. She didn't know whether he went smiling or went frightened.

He sat in the chair close to the fire.

The chair was as close to the fire as it could be without the legs scorching. The OC was hunched forward for the warmth. His wife watched the television and his kiddie played on the carpet with a toy. He didn't hear the television, he didn't see his kiddie. He looked at the jumping flames of the fire and felt the cold on his back and in his groin. He had been told that the Riordan boy had been seen getting into an unmarked police car, and that the Riordan boy had been gone for a full twenty-four hours and then turned up for work in Dungannon.

He no longer ruled on the mountain. Altmore was taken over by strangers.

A forty minute drive. No conversation in the car. Nothing spoken to Patsy and nothing said amongst them. The explanation had been curtailed in the garage beside his home, where they had found him crouched over the engine of the motorcycle. He was to be taken to a meeting. In the car he was not unduly alarmed. He had seen signposts lit by the headlights.

The journey took them beyond Pomeroy and out towards Carrickmore. In a village, just before they stopped, he saw illuminated over the driver's shoulders a sign that was strung from a lamp post. The sign was the silhouette of a volunteer with his head hidden by a balaclava and with the outline of an Armalite rifle in his hands. The slogan on the sign was 'Careless Talk Costs Lives'. He was still thinking of the sign and the slogan when the car came to a stop. In Coalisland or Cookstown or Dungannon, even in the villages of Altmore mountain, the army and police would have torn down the Provo poster. He was in the no-man's-land where the army and police chose not to patrol. The front passenger and the man who had sat silent beside him in the back of the car led him to the front door of a darkened house. They unlocked the door. Patsy walked inside, into the blackness. The door closed behind him. There was the blow on the back of his head, and his feet were tripped from underneath him, and as he fell there was the hard kick into his rib cage.

Mossie drove towards home that lunchtime.

It was not usual for him to go home for lunch from work.

He went home because the third and fourth steps of his ladder had cracked, and he kept a spare ladder in the shed at the back. After his injury he was always fearful of a further fall that might completely disable him.

He was two miles from the village when he saw her.

A lonely woman walking against the wind.

He slowed so that he would not splash her from

the road's rain puddles as he went by her. She had the collar of her coat turned up and a plastic rain hat was knotted tight under her chin. There was little of her face to see. It was only when he was on her that he recognized Mrs Riordan. It was a moment, fast gone, but time enough for her face to be clear to him.

The face was pain . . . and he was gone by.

She was a decent woman and her son had done him no harm.

There had been no tail on his car that morning.

He pulled into a farm gateway. The mountain, dark, stretched away above him. Distanced, small, he could see his own home. He could see the whitewashed walls where was Siobhan and his mother. He had switched off the engine. He was slumped in his seat . . . Who would be his friends? If he quit and ran, who would be his friends? If he stayed, who would be left to bury him . . . ? So many were buried. The day he had come back, on the Heysham to Belfast ferry, with Siobhan and the kids then born and the loaded car, the day the bitch had sent him back, that had been the day that Charlie McIlmurray, taxi driver from Belfast, had been found shot dead on the border. The day he had first found work had been the day that Tommy Wilson had been killed. Maguire had followed, and McKiernan and McNamee. The day Siobhan had gone into hospital to give him little Mary had been the day that Joe Fenton had been put to rest, and his Francis' birthday had been the day of the abduction of John McNulty before the torturing and the killing and the dumping. He could remember the day, bitter cold and bitter frightening, that he had heard on the vine through which whispered information flowed that

242

Paddy Flood, volunteer from Derry, had been taken from his home for questioning by the security team. Who would bury him, if he stayed? Siobhan was involved now and that was his weakness. She was as trapped as himself. They had shot Gerry Mahon, tout, and they had shot Gerry Mahon's wife, accomplice. Siobhan was no safer than himself. The nightmare spread in him. If he were pulled in, if he were worked on by the security team, then sooner or later he would crack, and when he cracked he would name his Siobhan as tout's accomplice . . . Who would hold the children's hands in a church-yard? And if he fled, then his friends in hiding would be the bitch and her minder. He would have no other friends . . .

Mossie started the engine. He drove home to collect the second ladder. He could not scour from his mind the pain-streaked face of Mrs Riordan, walking in the lane and walking against the wind.

He was blindfolded. He was stripped naked. He was tied at the wrists and ankles. He lay on the bed.

They searched his privates and his nostrils and ears and mouth, and between the cheeks of his buttocks, and he felt the cold touch on his skin and Patsy Riordan's numbed mind told him that they used a metal detector over his body.

He was lifted from the bed.

He was taken across the room. He felt the thin carpet below his feet. He was pushed down onto a chair.

The voice was in his ear. 'You know who we are, Patsy?'

So difficult to speak. The fear strangled the words. 'Yes.'

'You know why you're here, Patsy?'

'I done nothing.'

'You're a touting bastard, Patsy.'

'No . . . no . . .'

'And you're going to tell me, Patsy, that you're a touting bastard . . .'

The voice beat in his ears.

There was the quiet knock at the door.

Donnelly called out, 'Yeah?'

The door was opened. Donnelly had slid the paper under the pillow. He was putting the top on the pen and sliding it into the pocket of his shirt. The paper under the pillow was the plan he had drawn of the concourse of the railway terminus. The young man stood in the doorway and there was nervousness on his face. The young man's wife was behind him standing straighter and with her arms folded across her chest. Donnelly read them; she was behind him, the broom-stick up his arse. His eyes glinted. He was clearing his mind. It was the rubbish bin that had his attention. After the Victoria bomb they had taken away all the rubbish bins, but the stations had become so filthy and fifteen months later with no more main line stations attacked they had quietly, no fuss, re-introduced the rubbish bins. The rubbish bins were back, but he didn't know how often they were emptied, and how often they were checked, and he didn't know where they had placed new security cameras at the stations. He had drawn the plan so that he could better work out where cameras might

244

be placed, so that he could examine the possible fields of vision that the cameras might have . . .

'Hi, there, how you doing?' His mind was swept of the rubbish bin.

'We wanted to say . . .'

'Just tell him,' the woman snapped.

It was a soft accent, it was real Cork, being in London hadn't harmed it. The young man blurted, 'We wanted you gone . . .'

'Gone now,' she said.

'I've got work, there's another baby coming . . .'

'We don't want it going on . . .'

'We'll not have our lives ruined.'

He stood. Under his feet was the loose floorboard. Under the floorboard was a pistol and a timing device, and ammunition, and detonators and a circuit board. The anger was rising in him.

The young man said, 'So, we'd be glad if you were gone . . .'

'By tomorrow.'

He stood his full height. He sought to dominate with his physique, and he felt himself punched.

The young man said, 'It's averages, really, sooner or later they'll have you. If they have you then they have us . . .'

Always his wife, she reinforced him. 'The beginning and the end of it is that we've grown out of your games. We don't want them any more.'

The anger bubbled in him. He said, 'Wait, wait, easy, easy . . . Don't come in here feckin' telling me what suits you . . .'

'There's no call for language,' the young man said.

'. . . Don't think you can feckin' push me. Don't

245

think you can just throw me out on the street. What'll happen to you, you thought of that? What'll happen when it goes back to Dublin that a snivelling little prick, a snappy little cunt, have put me out on the street? You thought . . . ?'

'Don't threaten me,' he said.

'. . . you thought what'll happen when I pass the word?'

She looked at him. He could see that she was not afraid. 'Is that all you're at, making fear? I'll tell you something, this isn't home, this isn't where you run things. What are *you* going to do? You going to shoot us, because we want you out? It's a different place this, it's not your place. Your place is back where your bloody home is. You do what you bloody like where your bloody home is. I want you gone by tomorrow . . .'

'Or what?'

She gazed back at him. She met his eyes. Donnelly looked away. He turned his face from her eyes. He heard her voice.

'Try me.'

He heard the door close. He sat on the bed. He bent forward and pulled away the carpet and then with a savage strength he dragged up the loose floorboard. The ring of a voice in his ear. The voice of a brother. The voice of the brother who had gone away. Not even a Christmas card now from the brother who had been gone nine years. He took the folded sheet of paper, the plan, from its hiding place. The voice of a younger brother who now lived outside Albuquerque in New Mexico, and who was a big man and an executive in an electronics company, with a wife and

246

a bungalow and a pool and two young ones. The bell of a voice, 'I'm going, and I'm not coming back, because of people like you. People like you make a shit of everybody's world. You think you're the big smart bastard but you're just rubbish, and I'm going somewhere where people like you would just be squashed out of existence. You're not loved. All you have is the fear of your feckin' gun. I despise you, Jon Jo, and I am ashamed to be your family . . .' He tried to read the plan, but there were tears running on the face of Jon Jo Donnelly.

'What we could do, we could hang you by your legs, hang you upside down, and we could cut the balls off you. You could blather all you wanted, no one'll hear you. We'll get it out of you, you bastard little tout . . .'
    'I wasn't touting.'
    'What were you for at the barracks?'
    'They pulled me in.'
    'Why'd they send a car for you?'
    'To lift me.'
    'Why'd they let you go?'
    'Don't know.'
    'Who was they?'
    'Didn't give their names.'
    'Had you called them?'
    'I hadn't.'
Voices around him. The accusations dinning in his head. 'Why'd they send a car to collect you . . . Where'd the money come from for your bike . . . How many times you met them . . . ?'
    Patsy screaming. 'No . . . no . . . no . . .'
    The quietest voice. 'You knew, Patsy, you knew

247

what was planned in Dungannon. Good men, Vinny and Jacko and Malachy. They was set up, Patsy. They was shot down like dogs . . . And you got money for a bike, and they sent a car to collect you. You say they just lifted you. Why should they lift you? Why didn't they charge you?'

'I don't know . . .'

'I know, Patsy, I know because I can smell a tout when I'm close to him.'

He sat on the chair. The darkness of the blindfold was around him. The tightness of the binding cut at his wrists and ankles. Patsy Riordan knew no way to make them believe him.

She went to Sean Hegarty. Hegarty sat in the hard oak chair and his pipe smoke mixed with the scent of the peat blocks on his fire, and his sister brought in tea and then scuttled for the safety of her kitchen.

'I'm like everyone else on Altmore, Mrs Riordan. I know nothing and I see nothing and I hear nothing. I don't want to know anything, see anything, hear anything. There's an evil on the mountain, Mrs Riordan, and I live my life around it. I don't hold with murder, believe me, but I don't hold with touting either. If the police had your boy, had their claws in him, then I'm just sorry. I'm sorry for you, not for him. I can't tell you anything that'll help, Mrs Riordan. I'm just sorry, for you . . .'

She went to the house of the man she knew to be the OC of East Tyrone Brigade.

The OC let her no further than the kitchen door.

'I don't know why you came here, Missus, it's nothing that's my business. You go shouting your mouth round here, you go saying that I'm in the Armed Struggle, then you've got real trouble, Missus. I don't know who took Patsy away, I don't know why they took him away, I don't know what he might have done. No point in you, Missus, coming to me and asking that I speak up for your Patsy because I don't know who took him, why, what he might have done . . . only thing I'll tell you, Missus, if there's a tout from off this mountain and he's dead then you won't find tears on me . . .'

She walked in the rain up the lane spattered with tractor mud to the house of the man who had twice in the last three months called at her home for Patsy.

The Quartermaster took her to the back of his garage.

'It's not my business, Mrs Riordan, and you're making trouble for yourself by coming here. It's the business of the Organization, and I don't know anything about that. You'd best be asking them, Mrs Riordan, but don't be asking me where you'd find them. Not a clue, Mrs Riordan, I wouldn't have the first idea. I'll tell you this though, if your boy's clean then he'll come to no harm.'

The wind blew her coat hard around her as she came to the farmhouse far up the mountain slope.

Attracta Donnelly was in her barns and shovelling manure off the concrete and her brat was sweeping what she missed.

'You've an impertinence, Mrs Riordan, coming to me. What am I supposed to do? If your son's a tout, good riddance. Touts have destroyed fine men from here. There'll be no snivelling for the death of a tout in this house. You want to complain, well don't

249

complain to me. Get yourself down to Dungannon barracks and make a complaint to the Chief Inspector there, the 'Branch bastard, complain to him about the entrapment of good young boys to spy against their own community. I don't know what you think I could do, and I don't know where you'd the idea that I was someone to speak to. The people I mix with, Mrs Riordan, are patriots, they'd sooner die than inform on their own. Good evening to you . . .'

She sat in her wet shoes in the priest's office.

He had made her tea and she held the cup in both hands to control her shaking, and the cake he had brought her went untouched.

'I talk very frankly to you, Mrs Riordan. I speak in the knowledge that you will hold what I say in confidence. I am a person of convenience here. I baptize the children, I marry the adults, I bury the dead. That is what is required of me, to be a functionary. I venture to say that I have no influence in those areas of wickedness that afflict our society. I can stand in my pulpit and I can demand, or I can appeal, for your Patsy to be released. I would not be heeded. I would be ignored. It hurts me to say it to you, but I am as helpless as you are. The men who hold your Patsy would have no fear of God's wrath. They surround themselves with armour that is ignorance and hatred. And, Mrs Riordan, I have to tell you what you know already, that this community holds powerful feelings against those persuaded by the police to inform against the men of violence. I can only pray, I can only urge you to pray . . .'

She did not know what else she could do. Mrs Riordan walked home. She was not to know of the friend of the priest, who had grown up with him in a village in Antrim and who now worked high in the civil service administration at Stormont Castle, and who had the ear of the Assistant Under-Secretary, the Security Co-ordinator. She could not know that the priest would telephone his friend.

She could only go home to make her man's tea, to wait, and to pray.

The civil servant, the school friend of the priest, stood beside the Assistant Under-Secretary, the Security Co-ordinator. He heard the blustering anger as the Englishman shouted at the phone link to the Chief Constable.

'. . . There is a rule of law in this province, I don't care what Five says. I don't give a brass farthing for the *realpolitik* of Mr Hobbes, or how he justifies his sordid, dishonourable operations. I hold you account-able for the finding and rescue of that boy . . .'

'Patsy, I'm your friend . . .'

The voice in his ear.

'. . . I want to help you, Patsy . . .'

Hunger was in him, and tiredness, and, over-whelming all, fear.

'. . . Listen to what I'm saying, Patsy . . .'

There was the smell of cooking from downstairs.

'. . . You have half an hour, Patsy. You've that time to think on it. In half an hour I'll give you paper and a pen and you will write out all your contacts and all the money they've given you, and all the operations that you've told them about. If you write everything down then we will take you to a press conference and

251

you will read out the statement, and then you will be free to go . . .'

The breath beside his ear was of stale tobacco.

'. . . If you keep on with your lies, after half an hour, then you'll be given over to other men. We haven't treated you badly, Patsy, fair's fair, you'd see that. It'll be different if you get handed over to other men. They're animals, Patsy. There'd be cigarettes on you, there'd be electricity. I wouldn't want to reckon what they'd do to you, Patsy. You've a half an hour to think on it . . .'

'Wait.'

'You going to talk? That's being sensible.'

'Ask Mossie . . .'

'Ask Mossie what?'

'Mossie'll tell you. I worked to Mossie. I's no tout, Mossie'll know I's no tout. Go to Mossie, ask Mossie, Mossie'll speak for me . . . Mossie's a grand man, he'll tell you I's no tout . . .'

The voice was murmured close to him. 'It was Mossie that named you.'

A soft footfall slithering away on the carpet. He was left sitting on the chair and he thought his bladder would burst and his bowels would break.

There were a few times when he was told everything, and a few times when he was told nothing. Most often Colonel Johnny was given a partial truth.

He played host in his office to the Chief Superintendent from Division, and to Howard Rennie from Belfast and the Branch. He worked most days hand in glove with the Chief Superintendent from Division, but he had met Rennie only on a previous tour when he had served in the Intelligence section at HQ Northern Ireland. He thought that the Chief Superintendent from Division was present for form's sake. It was Rennie that he listened to. He remembered Rennie as a cheerful and no-nonsense man, and he was taken aback by the coldness of the Special Branch officer.

'. . . Against our better judgement, certain orders were given in the last forty-eight hours – the background is unimportant now – a boy called Riordan was arrested, questioned, released. I now realize that was an error of professional judgement, and I take no pride in my change of heart. Your intelligence and ours indicates a hunt on the mountain for an informer. Your most recent intelligence and ours indicates that the Riordan boy has been abducted by a PIRA security unit. He most certainly faces torture, and he most probably faces death. There is no way that Riordan is an informer, he is at worst a low-level courier. I now acknowledge that what we did was *wrong*, tactically and morally. I want that boy found before he is tortured. In Belfast a wasp's nest has been stirred up, and results are demanded. I need that mountain searched clean and I want that boy found alive.'

He gave orders for the movements of his duty company and his stand-by company. In the outer office his adjutant was calling up RAF Aldergrove for helicopter support . . . Faint hearts abroad, he thought . . . Her hand would be there, he had no doubt of that, Cathy's hand. Touts, informers, traitors, out on the mountain, that was Cathy's territory. Colonel Johnny was weak with words, but good at listening and evaluating. It was what an upbringing on the

Scottish moorlands had given him, that words of justi-
fication were usually the cover for the half-truth.
There were few words said on those high heathered
hills that were of value. 'Methinks he doth protest too
much.' The day a policeman, a Branch man, talked of
morality, well ... He thought it was pique, he thought
Howard Rennie might have been crossed.

Cathy was out on the mountain. Her radio signal,
her coded call sign announcing her presence had been
logged in Communications.

'Five minutes, Patsy ... A confession, signed. A press
conference and you go free ... Or ... you get handed
to the other men. Which is it to be? There's five
minutes of a half hour left, Patsy ...'

'I don't know anything.'

'God help you if you go to the other men. The
clock's turning, Patsy.'

'Don't know, can't say what you don't know ...'

From away below in the house, where the smell of
the cooking had come from, was the clamour of a telephone's bell.

They lay in the wetness of the hide. They had been in
the hide, by Bren's watch, more than five hours. They
had heard the helicopters scudding overhead, navigation lights lost in the low cloud. It was the way they
had been in the hide before, her half on top of him and
her leg thrown between his thighs. They watched the
bungalow alternately through the Night Observation
Device lens. There was the wind around them, and the
occasional bleating call of bullocks that were across
the far side of the field and huddled down against the

shelter of the thorn hedge on the far side of the field in front of them.

Bren whispered, 'Nugent's the key, isn't he?'

'That's what we'll tell Hobbes.'

'Song Bird's the jewel?'

So soft her voice, so calm. 'Always has been, always will be.'

'To bring back Jon Jo Donnelly? He was the star performer here, he was the best they ever had, is that it?'

'He's the stuff of their folklore, their bloody history. It's like they were lost when he went away.'

'And the Riordan boy saves Song Bird?'

'Right.'

The equations squirmed in his mind and spilled out the questions, and there was the deadness in the back of his legs where her weight pressed down on him.

'Because Jon Jo Donnelly's so important . . . ?'

'Donnelly's public enemy Number One right now in London. You know that.'

He heard the hoarseness of his own whisper. 'You can live with what happens to the Riordan boy?'

'It's just my job.'

'That's what they've always said, the people who ran the Nazi camps, the guards in Stalin's Russia, Saddam's torturers . . . They were just doing their job . . .'

'My conscience isn't bruised.'

'Should it be?'

'A tiger terrorizes a village, it's a man-eater. The villagers call in a marksman. He tethers a goat. The goat is sacrificed. The best moment for the marksman is when the tiger takes the goat. The tiger is shot, but that's academic for the goat. Tough on the goat . . .'

'You believe that?'

She shifted. Her face was beside his. He could see nothing of her. He could feel the warmth from her body and the breath from her mouth.

'You want my bible?'

'Give it me.'

'There's innocent people and good people, and they are suffocated by the killers. There's people out on this mountain who want nothing more than to lead *decent* and *honourable* lives. Agonizing is a luxury. Our job is to free them of the suffocation. It's just a matter of priorities. It's not nice and it's not pleasant, but it's the job I'm paid to do. End of speech . . . If I have another bloody question from you then I'll boot you out of here and you can walk home. Got me?'

'One more question.'

'One, only one.'

'What's it done to you, the job?'

He didn't know what she would have answered. The back door of the bungalow opened. It was his turn on the Night Observation Device. He saw Mossie Nugent come out of the kitchen door and go to the shelter of the back shed, and there was the small flash on the lens of a match striking. He saw Song Bird smoke a cigarette in the wind and the squalled rain of the night. Heh, Song Bird, are you feeling good? Should be feeling good because there's a poor young bastard out there who is keeping you safe by going through three pints of hell. Heh, Mr Nugent, you'll be safe because Miss God Almighty Parker up here has given you her promise.

* * *

256

'I can't write nothing . . .'

'It's your friends, Patsy, they's given us the story. They's out looking for you with helicopters. They's searching houses. They's got roadblocks all over Altmore. Would they be doing that if you weren't theirs? Would they, Patsy? They've told us, Patsy, that you's a tout . . .'

'It's bollocks. I's not a tout.'

'. . . They sent an army to find you, Patsy, and that's telling us. It's your feckin' friends, Patsy, that's told us you's a tout.'

Chapter Twelve

In sunshine, rain, snow, gales, he took his black and white cross collie bitch out onto the mountain. The dog's coat was never brushed, but the rushing and diving into bramble and along the rabbit trails in the gorse left the coat shiny and sleek. There was not an ounce of spare weight on the beast. Old Hegarty had the dog's nose and her wiry slimness and the same bright-eyed, questing appearance. They were inseparable. It was said in the community that Hegarty talked more to his dog on their morning walk than he ever exchanged words with any living being; his sister, certainly, had long since accepted that the dog took first place in his affections. The walk was brisk. Seventy-two years had not slowed old Hegarty's stride, and the dog all the time quartering the country around him.

When they were hunched down in the lee of a great rock or resting together on the cropped grass of a clearing in the forest, he shared the biscuits from his sister's tin and liquorice allsorts from the village shop with the dog, and he told the creature all that he had learned in the Library. The dog knew by now not all but much of what there was to know of the lives of the great architects of Ancient Greece, the highlights of the campaigns of Hannibal and Napoleon, and could probably have recited to herself the best part of the work of Samuel Taylor Coleridge . . . a well-versed hound, the cross-collie bitch.

This morning they were at the top of Logue's Hill, to the west of the summit plateau of Altmore, near the Telecom tower. The dog was ahead of him and it was the white flash on the chest of the dog that he continually saw and lost amongst the gorse and bracken and brambles. His eyesight was fine. He needed glasses only for reading. Fifty yards ahead of him the dog had crouched, belly on the ground, tongue lapping the lower jaw. It was the posture the dog would take if she had found a grazing deer or an unwary fox or pheasant. Old Hegarty had learned to move as silently as any of the mountain's creatures. He came swiftly forward. Beyond where the dog had crouched down, ahead of them, was the dark wall of the close-planted conifer forest. The track that the Forestry men used, past the Telecom tower and into the close-planted trees, was to the right of them. He came without sound to his dog. If it had been a deer and his movement had disturbed it then when they came to their next stop and the sharing of a biscuit he would have apologized.

He could do nothing about the smell of his body or his coat, but he could control his footfall. He knelt carefully beside the dog. Hegarty knew most of the cars that drove on the mountain lanes. He did not know this one . . . The car would have to have come down the gravelled track past the tower and towards

259

the forestry, and then it would have turned off. A car off the track was a hidden car. It was as if the dog knew that the car was covert business and its jaw was flat to the ground and its eyes were locked to the green and mud-spattered bodywork. They waited and they watched.

Hegarty was a man who said what he felt. In his youth his sharp tongue had made him unpopular and lonely. In his old age his reputation was of a harmless eccentric. The words were still in his mind. Later he might have justified them to the cross-collie bitch . . . 'If the police had your boy, had their claws in him, then I'm just sorry. I'm sorry for you, not for him.' There was a car off the track and hidden and there was a boy gone missing. The forest was a place they might have taken the boy. The day was clear ahead of him. His books were due back at the Library. He had only the Library to worry him and the woman there who gave him stick if his books were late. But the Library was not yet open. If he found the boy . . . or found those that held the boy . . . Well, that was something else . . . The mountain was quiet around him . . . If he found the boy, yes, he had his stick and he had his dog . . . Not to say he'd interfere, not to say he wouldn't, but it was Hegarty's pride that he knew everything of Altmore mountain . . . The dun brown of his coat merged with the frosted bracken stems. He pulled the collar up about his ears. He sat on the ground beside the dog.

They appeared between the undergrowth clumps, then were hidden again. They were careful.

He never saw the face of the woman, just the fleck of the gold in her hair.

Hegarty saw the face of the young man that was mud-smeared, and he saw the pistol that he carried and the camouflaged small pack. He saw that the woman carried a snubbed machine gun.

He watched. There was a whisper growl from his dog and his hand, fleshless and veined, dropped onto the dog's head to smooth the fur and quieten her. When they were fifty yards from the car the man and the woman separated. The man came close to him, not more than a dozen paces, and the woman made a circle round to the far side of the car. He saw the young man go down on his back and search underneath the car.

He heard the crisp English accent.

'You drive.'

Hegarty, who knew everything of the life of Altmore mountain, realized the pain of knowing more than he should have known, that there was a covert team on Altmore. He watched the man drive slowly back onto the track, he watched the girl try to erase the marks of the tyres with branches and lightly pushing the bracken into place over the path the car made. He stayed where he was a long time after the last sound of the car had gone.

She had left Bren in the corridor and she had gone to the door of Colonel Johnny's office and in response to her knock he had come to the door and there had been short words between them and then he had led her, Bren trailing, to the adjutant's office. Bren hadn't heard what was said.

Cathy dialled a number, let it ring briefly, then put down the receiver. Bren thought that she .was counting slowly to ten. She dialled again, let it ring, replaced the receiver. Another wait. She dialled the third time.

This was what infuriated him, when there were no explanations. They had come back off the mountain. They had driven to the barracks. They had gone their separate ways to shower and change. They had come to the officers' block to use the telephone. He was not told who she rang, why she rang three times. Since he had watched Mossie smoking his last cigarette out of his back door there had been seven hours of unbroken silence between them, except for the basics of the surveillance, before they had moved out in the half-light. And all she had said then was to tell him to drive . . .

They were in the corridor, and Rennie came out of an office and Colonel Johnny was with him.

She stood beside Bren. She was dwarfed by the three of them. She seemed to shake herself, to prepare for the challenge she could see coming. Rennie was the big man, she was the little woman. Where she stood she blocked Rennie's way down the corridor.

Bren could only admire her. That was her way, head on.

'Good God, look at this, Bren . . . It's the Eternal Flame, the policeman who never goes out. Heavens, Mr Rennie, not actually going to get mud on your shoes, are you?'

'Miss Parker, you are deep in shit.'

'Put me there, did you?'

'And I won't be around to lift you out.'

'We haven't been telling tales out of school, have we? I gave that up in the fourth form . . .'

262

'You're running out of time, Miss Parker, and don't say you weren't warned . . .'

Cathy stood four-square across the corridor, tiny and implacable, the tired bloody-mindedness that was all her own set against Rennie's rising temper.

'. . . Don't push me, not one inch further.'

She mimicked his accent. 'Would you fall over?'

She stood aside. She let them pass. Rennie and the colonel strode away and then turned for the Operations Room.

It snapped in Bren. 'That's just terrific, Cathy. Bloody wonderful. That's a man that would go to the wall for you. Don't mind me, I don't matter, I'm just here to do the chores. But that man matters and you've lost him. By God, I'm learning the lot today, really sophisticated, top operative stuff. Come off your high horse, Cathy, for Christ's sake.'

She walked away from him. She swayed once and he thought she might just have been half asleep.

They were outside the block building, deafened by a helicopter floating down to land. There were soldiers with their kit and their weapons kneeling in a line, ready to board. Her voice was drowned but shouting at him.

They had time to kill.

How long to kill?

Six hours, seven.

What should he do?

They were going to be eating, sleeping, drinking east Tyrone, he should learn about the place.

How to do that?

Start where everyone starts, in the Library . . .

Where was she going to be?

She was going back to Belfast, she would collect him in six hours in the Market Square.

Shouldn't he be with her?

'Mooning around after me like a bloody sheep on heat? No, thank you.'

She might have punched him.

'I'll see you,' Bren said.

Two roadblocks on his way to work. Because he was Charlie One, Stop and Search, he had been out of the car both times and half stripped down at the side of the road, and both times every piece of kit that he took to work, tins, dust sheets, brushes, ladders had been emptied out of the back of the estate for examination. If there had not been a uniformed police constable at both roadblocks then he might have been roughed over by the soldiers. Bitter, snarling taunts from the soldiers, like they were trying to wind him, like the best they could hope for was that his temper would crack. 'Heh, you cripple arsehole, why are you making war on your own people, eh?' 'You must be fucking perverts, torturing some little kiddie for your kicks.' 'Got a tout in your knickers, have you? Giving out the inside story, is he?' 'Steady on, Sar'nt, better be nice to this one, maybe he's one of ours.' 'Nah, this one's a kiddie-torturer . . .' It was what they wanted, that he would flail out, and then they could have taken him behind the hedge and given him the real kicking, the hard belting. It was Mossie's secret, and he could hold his temper. The whole of the mountain community had known that the roadblocks ringed the villages. At home, under the false floor of the wardrobe beside the Building Society account book,

264

was the bleeper. Couldn't have the bleeper strapped between his legs if he were to be stopped and searched by the army and police. It was his secret, one he shared with the bitch.

So he had been late to work. He had been there an hour when there was a message, he was wanted on the telephone.

Siobhan told him there had been three calls, close together, twice she had picked it up, no voice.

He told her he would be late home.

It was the first time he could remember the bitch using her emergency code to call him to a meeting.

The man from Lurgan had the reports. More troops on the mountain than there had been the evening before, more police blocks, derelict buildings had been searched, houses had been raided. The reports came by telephone and by courier. It was confirmation of what he had earlier thought.

The house where they held the Riordan boy was outside the cordon that had been thrown around Altmore. He knew the way the army and the police worked. They would first satisfy themselves that the boy was not inside their present net, then they would expand it. He didn't reckon he had much time left.

If 500 soldiers and police with helicopter support were searching the mountain then it was because of *obligation*. They had lost one of their own. The man from Lurgan was without remorse, without compassion. Many years before, when Patsy Riordan who was now upstairs and blindfolded and bound had been in nursery school, the man from Lurgan had been interviewed by a psychiatrist. He had been in custody, charged with murder. The psychiatrist had declared him to be without mental illness, not reliant on alcohol, emotionally stable and of average intelligence. The forensic evidence against him had failed. The man from Lurgan was quite normal, quite loving, in the company of his family and the friends he acknowledged who were outside the Provisionals. He could handle, effortlessly, the irreconcilable compartments of his life . . . He would have preferred a confession from the boy. He would have wanted it on tape so that it could be played to the tout's family.

But time was against the man from Lurgan.

On the telephone he named a rendezvous, and he asked for a handgun to be brought to the rendezvous.

'Do you want leave?'

'I do not.'

'Do you want transferring out?'

Cathy said, 'All I want to know is that you'll stand my corner.'

Hobbes thought she was magnificent. He thought she was the sort of young woman who would be found at hunter trials or working her own big estate, or who would very occasionally take time off to be at one of those Sunday drinks in the country where his wife was so happily at home and where he was the abysmal stranger. Darling Charlotte had flatly refused to join him in Belfast, stated right off the bat when his transfer had come through that life was too short to be wasting it in the provinces.

'Damn you for thinking you even need to ask.' She grinned. 'Their nerve's going.'

'It's what you'd expect, policemen, civil servants,

politicians. I'll stand your corner, always.'

He had never understood from where she quarried her strength. She looked to him to be worn out. She obviously needed leave and she probably did need transferring out. Nor could he grasp what seemed to be her compulsion to stay in Northern Ireland. Perhaps it was not his job to understand, just to be thankful that he had her on his payroll. He ran six teams in the Province, three in Belfast, three for the rest of the territory. She was unique. He would never again be surprised by her, not after the Christmas party the year before last, where all the teams came together. Fancy dress. Cathy, the only woman there, on the table. Cathy dancing a belly dance to the frantic hand-clapping of the men around her. Best Christmas party anyone could remember. She hadn't come last year, hadn't even answered the invitation actually . . . She wouldn't be transferred out, they'd need a blow torch to move her. He did not understand what was the compulsion.

'You go careful.'

'And you keep those bastards off my back – till I've got Donnelly here, till I've him stitched.'

He showed her out. He went back to his desk and sat beside his telephone and waited for the Triple A, anti-aircraft artillery, to begin to detonate around him.

Mrs Riordan stayed at home. Her man was away at the farm. It was too stressful for him to sit with her by the small fire and while away the uncertain hours. No neighbours visited her. If she had gone to the village shop, all the talk would have stopped while she made her purchases and paid for them, not started again until she had gone back out through the shop door. It was no more than she expected, that her neighbours would shun her, abandon her. It would be known across the mountain that her Patsy had been taken for questioning as a tout. So confused . . . She had known he was junior with the Provisionals, but through the pain, the agony of imagining her son, screaming in fear, she could think of nothing that might have told her he lived the double life, couldn't, couldn't, couldn't believe it of him. She had said as much to her man. She had gone so far as to say that young Patsy wasn't up to it, not bright enough, but her man wouldn't meet her eye, couldn't bring himself to speak the boy's name. She was so alone she thought her heart would just break.

It would be the priest who would bring the news of the finding of a body.

There was no note taken, no stenographer was present. The Assistant Under-Secretary was on secondment from London. The Chief Constable had been transferred from a northern English force. They were blow-ins. Competing voices because each man sought to preserve the sanctity of his position.

'It's down to Five. Five thinks it can ride roughshod over us. They're unaccountable. They have no place here . . .'

'They demand support and facilities, and they share nothing.'

'It's the arrogance of their people that infuriates me, the constant implication that no-one else is prepared to prosecute the war with sufficient ruthlessness . . .'

'This time they've gone too far.'

The Assistant Under-Secretary said, 'But your people are involved. Your people arrested the Riordan boy, directed the finger of suspicion at him . . .'

The Chief Constable said, 'Not at my rank, not at the level of my Deputy, nor my Assistant Chief Constables – way below that.'

'All they talk about, Five, is winning the war, they have no comprehension of winning the peace . . .'

'It's to be stopped. They're to be put out of here. They're a nuisance and an impediment. What I hear, not from them of course, I'm told nothing by that dreadful little Hobbes, what I hear is that all of this fiasco can be laid at the door of just a slip of a girl.'

The Assistant Under-Secretary said, 'If my Secretary of State backs down in front of them, I'll take it to Downing Street . . .'

The Chief Constable said, 'You do that. You will have the gratitude of every senior man in my force, just rid us of them.'

The voice of the Assistant Under-Secretary dropped, 'Did I hear you right? Did you say, a girl . . . ?'

Bren sat in the Library on the town's Market Square.

He was on the first floor, in the wide well-lit room that was the reference section. It was the type of library rarely found at home. Probably a bomb had done for its predecessor, this was new and clean and warm. Most of the square outside, round the cenotaph, was recently built, as if the old centre of Dungannon had been blown away, a chunk of used history.

He had started with the back files of the local paper. All of life's tapestry spread before him. Road deaths, local thieving, drunk driving bans, industrial accidents, assaults, vandalism. Jobs hopes and jobs despair, fashion shows, advertisements of Christmas menus at the hotels and restaurants, property for sale. Quite like home . . . Bullshit.

'. . . he died after being shot by gunmen as he worked in a friend's garage on the outskirts of . . .'

'. . . the chairman of the District Council went on to express sympathy to the family and relatives of . . .'

'. . . he called on the RUC to take action following the UVF arson attack . . .'

'. . . the Presbytery of Tyrone expresses its deep concern at the campaign of vicious terrorist violence that goes on unabated . . .'

'. . . the two police officers suffered minor shock when the car in which they were travelling was . . .'

Stories tucked away, given no special prominence, in the local newspaper. He turned to the current rates at the Farmers' Mart, and the organized day tour to show off a new flat-deck weaner house for pig breeders. He checked the local gaelic football results and the property prices. The killings and the burnings and the ambushes were given no particular priority. All new to him, and all old and sickening and *ordinary* to the people of the community . . .

He looked up. She was a pretty girl. She carried four volumes of old books. She was sorry she had not been quicker. They would cover the history of Dungannon and the history of Tyrone. She wore bright clothes and careful make-up. He wondered how she closed her mind to killings and burnings and ambushes. She

270

took away the bound files of the newspapers. There were five tables in the room. Three were taken by sixth-formers, quiet and dedicated in their reading.

Dungannon . . . Dun-Genan . . . Dun was fort on the hill, Genan was the son of Cathbad the druid. Genan, son of Cathbad, had built his strongpoint on the hill that was above Market Square. He gutted the pages. Saint Patrick had built a religious house here. Time slipping by Bren. Shane O'Neill, with his seat at Dungannon, launched rebellion against Elizabeth the First of England, defeated in battle, trapped, killed, his head worth £1000. Fine print straining his eyes. Hugh O'Neill, uncrowned king of Ireland and ruling from Dungannon, defeating the English at the battle of the Yellow Ford. Feet shuffling towards him on the parquet floor. Hugh O'Neill destroyed by the army of James the First of England, and the start of the plantation. A chair at his table scraped back. The good lands planted with English and Scots settlers, and the Dungannon Irish driven to the mountain slopes of Altmore, castles built and Dungannon fortified, and seditious speaking a capital offence. The smell was stale rich, of an unwashed body and clothes. The rebellion of Sir Phelim O'Neill, and the English slaughtered in Dungannon and Tullyhogue; a battle-ground for Cromwell; a campaign land for William of Orange and the deposed James the Second; at the top of the Market Square, below the walls of the castle, had been the high gallows. There was a guttural cough and then the sound of phlegm spat into a handkerchief. He read the name of Shane Bearnagh Donnelly, the dispossessed, the man without teeth whose gums were tough enough to bite through a tin

271

plate who was hunted by the English dragoons, and who . . .

'They's fine books.'

Bren looked up. He saw the strong country face and a thin chin not shaven that day. Behind the man was the sign requesting 'Silence'. The old man wore a rain-stiffened overcoat and under that was a grey jacket and then a shirt without most of the upper buttons and then a high-necked and yellowed vest.

'Yes.'

'It's the book I like the best here.'

'Is it?'

'It's the book that tells best of the injustices done to us.'

'Really?'

The hand, grimed fingernails and bloodless knuckles, snaked out over the table. The old man pulled the book to him.

'So, you's reading of Shane Bearnagh . . . ?'

'I am.'

'Gave the English a great dance. A whole barracks they built for the soldiers hunting him on the mountain. Is you's English?'

'Yes.'

There was a cackled laugh. 'You've not much of a tongue.'

Bren felt the colour in his face. The book was pushed back towards him. 'Well, . . .'

'So, what brings an Englishman to Dungannon to read the history of Shane Bearnagh Donnelly, rebel and patriot?'

'I had time to kill. I've always been interested in history.'

'You won't mind me, course you won't, what's your business?'

Bren tripped it out. 'Department of the Environment.'

'Ah . . .' As if so much was explained.

'Just learning about this community . . .'

They were clear and pale blue, the eyes were on Bren's. Bren thought that it was like play at the surface of the eyes, and only mirthless cold behind. To leave now would be to draw attention to himself. It was harmless enough. The eyes followed Bren as he shifted his head.

'Have you's found a fine welcome here?'

'Only just starting.'

'You'll find a grand welcome. We're friendly people.'

'Yes.'

'Even friendly to an Englishman from the Department of the Environment.'

'Good to know.'

'You'd not get a welcome, but you'd be knowing that, if it was thought you were of the Crown Forces.'

'The Department of the Environment has nothing to do . . .' Bren said.

'Crown Forces aren't welcome, nor their spies.'

'I wouldn't know,' Bren said.

'There's a way round here of showing people they're not welcome, if they're spies.'

The page was blurred in front of him. 'They're difficult times.'

273

'They don't last, young man, the spies.'

Bren looked up and saw that four girls at the next table, trim in their school uniforms, seemed to hear nothing.

'There's a nose for spies in this town, on that mountain out there. Spies smell.'

'If you'll excuse me . . .'

The sudden smile splintered the weather-beaten face. 'Talking too much again, always Hegarty's problem, talking too much. You'll be wanting to be back to your reading.'

Bren stood up. He gathered the books from the table. The old man had hunched himself over the day's newspaper. Bren returned the books to the pretty girl downstairs. He thought he might be sick. He walked out through the wide glass doors of the Library and into the end of the afternoon. The wind caught at him and the sweat ran chilled on the back of his spine. A stupid old fart, just a prattling old windbag . . . So they wouldn't last, the spies. He thought of Cathy, tired and sweet and lovely Cathy. Cathy who would be there tomorrow, and the next month, and the next year, in the town and on the mountain. He had time still to lose, so he walked briskly away from the Library, forcing himself not to look back at the first-floor windows, and he believed that every eye in Market Square was on him.

On the site, two heavy packets of nails and screws and bolts and nuts had been delivered. Nothing out of the ordinary. A van driver unknown to Mossie had called at the foreman's portacabin for a signature. A trainee chippy had been sent back to the van to fetch the

274

delivery. Nothing there to disturb Mossie as he got on with brushing the undercoat onto the fresh plasterwork. But he had seen the sullen expression of the apprentice. Next time he passed, he called the boy, quietly, not drawing attention to himself, and asked him why so cross, laddie. The boy had spat it out. The driver had been the lippy one at a vehicle check point three nights back when the boy had been tipped out of his old car, and his girl, searched down to his bollocks, given the chat that was always roughest when the UDR part-timers were flaunting their bullet-proof flak jackets and their high-velocity rifles. The boy had recognized the driver as the soldier who had humiliated him in front of his girl. And Mossie had noted the smart new logo on the side of the van.

He had left work early. He had no problem getting away early because he was on piecework and he had already achieved the amount for the day for which he was paid.

He sat in his car. He was down the road from the gates to the builders' merchant's. He saw the van come back, checked the number plate against his memory. He wrote nothing down. His memory served him well. He recognized the driver. It was his task, that of the Intelligence Officer of the East Tyrone Brigade, to identify targets for the Active Service Units. He was way off safe territory, he was up past Stewartstown, and that was danger, particularly for a man who was Charlie One, Stop and Search. He watched the man, changed out of his overalls, drive from the yard in a dark blue saloon car. He followed cautiously. Most often he would have left this work to a young volunteer, a kid, even a girl, who was on the edge of the Organization's operations, who was being tested. Not always. Mossie thought that it was only sometimes possible to involve the kids, but the time always came when it was necessary for him to take the risk himself. On the far side of Stewartstown he saw the car pull up outside a small and clean-painted bungalow. That was when he held back. A part-time soldier in the Ulster Defence Regiment would have been briefed, had it pounded into his skull, that he was most in danger from ambush when he left his home and when he returned to his home. When the man was inside, through his front door, Mossie drove past the bungalow. He could do that once, only once. He saw an elderly woman, the hem of an apron peeping from under her raincoat, sweeping leaves from the front path, he saw the glower look that the mother of a UDR part-timer would reserve for any car going slowly past her home.

It was a nugget of information. It was a beginning. There was no race to kill a man who was a part-timer with the UDR. The critical moment was already past, the linking of the chain, the identifying of the bastard. He drove away. He looked for the proximity of the part-timer's neighbours, and for the cover that the winter hedgerows would offer, and the fall of the trees back across the first field on the far side of the road. It might take weeks, months even, to learn the habits of the soldier, whether he always left home and returned home on his own, whether he was sometimes collected by a work colleague or a soldier colleague. He would learn at what pub he drank, where he worshipped, his shift pattern at the barracks. He would learn whether his mother always made it her business to be in the garden when he left and returned, and whether he drove away fast, and whether the car was securely locked into the garage at night. He would find the name of the soldier and the history of the soldier. And he would never speak of him to the apprentice boy at work.

A man was marked.

Only when he was quite satisfied would he present his plan to the OC. That Cathy might then throw away the plan, because he would report all of that business faithfully to his handler, that was of no importance to him. It had grown to be the miracle of Mossie Nugent, that he could live with a life divided.

He was the stranger and he tramped the pavements of the town.

Two great religious buildings, and their matching magnificence to emphasize a community's separation, St Anne's for the Protestants and St Patrick's for the Roman Catholics. Two great school complexes to hammer home a community's division, the Royal for the Protestants and the Academy for the Roman Catholics. Two main shopping streets to bring home the opposition of the cultures, Scotch Street for the Protestants and Irish Street for the Roman Catholics. Two spreading sports complexes where the people of the town were split, the rugby club to the east for the Protestants and the gaelic pitches to the west for the Roman Catholics.

Bren walked through the town community that was separated, divided.

He was the stranger.

He was the spy . . .

An old man had frightened him.

He walked because he had been frightened by the queer crack of an old man. God, and he wouldn't be telling Cathy Parker that he had run, tail between the legs, from an old man in a library. They were gathered on each corner of Market Square, the men who watched him. He would have sworn that every eye was upon him. Old men and young men, cupping their hands across their faces to light their cigarettes, lounged against walls on the corners where Irish Street and Scotch Street and Church Street ran up into the Square. Eyes piercing him and stripping him.

He was trained to move on a street without attracting attention to himself.

It was just idiotic that he should feel fear.

He thought the training was nothing, the reality was the peering eyes from each corner of Market Square.

It was the separated and divided town. There were no high barriers of corrugated iron to divide off each community's ghettos. He learned, as he walked, the unspoken boundaries. The soldiers patrolled the streets that were set aside for Roman Catholic homes, laden with backpacks and radio sets and machine guns, marked the territory of the Roman Catholics. Young men, whipping orders in the *patois* of the north of England, questioning and frisking kids in a tongue that was foreign and hostile to the town. The police ruled the Protestants' roads and avenues. Crisply turned out, bulged by their bullet-proof vests, powerful with their carbine rifles and sub-machine guns, ties knotted neatly under their laundered collars ... Each pace he took, so he felt the growing of the fear.

A community divided by history, tacked together by firepower, separated by suspicion. He thought he could have read for a year in London and not have known the half of what he had seen for himself in an hour. A town that was no place for strangers.

'. . . They don't last, young man, the spies . . . There's no safety for spies . . .'

'When did it happen?'

'It was two days back, they was here four hours.'

It was still daylight outside. The light was filtered through the coloured glass of the old door and magnified the pattern on Jon Jo's back. He thought the man must have been watching as his car arrived because the door had been opened even before he reached the porch. He had been hurried inside and the door had been pushed shut immediately.

'There was nothing to find.'

'But they came . . . I don't know how long they'd the house watched, and I don't know whether they still have us watched. I was talking last night to friends, they're the other end of Guildford, they're the only other Irish I know in the town, they were turned over two days back as well.'

'It won't be for long.'

Jon Jo saw the shake of the man's head. 'Oh, no . . . no, no . . . don't get me wrong, it's been my family's cause more than a century; I stand by it; but, my friend, you don't come back . . . Perhaps it's just that they're searching everywhere, how do I know? You don't come back to a house that's just been searched. It's not right for you, it's less than right for me. It wasn't just uniformed men that came, it was detectives . . . Whose

279

was the empty room? For any of the family from over the water . . . Was anyone expected? Not just right now . . . Why was there fresh bed-linen if no-one was expected? Always clean bed-linen . . . If no-one's expected, why is the room kept free, don't I need the money? Any time, any of the family might decide to come over . . . When was there last someone from the family over? Difficult to remember . . . They searched hard. I don't know, maybe it was just routine, they were four hours going over the place. Jon Jo, hear me, I'm not giving them reason to come back.'

'I have to have a place.'

'You have to sort it yourself, and Jon Jo . . .'

'Do you feel no shame?'

'Listen, damn it, they showed your photograph . . . they showed it to the English that lodge . . .'

He swayed against the wallpaper in the hallway.

'. . . I saw the photograph, what they were showing. It was you. Didn't put a name to it, but it was your photograph . . .'

He felt the shock and the sickness that followed.

'I'm sorry, Jon Jo.'

He didn't help the man. He didn't say that he understood. There was the tightness all across him, like a noose at his neck, like handcuffs on his wrists.

'Jon Jo, my advice, get yourself out of here, get yourself home. Get yourself where you're from.'

'I might, I might just . . .'

He was wanted out and he went. Only on the mountain would he know friends.

They took Patsy Riordan, after it was dark, they turned the lights out and carried him out of the front

280

door and they tipped him into the boot of the car that had been backed up close. They had dressed him upstairs. Vest, shirt, sweater, underpants, trousers, socks, anorak. His trainer shoes were carried to the car by a man who wore plastic gloves.

It was the old Irish custom from the dark past. A man with his shoes taken from him is a man disgraced.

His wrists were bound at his back. He was blind-folded. There was a gag at his mouth. The blindfold had been tightened and knotted again.

He was a young man who was going to his death and there was no love around him and no comfort.

The boot lid shut above him. He kicked and writhed and tried to scream. There was no-one who would hear him. He was thrown against the spare tyre and bounced as the car hit the pavement edge as it turned out of the drive and made for the open country lanes. He struggled to free himself, to draw attention to himself, until he was too weak to move again. He prayed, mumbled words that were muffled by the gag, for the sound of the English soldiers' voices, for the knowledge that the car had run against a road-block. He knew they went on winding and potholed roads. The Provisional wing of the Irish Republican Army had been everything that he admired, every-thing that he had sought to be part of. He heard no talk in the car, only the music from the Downtown station. He had lost all sense of direction. He began to lose the sense of time. The blindfold on his eyes was wet from his tears. He had done nothing, he was without guilt . . . he was to be killed as a tout.

Patsy Riordan was already dead, his mind blown

away by terror, when the car stopped.

He was dragged from the boot.

A bin liner bag was forced over his head and he lay on the wet, cold grass of the lane's verge as hands reached under the bag to remove the gag and the blindfold.

He heard a voice. 'Get it done.'

He heard the splatter of the rain on the plastic of the bin liner bag that was over his head.

He heard the arming of the pistol.

The darkness was all around him. There was the weight of a boot in the small of his back, as if to hold him steady.

Chapter Thirteen

'They've shot the Riordan kid.'

Bren winced.

Cathy said, 'It's not your problem.'

'The little bugger had no chance.'

Bren was just the minder, and the man with the gun, the protection.

Cathy said, 'Don't give me any crocodile tears, Mossie. I don't want to hear "it's a rotten old world". You're safe, and you get paid.'

'The body's down by the border.'

Bren held the Heckler and Koch. It was set to semi-automatic, and his finger lay alongside the trigger guard.

Cathy said, 'It's gone and it's past and it was never your problem. I told your wife I'd look after you. I keep my promises, don't forget that.'

'You's a feckin' awful woman.'

Bren felt the muscle tightening in his arms. If Song Bird touched Cathy he would belt him with the stock of the weapon, straight across the back of the head. That was just ridiculous. About half a light year before he could have hit the tout she would have had him flat

283

on his face . . . He could hear the music from the bar.
They had left the car in the parking area, an expanse
of weeded gravel, they had gone to the darkness
behind the propane gas tanks at the back of the bar.

Cathy said, 'If you've had your whining time,
Mossie . . .'

'He'd done nothing, that Patsy.'

Bren was the voyeur. He just watched her at work.
Tough and soft, stick and carrot. She had him in the
palm of her hand, and she knew it and her hands
dropped off his shoulders as if there was no more
need for her to shake the hardness back into him.
'You're not a bloody kid, Mossie, you are the best man
I have. You are just bloody brilliant, Mossie, and
you're *safe*. Got me?'

'What do you want?'

Bren glanced down at his watch. Near to closing
time.

Cathy said, 'I want Jon Jo Donnelly back on the
mountain . . .'

The bar was a roadhouse between Portadown and
Lurgan. The bar was on a main road and there was no
backup in position. A group spilled out of the bar and
Bren went to the edge of the wall that cut off the gas
tanks from the car park. He watched the men coming
out of the bar and one was staggering and two were
helping him. He had his back to Cathy and her Song
Bird. He could only hear short snatches of what was
said behind him. He ducked back behind the wall
as the arc of the headlights swept the car park when
the vehicle turned. She talked about money, big
money, for Song Bird. He told her that Jon Jo Donnelly
was a hero on Altmore. It was what they wanted, she

284

said, Donnelly back home. He said it was all the talk of the Brigade that Jon Jo was needed. Bren listened. The car park was quiet again. She dominated him, took no hesitancy from him. She said that they wanted Donnelly back soonest, and he said that the OC would back it. She said it wasn't to be in a month, but a week, and he said that the OC would go down to Dublin and ask for it, sure as hell. There were more men tripping from the bar. God help you, Mossie Nugent, because no other bastard would. More talk of money from Cathy, always she returned to the money.

Then Mossie was gone, away round the gas tanks behind the bar, walking back into the lights of the car park, pulling up his trouser zip and walking unsteadily. Back into his real world. His real world was touts, and a bullet in the head, and money that he couldn't spend, and Patsy Riordan's mother, and his fear for Siobhan and the children, and the meetings in the darkness at the back of a bar's car park.

She was very close. He saw that she was grinning. He could feel the tension rising in him, perhaps she saw it and it amused her.

'How long, Cathy?'

'How long what?'

'How much longer do you go on like this?'

'What sort of drivel's that?'

'It can't last.'

'You're going soft.'

'Like tonight, no back-up.'

'Losing your bottle?'

'You've no back-up because you've fouled with Rennie and you're too proud to ask it of the military. You're buggering about on the end of the bloody

285

branch, Cathy, and you're going to fall off. Luck is going to run out on you because you're taking short cuts. No back-up tonight. No back-up on the mountain last night.'

'Why don't you just get on the plane out?'

'You're starting to make mistakes, Cathy. It's a mistake to come to a meeting without back-up. It was a mistake to lose Rennie. And most of all, it's a mistake to think you can operate alone here.'

'I think we'll have to tell little Mr Wilkins that you're not quite up to it, why not?'

'You're running out of friends, Cathy . . .'

'Have you finished?'

Bren stood his full height. It was his mistake. He had his back to the car park. He looked down at her. 'You go on like this and you go home in a box. Is that what you want? Are we playing the little heroine game? Are we too clever to take the precautions that everyone else takes?'

She looked past him. She hissed, 'Behind you . . .'

He swung. He was wrenching the cocking lever of the weapon.

His eyes traversed the emptiness of the car park. There was the chuckle of her laughter.

'When I'm ready, Bren, then I'll go home.'

Bren said, flat, 'You won't last.'

She was still laughing. 'Watch me . . .'

Mossie shut the door quietly behind him. His car might have woken them all, his Siobhan and his mother and the children, but he paused on the balls of his feet in the hall of the bungalow. There was the light in the hall that was left on so that the children would not be afraid. Right to leave it on all night, because there was no call for the children to be afraid . . . God . . . no cause for his children to be afraid . . . Mother of Mary . . . like they would have been afraid if they had known the half of their father. He went into the living room and closed the door behind him and he went to the window and eased back the joined curtains, enough for him to see out. He looked up the lane for the flash of a match, for the low glow of a cigarette. From the living room he went to the kitchen and again closed the door behind him and stood in the darkness to look over the fields behind the bungalow. There was faint moonlight. He might have seen a movement if it had been there, he might not. He saw nothing, no sign that they were still watched, that his children had cause to be afraid . . . Jesus . . . He wondered if in her house Mrs Riordan slept.

He took off his shoes in the hall and went in his socks into their bedroom. He undressed in the dark. He laid his clothes silently on the chair. He took his pyjamas carefully from under the pillow on his side of the bed. Just as any other night when he came back late and his family were asleep. He lay down beside Siobhan.

She hadn't slept. He whispered that they wanted Jon Jo Donnelly back.

'That's a bad boy,' Siobhan said softly.

'I's to do what I can to get him back.'

She was dragging his arm around her shoulder, nestling closer to him. 'She's a stuck-up woman, his.'

'He's bombing and killing across the water. They can't find him there, so they wants me to bring him back and mark him for them.'

287

'You do that for her, what'll she do for you?'

She was against his body. He held her closer. 'She said I'd have more money.'

'What'd we do with the money?'

'What we done with it so far, nothing.'

'How much money?'

'She didn't tell.'

'You didn't ask her?'

'She just said that if I got Jon Jo back there would be more money.'

'I'd have wanted to know how much money . . . I never could take Attracta Donnelly . . .'

He pitched his body up on his elbow. He glowered over her. 'Does that make it right? More money? That you don't like Attracta Donnelly?'

'Makes it right enough for me.'

No way out and no way back. He didn't tell her what he knew of Patsy Riordan. The sweat was on his body. The corpse lay at the side of the lane. The hands were tied and the head was hooded. The corpse wore his own clothes, Mossie's clothes. Not a dream, because sleep was far from him. The head of the corpse that was covered with the plastic bag hung down into the rainwater ditch, and the body that wore his clothes was across the grass, and the feet from which the shoes had been taken were splayed on the tarmacadam surface.

Mossie's body.

The Lynx circled at three thousand feet.

The camera's screen showed them the black of the plastic bag, the yellow of the shirt and the grey of the pullover and the green of the anorak. The jeans

288

on the body were pale blue. White socks on the feet, and the helicopter's crewman wondered why they had taken the shoes from the body.

They had lifted off at first light, within an hour of the first report.

The crewman looked away from the screen and to the helmeted head of the pilot. He flicked his intercom switch.

'Tell you what, Barrie. Seeing what they do to their own sort of shrivels my pecker at the thought of what they'd do to us if we came into their loving hands.'

The distorted voice in his ear. 'Fly high, fly safe. Best answer to the problem, let the bastards butcher each other, faster the better, more the merrier.'

When they had photographed the body, they turned to the other equipment they carried, the infra-red that could show them the path of a buried command wire to a booby trap beside the body and they switched on the high-frequency radio signals that would detonate a bomb laid for the recovery team.

They had been up an hour, and from that vantage point they could see across the rolling hills, the steep escarpment mountains, meadow lands, scattered farmhouses, villages, and tiny spires reaching a very little closer to God . . .

The crewman said, 'Forget the body, Barrie, it's a pretty lovely place down there.'

The voice crackled in his ear.

'Listen, my old darling . . .

  MacDonagh and MacBride
  And Connolly and Pearse

289

Now and in time to be,
Wherever green is worn,
Are changed, changed utterly;
A terrible beauty is born.

. . . That was Mr Yeats for you. "A terrible beauty is born", but it's an evil beauty. It's beauty best seen at altitude.'

The helicopter circled and its shadow flitted over the discarded body.

The priest came early to the Riordans' house. It was the priest who brought the news when a volunteer was killed in action or by the explosion of his own bomb, it was the priest who called when an outcast was executed.

The priest sat in the chair that was usually taken by Patsy's father. Patsy's father, wrapped in an old dressing gown, slumped on the settee in the place that was Patsy's mother's. Patsy's mother was on all fours in front of the fire, cleaning it and lighting it, and refusing to ignore it.

'They think it's the dear boy, but it is the sadness of these times that it is not yet possible for them to approach him. It's down in Armagh, a priest has already been to him, that should be of some small comfort to you. We cannot be positive yet because the military have only allowed the local parish priest forward, and briefly, and I am afraid to say that I am advised it may be a long time before he can actually be recovered and identified. There may be bombs put in that place for the military, one shudders at the wickedness of these days we live in. We have to be brave and we have to be patient . . .'

Patsy's father lit his third cigarette of the morning. 'We're disgraced, right, Father? We did everything for the boy. His mother worked her hands to the bone for the little bastard. How does he repay her? He touts . . . How'll I hold my head up again, the man who fathered a tout, how?'

The priest clasped his hands across his chest. 'We are not to feel bitterness, Donal'. We are all to be judged, in time, by God . . . I offer you this thought. There are many today who will carry the burden of guilt. Those who foully murdered dear Patsy. Those who cynically led him into mortal danger. Take pity on them for their wretchedness . . .'

'The Brit feckers.'

'May they live with their consciences, those who inveigled dear Patsy to renounce his own people for their false gold.'

As Mrs Riordan had the fire alight, the priest was already hurrying away.

He was woken by the sound of broken twigs, scuffed wet leaves and voices and dogs.

The hide he had made was an angled strip of dark green groundsheet tethered by stones and tied with green garden wire to a low branch. There were voices and then the barking of dogs. There were dead branches laid against the groundsheet. Jon Jo lay very still. He held his breath. A few inches from his hand was the Kalashnikov assault rifle. The voices moved closer.

He had been warned away from the safe house in Hackney, flatly rejected from the haven in Guildford.

It was the first time that he had felt truly threatened. He was more than ever before alone. In darkness he had made for the weapon cache. There had been a man before, one of the finest, a man who had taken the war to the heart of the bastards, and he had been turned away, rejected, when the going was fierce, and he had been alone enough to turn his own gun on himself . . . Jon Jo had gone to the cache because there was no alternative . . . He had taken no decision yet as to whether he would go back to the Torbay digs. They had his photograph, they were checking wherever there were Irish. Not the time to make the decision.

He had fashioned the hide a dozen paces from where the dustbin was buried with the weapons and the explosives.

He had slept for five hours. There was clear light falling between the trellis of the upper branches of the trees. The rifle was within reach, the magazine was loaded. He had often slept rough. In the weeks before he had gone away to England, when he was hunted on Altmore, he had made that vast expanse of forest his home, and slipped down to the farmhouse only in darkness, and evaded the surveillance . . . when he was younger, before marriage, before his first arrest and imprisonment in the Kesh. He could live rough as well as any soldier. Now the voices and the movements were nearer. He edged his body to the front of the hide.

He saw the boots and the bright-coloured stockings and the corduroys and the waterproof coats. He saw men and women. He saw stout walking sticks. He saw the leashed dogs. Thank the Lord. He pushed the rifle sideways under the groundsheet to hide it.

'God Almighty, look at this . . . It's not allowed, is it, the ranger would throw a fit . . . get one in and we'll have a whole camp of these people . . . next thing they'll be lighting fires, short cut to mega-problems . . . Who the hell are you? What the hell do you think you're doing here?'

His mind raced. His tongue seemed to flap and his lips moved, and there was no voice. He had the idiot smile on his face. To speak was to give himself away. His arms moved with his mouth, as if that were his communication. To show fear would be a catastrophe, to show aggression was disaster. He was thinking well. Irish accent, frightened, aggressive, a hide deep in forest . . . He gave the whole party the mad grin, and he said nothing. There were seven of them.

One of the women spoke as if he could not hear her, as if he were an imbecile.

'It's really just scandalous, these people should be in care. They've closed down all the sort of places where these people should be. They're just put out on the streets to fend for themselves. It's criminal. We've probably frightened the poor man half out of his wits. Sometimes I look at the new face of Britain and I'm ashamed.'

They made a collection. There were 50 pence pieces and pound coins, and the woman gave them to Jon Jo, and he cupped his hands together to receive them from the woman.

'But you've no right to be here.' She spoke slowly and loudly. 'We don't expect to find you here again.'

They moved away. They left him shivering, huddled under the groundsheet.

*   *   *

They met in a house that was on the plateau of the mountain, on the road to Pomeroy. Only Nugent and the OC, in the back bedroom upstairs. The warmth of the OC gushed over Mossie. Not a word of what had happened in the barn. That was past history, forgotten by the OC.

What Mossie noticed was the number of times that the OC touched him. They drank a pot of tea together. They talked of a UDR man who drove a school bus by day, and the new route he had been given. They spoke of a policeman said to be Catholic who had joined the Special Branch unit at Dungannon. They looked, on a map, at what seemed to be a regular helicopter landing zone where troops were dropped off or collected after forty-eight-hour patrols. Patsy never mentioned, and his body cold on the side of a lane in South Armagh. The man from Lurgan never mentioned, and gone home to his own town.

'We have to show them we's alive,' the OC said. 'We have to hurt them so's they know they's won nothing . . .'

Mossie breathed deep. 'We need Jon Jo back.'

He had interrupted the OC. 'What's that?'

'Jon Jo was the best that ever was on Altmore. The way they'll know that they've won nothing is if Jon Jo's here to hit them.'

The OC stared at the drawn curtain. 'He was great, the best there's been . . . remember when he took the police in the Market Square? . . . remember when he was on the big machine gun, 12.7-calibre, Russian job, and he took the helicopter?'

And Mossie hadn't thought it would be so easy. 'It's not the big scene down in Armagh now, they're just playing at it. Belfast's all talk. Derry's gone, lost the soul. East Tyrone Brigade, no equal, but with Jon Jo back . . .'

'How does I do that?'

'You'd be top cat, but you'd have Jon Jo for the hitting . . . You takes yourself down to Dublin, and you tells them that's what you want. You *tells* them.'

'He's identified, what they did to his house shows . . .'

'Jon Jo knows the mountain better than any.'

'Worth thinking on . . .'

'Worth acting on,' Mossie said, and he squeezed the OC's hand in friendship.

It wasn't quietly smart like Cathy's; it wasn't where Hobbes lived, but Bren thought it was fine.

It was one bedroom and a dining room/living room with kitchen off, a bathroom, and use of a lawn outside. There was an older woman who showed him round the flat, then made him count each last plate, glass, saucepan, and fork and then sign the inventory. When she'd gone, when he had the place to himself, he sat in the easy chair and the pleasure beamed off him. Gone from Malone Road without a backward glance, without even checking to see if the cardboard city man was in his room.

Flat 3, Creagh House, 43/49 Amsterdam Gardens, Lisburn, Co. Down . . . home, with an easy chair. A place of his own. Up from the chair. Into the kitchen to check again all that was his in the cupboards. It would be home for two years. Back into the bedroom to unpack his cases, folding his shirts again and laying them neatly into drawers, hanging his two suits in the wardrobe and his slacks and his blazer, lopping his ties onto the hooks. The central heating was on. He was warm. He felt comfortable. He reached for the remote control beside the television, and flicked through the channels.

Bren saw the picture. It was a telephoto of a winding lane. '. . . believed to be that of Patrick Riordan, aged eighteen, from the Dungannon area, reported taken from his home three days ago. A police spokesman said within the last hour it would be at least another day before the ground round the body was declared safe of booby traps and the body could be recovered . . .'

Bren was slumped in the easy chair. He could hear the righteous ring of his own voice. '. . . luck is going to run out on you . . . You're running out of friends, Cathy . . .' It wasn't a day trip, it was two bloody years. How much luck would he need for two bloody years?

He snapped the television off.

He locked the front door behind him and went to his car to drive to the shopping centre to buy food and milk and bright indoor plants for his home.

'What I am telling you is that they have to be curbed . . .'

The Secretary of State for Northern Ireland was the last viceroy of the whittled empire. He rejoiced in his tiny fiefdom. There were Cabinet colleagues who had turned down the position, others who had previously gone to Belfast sulking and in poor grace. But he loved it, and his wife adored it. They were the great fishes in the small pond. He was a small man and, to emphasize his point, he strode up and down the

Home Secretary's carpet, jabbing his finger like a hell-fire preacher.

'. . . I will not permit the Security Service to run riot across the Province . . .'

The Home Secretary scratched at a trimmed moustache. 'I hope you will allow me, as an old friend, to say that your reaction may be slightly excessive.'

'A young man died. He was as good as murdered by Five. That is not tolerable.'

'We should all be pulling in the same direction, even if different arms by their very natures, by their very specializations, are using different methods.'

Nominally the Home Secretary was considered responsible for the Security Service. The early meetings, when he had first taken the appointment, were etched on his experience. Two men, Director General and Deputy Director General, sitting in his office, drinking his sherry, letting him know that they had forty-two years of service and wisdom between them, making it so clear that in the two or three years he might spend as Home Secretary before electoral defeat or a ministerial reshuffle he would not be welcome at the workface. Done with great politeness, quiet chill, the slamming of the door on his foot. He hadn't made a fuss there and then and oddly enough he had found as the months went by that, well, the inner workings were indeed perhaps rather less interesting, less of an urgent anxiety than a good deal else crossing his desk.

'I want them out, gone.'

'I understand your feelings, but I doubt that's possible.'

'I'll go to the Prime Minister over it.'

'I'm not sure that's wise.'

'I will not allow a young woman to run round Northern Ireland, in the name of this Government, deciding who lives, who dies . . .'

'I don't think . . .'

'You never have done . . . I will take your refusal to the Prime Minister. I'll have Five out by the end of the year, and that young woman out by the end of the week.'

'I'm sorry you feel . . .'

'I'll fight you and I'll win,' the Secretary of State said.

Young Kevin had changed out of his school uniform and into his farm clothes.

It was dark when he returned to the farmhouse, the clear beam of the torch guiding him.

'They's fine, Ma, they's finding good grass at the top.'

She thought him a great boy. She had been too busy that day to hike up to the Mahoneys' fields to check the beef stock. Attracta Donnelly had shopped, mended a skirt torn on barbed wire when she had tried to repair a length of broken fencing, and she had scrubbed through her kitchen. He was a great boy to go away up the mountain slope to the field where the bullocks were. He was a boy that Jon Jo would have been proud of. Each day, just as the satisfaction rested on her, she thought of Jon Jo, and she was flattened.

He had made his cryptic calls, he was expected. He drove fast on the winding lanes as he headed for the open road that would take him across the border and into the south. He would still be the OC, he believed that, otherwise he would not have countenanced it. He had told Mossie Nugent that the meeting was set up. As he drove into the night he felt the warm glow inside him . . . if Jon Jo Donnelly were back, the mountain would burn bright again.

Wilkins had been tidying away the papers on his desk for the night when the call came for him. His annoyance cut him, not because of the call that would delay his journey home but because the matter of the day was unresolved. It would have to be a direct order, the way Penn was playing it from Nairobi. The time for suggestion and request was gone. The man was stalling. Another day gone and the decision had been further postponed. The decision was whether to demand the immediate return of Penn from Kenya, and to further demand his prompt transfer to Belfast . . . it would be a shame for young Brennard.

The call had come from the Director General's outer office, could Mr Wilkins be so kind as to spare five minutes?

His own area was deserted. Carthew already gone, and Foster. He had missed Bill that day, but then Bill was becoming erratic in his attendance, and Charles was sick, and Archie had been telling anybody who cared to listen since the early morning that he had tickets for the National Theatre and had needed to leave before the tea trolley had reached their end of the corridor. Most evenings, after seven, when he cleared his desk, locked all the papers away in his safe, at least Brennard would still have been working. A good young man that. Hobbes was over the following

299

week and he made a note to enquire how Brennard was making out over there. Archie had got hold of some quite extraordinary story of how Brennard had run PTI Terry off his legs and had actually shot at Jocelyn and winged his combat jacket. That would let some of the hot air out of the pair of them . . . He climbed the darkened staircase to the top floor.

The Director General painted a rapid picture. Five was at war. The RUC at Chief Constable level were clamouring for blood. The civil service at Assistant Under-Secretary rank were demanding a head. And the Secretary of State seemed to be blundering round Whitehall, boring little man, preaching morality. Five was back against the wall.

'These bloody people, Ernest, they're going to the Prime Minister. What defence do we lay out?'

Wilkins stood in front of the Director General's desk, hands clasped in front of his stomach. 'The young people I send over to Northern Ireland, and I include Hobbes, are all committed completely to the work there. Those young people, sir, are the finest that the Service can offer. Sometimes I feel humble, privileged, to know them . . .'

'Ernest, I know that speech. Can we come very quickly to the point?'

It was his usual stance. His wife had told him, not once but frequently, not to look like a waiter attending on an order. 'I just want to point out, sir, that they are the very front line. We must trust them to interpret the evidence as they on the ground see it. They are forced to make exceptionally finely calculated judgements. These involve their own lives as well as other people's . . .'

'Thank you, but I can do that one, almost word for word. I want you to come clean about this killing of an apparently innocent young man. Tell me the truth.'

So Wilkins told him as much as he knew and what was at stake.

'You'll have to convince the Prime Minister . . .'

'Not a man of fibre, sadly.'

'You had better stand by to do that. I like the bit about only being able to supervise the sewer cleaners if you're prepared to climb down into the tunnels yourself. Keep the sermonizing to a minimum. And the young woman, can you save her?'

Wilkins shook his head. 'Save Cathy Parker? I don't know, sir, and I won't know until I have tried. I can only do my best.'

Jon Jo sat in the pub on the Harrow Road and was passed the sealed envelope.

He read the message of approval.

He had moved his hide in the morning and reset his groundsheet in deeper undergrowth further from the buried dustbin. He had stayed in the hide through the day and only emerged from the forest as night had fallen. In the pub he could smell himself, the dank wetness of his clothes and the dirt of his body. The courier was going back on the last flight. Donnelly told the girl, perhaps eighteen years old, that two safe houses were now denied him. The girl was from County Armagh and there was the softness of her accent in his ear, and there was the longing in him for his home. When she had gone, hurrying for Heathrow, he tore the message of approval into small pieces and flaked them into the ash tray and took them to the pub's open fire to burn them. She would carry back with her a sealed envelope. He had been a long time writing the letter it contained.

He had approval to place a bomb in a main-line railway station.

The smells merged over Bren. There was the smell of the polished flooring and of the newly painted walls and of the webbing of the men who passed him in the corridor and the damp of their uniforms and of baked beans heated near to him, and always the tang of cigarettes.

The sounds of the barracks played around him. Helicopters thrusting for elevation and the crack of gunfire from the floodlit small-arms range and the bark of out-of-doors orders and the mutter of conversation from civilian clerks and the Orderly NCOs whose voices dropped further when they used the corridor where Bren waited.

He had been an hour in the corridor outside Colonel Johnny's office. He had arrived without an appointment, he had been told the colonel was engaged and that he would be fitted in when it was possible. He had read an article in *Soldier* magazine about tank warfare and the lessons of the First Armoured Division in the Gulf, and discarded it as quite simply irrelevant. It was an impulse that had brought him from his new flat to the barracks at Dungannon, and with each jerk on the hands of his watch he had thought the impulse more stupid.

The door at the end of the corridor opened.

Colonel Johnny ushering out a middle-aged woman.

302

The colonel speaking quietly to her, bringing her down the corridor towards where Bren sat. 'Don't apologize, please, absolutely not. You had every right to come here.'

A small voice, 'You've been kind . . .'

'I wish I could have done more. We did everything we could do to find him and save him. I'm very sorry that we were unsuccessful.'

Bren stood. The colonel looked through him. The woman ignored him and was pulling a rain hat from her bag.

'It helps me to know that you tried . . .'

'Now, how will you get home?' Said kindly.

'My man's in a bar in the town, down Irish Street. I left him there because he wouldn't drive me to the barracks, said it wasn't right.'

They were at the far door of the corridor, where it opened onto the parade ground.

'Good night . . . I'm sorry we couldn't do more. Safe home, Mrs Riordan . . .'

Bren's head twisted. His eyes raked down the corridor. He saw the back of the woman as she went down the step and there was the howl of a night gale to greet her. He saw her face when she turned, the few seconds, to shake the colonel's hand, and then her face was gone and her head was wrapped in the rain hat, and she followed the escort soldier away . . . Christ . . . she was the debris he scattered, that he and Cathy Parker threw over their shoulders . . . He stood his ground and faced the colonel. There was no warmth, only crisp recognition. The colonel waved for him to follow him back towards the office.

He was gestured to a chair.

Bren said, 'I wanted to talk to you.'

'Well, I'm here, you're here, so talk.'

'About Cathy . . .'

'What about Miss Parker?'

There was no sympathy. Bren said, 'It's just that I was worried . . . I don't suppose it matters. Forget it. I was just worried about her.'

'What way worried?'

'The way she is . . . you've seen her. It's like people are when they start to make mistakes . . .'

'Mistakes, oh, that's very good. Going to make mistakes, is she? Over here, it gets to be a habit, making mistakes. A police inspector I used to know made a mistake, went to church on a Sunday morning with his family, that was a mistake because he was shot dead on the church steps, silly mistake going to worship. One of my soldiers last year made a mistake, went through an open gateway between two fields when he should have pushed through a thorn hedge, a mistake because there was a pressure plate in the gateway, elementary mistake going through a gateway when there was a perfectly good hedge to push through. A little kiddie made a mistake two years ago, my first week here, picked up a box left in a ditch, didn't know that we'd had a call out and hadn't moved, didn't see the fishing wire from the box to the bomb, dumb little kiddie to be making a mistake like that. Nothing special about making mistakes, gets to be an occupational hazard when you stay around too long. There's no way of stopping Miss Parker from making mistakes either. Mistakes are a part of the job . . .'

'How can I help her?'

'I doubt you can,' Colonel Johnny said. 'I doubt any of us can. It's what makes her special to us, all of us, that she's not looking for bloody help, and it's her strength that she's not frightened of making mistakes.'

Bren stood, 'Thank you for your time.'

Chapter Fourteen

It was the dawn.

The start of another day.

The dawn was the start of the 342nd day since Jon Jo Donnelly had taken the Aer Lingus to Paris and been in transit two hours and then been carried on a Lufthansa flight to Munich and then caught the British Airways aircraft to London's Heathrow.

The rain came with the dawn.

It fell hard against the upper branches of the forest.

The rain careered down onto the roofing of the groundsheet. There was the spatter of the rain above his head.

Jon Jo sat under his cover.

He was cross-legged and his arms were folded over his stomach. Beside him was the torn wrapping paper of a biscuit packet. He had eaten the whole of the packet of shortbreads.

Perhaps it was because of the rain but there were few birds calling the dawn's arrival, only the robin to which he threw the last of the biscuit crumbs. The robin was without fear of him and strutted close to the hide and challenged him for more of the shortbread biscuits. He watched the robin. He saw the proud freedom of the little bird, and he saw its bravery in advancing on him. He wondered, if he had not wolfed down the biscuits, if he had filled his hand with crumbs and stretched his hand out whether the bird would have had the courage to come to take crumbs from the palm of his hand.

It was as if he sought to find a peace for himself.

He was still. He sat quite motionless. The robin danced in front of him.

For 250 of those days since he had come to London he had prepared himself for the campaign that was his own. He had found the safe houses, he had bought the cars that were paid for in cash. He had accumulated the documentation that came from the forgers in Dublin. He had received the dribble of weapons, and the timing devices, and the detonators, and the explosives that were sometimes hand-carried on the cross-Channel ferry and sometimes landed from a fishing boat on the remote stretch of the north Cornish coast in a cove near Gurnard's Head. For 90 of those days he had fought his war. He sat without movement to find again the strength that was needed of a soldier. He took his strength, bled it, from the home that was his, and the woman that was his, and the boy child that was his. He took strength, leached it, from the mountain that was his. They would none of them know, the mass that would flow through a main-line railway station, of his home and his woman and his child and his mountain. Only the fall of the rain around him and the cheerful strut of the robin. He thought of the bar in the village, where there was singing and where there were his friends. He thought of the land around the small farm, where the bracken and gorse had been driven back first by his grandfather and then by his father and then by himself. He thought of the church in the village where he had made his first Communion, and where he had stood awkward in his suit and tight in his collar and held little Kevin for baptism. He thought of the neighbours that he had known, who had never left him to feel alone, good men and good women, Mrs Riordan and Mrs Devitt and Mrs Nugent, and Pius Blaney who drove the milk cart and never cursed not even when there was snow on the mountain slope, and the difficult old bugger who was old Hegarty. He thought of the good times, when the Armalite had pounded against his shoulder, when he had watched through binoculars as the road to Aghnagar had lifted under the unmarked police car, when they had taken over the road from Coalisland to Stewartstown and there had been more than twenty of them and they had blasted the barracks at Stewartstown with machine guns and the RPG7 rocket launcher and sprayed the roof with diesel oil and petrol to get the big fire going . . . good times. It was his place, they were his people. It was Jon Jo's place, the place of his family's graves. It was Jon Jo's home, the home of the war.

The strength grew in his body. The peace settled on his mind.

For the first time since the dawn light had come he shifted from where he had sat. He crouched over the flattened ground beneath the cover of his hide. Among the dead squashed leaves, among the grass stems, he found more crumbs, and he tossed them out to the robin and he willed the bird to find them where they had scattered.

He moved away from the hide.

Three times, between the hide and the cache, he stopped and froze against a tree trunk and listened to the rain falling in the forest. He listened for voices and for footsteps, and for the sound of a command whistle to a dog. There was only the clatter of the rain dropping from the upper branches.

He lined up the position of the cache. The uprooted base of a tree and away from it the dead elm disfigured with ivy. That was how he always found the holly tree where the dustbin was buried. He dug with his hands, pushed aside the mulch and then the soil. The lightweight kitchen gloves were on his hands. He took the Semtex explosive and the detonator and the wiring and the timer from the dustbin, and the ice-cream box and the adhesive tape. It was difficult to work at the assembly wearing the gloves. He was too careful ever to take off the gloves; Jon Jo could have reeled them off, the names of the men who had made bombs and who had not worn gloves, and who rotted in the mainland gaols.

It took him half the morning to make the bomb.

He scraped the earth and the mulch back over the dustbin. He used a dead twig to scour his footsteps and the indents of his body weight from the ground close to the cache.

The rain had eased.

She hadn't telephoned him, and he wouldn't ring her.

She had the number of the flat and the number of his office at the back of the Department of

Environment building, and she hadn't used either.

If she didn't want to ring him, her problem. If she thought he was not up to the job, so be it.

All the while Bren had dressed, and all the while he had eaten his breakfast, he had looked at the telephone in the flat, willed it to ring, cursed it for its silence.

All the while he had sat in his office, turned file papers, made coffee, tried for the hell of it to master the intricacy of the dual carriage projects and the salary restructuring programme for clerical workers, he waited for any of his telephones to ring. The quiet burgeoned round him. Nothing on the receiver that was linked to the building switchboard, nothing on the telephone that Song Bird would have used, nothing on the line that was Cathy's alone. Always talk and always movement in the Curzon Street complex of desks where the Irish unit was housed. This was bloody. Being stuck in a room at the back of a building, where no-one came and where the telephone didn't ring, that was a sort of hell to him. He had cracked by the middle of the day. He had rung Hobbes. He'd marked Hobbes down, supercilious bastard, and he was most certainly not going to be spilling to Hobbes that Miss Cathy Parker had cut him out. Trying to be casual. Had time on his hands. Any suggestions as to where he might go, what might be useful? Hobbes hadn't sounded as if he cared and hadn't sounded as if he was surprised. Just curt. He should try Mahon Road. He should get himself to Portadown. He'd be expected. He was given a name. Hobbes sounded like there was a crisis that he wasn't prepared to share, and Portadown was the sort of

310

place to dump a bored kid. He did as he was told. He drove to Portadown, and the barracks in Mahon Road, and all the way down the motorway he sought to obliterate Cathy Parker from his mind, and the failure hurt him.

High fencing of rusting steel. Black painted watch-towers. Screens of chicken-wire netting that would prematurely detonate an armour-piercing missile. A call on ahead from the taciturn police at the gate check.

It was indicated to him where he should park.

The parking area where he went was separate from the main mass of vehicles. The big area held the shined, washed Cavaliers and Sierras and Escorts, policemen's cars for driving to and from work. Where Bren parked was a junkyard. Old vans without side windows and with convenient mud masking the number plates, and beaten Fords that were scraped and dented, and what might have doubled as a removal lorry, and a Telecom van and another that had the logo of a bakery with a home delivery service. He went to the weapons pit and cleared his Browning and pocketed it again. From the gate, the two-storey building, dull brickwork, had been pointed out to him.

Bren went inside the outer door. He was stopped. The man was younger than himself and dressed casu-ally and there was a short-barrel machine pistol on the table. Identification . . . Another phone call through . . . Passed on.

He went up the stairs, past bare walls. He walked into the big open area. He gazed around him. Half a dozen men and three women bowed over computer

311

consoles. Two men and two women at banks of radio equipment, smoking and reading newspapers and talking quietly and with head sets over their ears. Five's place, Five's back room.

'Hello there . . .'

A quiet voice close to him. Bren spun on his heel.

He saw the cardboard city man.

'Hello again.'

'Jimmy's had to pop out, I said I'd field you.'

'Oh, I see . . .'

There were two others sitting with the cardboard city man. They were all three sprawled on chairs at the far side of the big room to the consoles and the radio and their ashtray was filled and a low table near them was cluttered with their boots and their used coffee beakers. Bren saw the weapons laid on the floor. They'd have done for farm workers, any of them.

There was a printed sign on the wall above their chairs and their table.

'Hereford Gun Club. No Entry. Trespassers Will Be Shot'.

Bren could smell them from five paces.

'I'll do the introductions. The ugly one's Jocko, the really ugly one's Herbie . . . Don't bloody eat him, guys, he's Cathy's latest . . .'

'Pleased to meet you all, I'm Bren.'

He felt the pillock. He stood in his slacks and his jacket and he looked down at three men who wore the mud on their jeans and the dirt on their shirts. He felt the daftness of the name he had given himself, could have crawled away.

The cardboard city man said, 'Jimmy'll be an hour or so. It's a bad time for him, this, tends to pop off out

312

for a drop of nookie in the middle of the day. How long have you?'

'I've a clear afternoon . . .'

'When's Cathy picking you up?'

'I'm not meeting her.'

He saw the puzzlement cross the face of the cardboard city man. 'You don't . . .'

'I don't know where she is.'

After the puzzlement, the frown. Bren saw the hardening of the face. 'She was here four hours ago, half drowned from being out all night. Changed, and pushed off again . . . You're not meeting her?'

'That's what I said.' He should have stayed in the office in Belfast. He should have pushed paper.

'And you don't know where she is?'

'She hasn't told me,' Bren said, tried to closet the humiliation.

'I thought you were minding her.'

'When I'm allowed to.'

'Christ, old sunshine, you don't stand on bloody ceremony with her. You don't let her just bloody wander off alone out there. You bloody handcuff yourself to her. You're here to mind that woman . . .'

The two others, the one called Jocko and the one called Herbie, gazed up at Bren, like he was beneath contempt.

The cardboard city man said, 'When Jimmy's shown you round his box of tricks, we'll take you for a drive round, show you the sights, Cathy'll be back by then. Like I said, you tie yourself to her. You don't put up with her shit. You mind her. You don't allow her out there on her own, not ever.'

'I'd like the drive round,' Bren said.

313

*   *   *

The OC had been and gone the previous evening.

The four men and the woman stayed on in Cavan town, slept on what had been proposed, met again in the morning, thrashed round the proposal that had been brought them from County Tyrone.

'He's a major asset where he is, he should be let be,' the woman said.

'Be harder for him back in the North, but it's where he knows.'

'To be charitable would be to say that he's done his time over there, and done it well.'

'Not done as well recent as before, my thought is that he's slipping.'

'If he's slipping then he needs out, it's what we'd owe him.'

'Was never said it would be easy over there, why he was chosen, take months to get another in place,' the woman said.

'Jon Jo's not one to shout, never complain, but the strain on him'd have to be fierce.'

'You keep a man in place too long, and you burn him out, gone for ever.'

'Leave him there much longer, so's he burned, and he'll be lifted too.'

'He'd have had the colonel if he'd been fresh, not have had the kiddies if he'd not gone stale.'

'If you pull him out then you chuck away what he's won,' the woman said.

'I say he's ready for out.'

'The railway bomb, that's the last.'

'Let him back.'

'Worth gold to have him hitting where he knows.'

314

She fought it to the end. She had never met Jon Jo Donnelly. She had a sociology degree gained from University College, Cork. She came from wealth, a prominent Galway legal family. She had never been accepted quite totally. She was a woman. The Organization was of men. She had the intellect and the fervour and she had climbed in rank on the back of the quality of her planning. She was credited with setting up a gun team in the German city of Hanover that could roam the autobahns in search of off-duty British soldiers. She had seen the vulnerability of a Special Branch computer installed in the Monaghan police station and rented the house on the opposite side of the street and found the man with the design skill to build the scanning equipment that could monitor the computer's transmissions. She possessed the ruthlessness to travel to Belfast, take a bedsitter, search out a soldiers' bar, bring a squaddie on a promise back with her, and shoot him dead between the eyes. But, she was a woman, and the Organization was of men.

'Jon Jo's done his time.'

'There'll be hell after the railway.'

'Too hot for him, better for him to cool.'

'He should be let to rest, after the railway.'

The woman said, 'You're frightened, you're scared of real war. So, you have Jon Jo back . . . So, it'll be the Brits that are thanking you . . . There'd not be any of you, I hope, looking for the soft way, talks and conversation and dialogue? There'd not be any of you thinking bombings in London block crap negotiation? There'd not be any of you that's weakened . . . ?'

'That's treason talk.'

'No call for it.'

'We're strong as we ever was, to fight on.'

'It's owed to Jon Jo.'

He sat in the coffee shop. He nursed the mug in his hands. He could see right across the concourse where the crowds flowed. There were two uniformed policemen on the concourse and he watched them. They walked and they stood and they answered tourists' questions and they checked a youth who Jon Jo thought might have run from home to the capital. He waited for them to be gone. He could see the rubbish bin, and he could see the crowds that swelled near the ticket hatch as the afternoon wore on closer towards the evening rush.

He felt at peace.

There was a plastic bag on the floor, held upright tight between his ankles.

A woman asked him if he would be so kind as to pass her the salt and pepper that was on his table, for her sandwich, and he smiled and obliged her.

They split at Cavan town.

The woman travelled west for the wild Sligo shore-line that was her home.

Two of the men went due south for the Irish midlands.

The remaining two drove on the Dublin road. It was the way of the Organization that age counted for little. The youngest at the meeting had been a Belfast man, not yet past his twenty-fourth birthday. He had laid bombs in his home city and in Holland, and he had twice travelled to the eastern states of the USA to obtain more sophisticated and advanced electronic equipment. The youngest was the passenger in the car headed for Dublin . . . He had loathed the woman at the meeting since he had first realized that she wanted to bed him, and he thought her hair hideous, and her underwear dirty because he could smell it, and her breath foul, and her politics patronizing . . . Jon Jo was gone from his mind. Jon Jo would telephone after the railway bomb, and would be given the decision of the meeting. A greater problem concerned him. Under his guidance the Organization had known months of success. The success had come because they had used for the detonation of bombs the combination of the radar gun that was standard issue to the highway police in the United States, along with the detection devices that warned motorists of the use of the gun and that could be purchased at any Radio Shack store, good and cheap. The army could block them now . . . It was the laser that was wanted. The army could match the wavelengths; two men dead, their car blown up, to prove it, and the crowing of the Lisburn HQ Press Desk for another 'own goal'. A laser signal from the command hide to the bomb, instant detonation . . . A real problem, and the one that concerned him now that the matter of Jon Jo Donnelly was settled.

His view, the war at home mattered. His opinion, the war in London was a sideshow. His intention, if that bitch from Sligo ever again accused him of running frightened, going scared, he'd smack the gob off her, break her jaw. His doubt, that the war, wherever, could be won, any time . . . he dozed. That a bomb rested between Jon Jo Donnelly's ankles in the coffee shop of a London station was not enough to keep him from his sleep.

He wrote a terse note.

'Ernest, the Prime Minister will see you at 4.45 p.m. today. I understand Sec. of State NI bent his ear this morning. Probably tin hat required. No concessions, please, DG.'

The Director General of the Security Service usually sent men such as Ernest Wilkins to face Downing Street flak. He seldom attended himself. Not cowardice, of course not. He believed, and he was right, that the operations of Curzon Street were best defended by those who knew most about them. The Prime Minister would know nothing, the Secretary of State would have rehashed a brief given him. Ernest Wilkins would baffle them with detail, perhaps. There was a difficulty, the matter of Miss Parker and a boy tortured to death was most certainly a difficulty. But then, Wilkins was so accomplished in the art of plausible deniability. Accomplished enough? It would depend on the Prime Minister's mood, and it was a pity that the man had as yet shown no recognizable sign of steel.

And if Wilkins failed? Well, time then for further consideration. His brother knew Miss Parker's parents, good landowners. He would stand and fight on the future deployment of Five in Northern Ireland, but the young woman . . . There was always a good home for Miss Parker to go back to.

He buzzed for his secretary, asked her to take the folded note down to Wilkins, Irish Desk.

*   *   *

Jimmy was bald with a monk's ruff of hair sand-wiched between his shined scalp and his ears. He wore thick glasses and Bren would have expected him to be working in a university laboratory. Not the sort of man that Bren had met in Curzon Street. Jimmy rattled through a brief precis of the work on the second floor of the detached building on Mahon Road as if it were unsatisfactory to be sharing secrets with a mere handler. The computers logged 'traces'. Traces came from police and uniformed military. Who had been seen, with whom and when and where. Jimmy said that the computers built patterns of behaviour and associates and routines. The radios controlled the bleeps that were issued. The bleeps were carried by informers and by operatives. The channels were monitored twenty-four hours a day and an emergency transmission would be acted on immediately, the necessary information flashed to police and army barracks for Quick Reaction back-up. Jimmy said that in another area they controlled remote cameras and also the listening bugs that were planted in known arms caches and where it was thought meetings might take place; he didn't seem to want to take Bren to that area, and Bren didn't push. It was the world of back-room men. Bren asked Jimmy if he ever went out into the field and was left with the impression that it would take half a troop of the Special Air Service to be in position as escort before this academic and vague creature would even consider getting cow shit on his shoes. He had gazed around the room. He had wondered which of the technicians monitored Cathy Parker's emergency bleep . . .

319

He left with the cardboard city man and the others who were Jocko and Herbie.

The bodywork of the car was dirty, rusted, dented and scraped. The engine purred, ran smooth.

He was given a flat cap to wear and it was pointed out to him that the sooner he got his hair growing long then the happier they would be. He pulled off his tie and buried it in his pocket and wrapped himself in his anorak. Herbie drove and had armed his pistol and laid it on the seat under his thighs. The cardboard city man and the big fellow, Jocko, had Heckler and Kochs.

They drove out onto the street.

Jocko said, North-Country burr, 'We're not used to passengers, we don't do the guide book bit. You don't talk unless you're asked to, and what you don't do is anything that might distract us . . .'

They skirted the shore of Lough Neagh.

They drove flat and straight lanes. They passed small hedged fields that sprouted bog reeds. They went by little and isolated communities of bungalows and Housing Executive homes. They had the rain wipers clearing water from the windscreen . . .

The cardboard city man said, 'We get called to a stake-out, but we may not have time to do the recce the way we'd like. Ideal world, we'd have three, four, days to know the land. Most times we don't get what we'd like, it's hassle and hurry. We spend as much time as possible cruising, getting familiar with the ground. It's what we're at today . . .'

Going by a pair of semi-detached bungalows, each with a cattle barn at the back.

Jocko said, 'Right-hand home, two boys, one's doing

fifteen and the other's got eight years. Next door's two decent kids, no trouble, never. Left-hand side won't touch violence, but they wouldn't interfere, wouldn't even consider picking up the Confidential phone . . .'

Going by a woman driving a speeding Mini car, seeing fast the throw of her fine black hair to her shoulders.

'. . . Bloody hard case, that one. Started as a teenie bop at the barracks gates collecting detectives' car registrations, moved up to running messages, on to shifting hardware. She'll kill. She's bad and going to get worse. She'll take stopping, that one . . .'

Going by a big house, new, white painted rendering, double garage.

Jocko said, 'Six times in the last ten years they've had a car pinched for a PIRA hit. Rings the Organization to ask for it back, gives 'em hell, wouldn't ever ring the police. If he rang the police and the car was stopped and the boys lifted then he'd be dubbed a collaborator. Collaborators get nutted. Who'd blame him . . .'

Going by a young man who drove a cow and three calves on the lane, and who didn't look up at the car as it waited for the road to clear.

Jocko said, 'He did nine years, Attempted Murder and Possession of Explosives, served his time and came home. He's one of the best in the community now, does a hell of a good job with handicapped kids. He's never been involved again. They leave him alone because they know he hates them for what he went through in their name, but he wouldn't cross the road for you, me, or a policeman if we were half dead in a ditch with gunshot wounds . . .'

Going by a bar with a Harp sign above the door and a security camera and big rocks in the forecourt to prevent cars driving against the outer wall and heavy mesh on the windows.

Jocko said, 'It got hit by the Protestants, went in and shot two Provos. The Scenes of Crime guys and the detectives weren't allowed inside. A UDR man was shot in retaliation. They did it their own way. They'll remember for ever that two of their blokes were killed here, they'd have forgotten the day after that a UDR man was killed . . .'

Going through a crossroads, where the high-hedged lanes met.

'History doesn't go away here. Stories lose nothing by the telling. Stories are handed down, father to son, family to family, close as frogs in a drain here. Listen . . . This crossroads, anyone'll tell you, was where the Auxiliaries shot the Catholic postman in 1922 . . .'

Going by a farmhouse, three hundred yards further.

'. . . Two lads, one from the farm, best Sunday clothes, go to check a weapons cache, our boys mashed them, middle 1970s . . .'

Going by a copse, and the road falling away towards a cemetery, bright with white headstones and fresh-cut flowers.

'. . . That's the wood where the guns were, that's the graveyard where they are, and there's a prison escaper in there with them, shot in the early 1980s . . .'

Going away from the graveyard and towards the bridge where the lane joined the main road and where the fast stream tumbled dirty underneath.

'. . . The Protestants came to burn down the RC

chapel here, there was a hell of a fight and about a dozen Catholics were beaten to death. They call it the Battle of Black Bridge. They know it like it was yesterday, but yesterday was 1829 . . .'

Going by the shops at the main road junction.

'. . . There was a UDR man, drove the school bus, shot here a few years back. Nobody remembers when because nobody cares when, but they'll tell you the day and the hour when the postman was shot, and the boys at the cache, and the lad breaking out from the Kesh, and they'll tell you whether it was wet or fine on the day of the Battle of Black Bridge . . .'

'You trying to depress the poor bugger?' A sly grin from the cardboard city man.

Jocko said, cheerful, 'It's better he knows, safer.'

Bren sat huddled in the back of the car. He wondered where was Cathy. They had been gone more than two hours before Herbie accelerated for home base. He wondered why she had not allowed him to be with her. They drove fast away from the low wetland beside the Lough. And he wondered how it was possible to survive, on the ground, alone, out there, and he thought the mountain of Altmore was worse than what they had shown him.

They returned to Mahon Road.

Cathy hadn't shown.

Bren asked if he could wait for her.

They thought it was where she would come back to. He should please himself.

Wilkins stood.

He had thought the man feeble. He was lashed with the Prime Minister's tongue.

Wilkins was the chastized labrador dog and the beating was savage. He thought he could accept it, it was why he had been sent. He would never, ever, answer back. It was why he had been sent from Curzon Street, to absorb a verbal thrashing.

'. . . I have to tell you, Wilkins, that I had expected your Director General. On a matter of this importance I had not thought it necessary to stipulate the attendance of the Director General. What I most certainly do not require is a potted and imprecise lecture on the work of the Security Service in Northern Ireland, a golden petal. I am not in need of generalities, but of some very clear specifics. The charge brought to my attention against the Security Service operations in the province is of the gravest type. It smacks to me of a total disregard on the part of the senior officials for the close supervision of juniors. The charge laid against you, and one that should have been answered by the Director General, is that a young man was set up, the correct vernacular I believe, so that the Provisional IRA might consider that young person to be an informer. He was not an informer, never had been, and was unlikely to be one in the future. The young man was quite directly pitched into a most hideous danger, from which he unhappily did not survive. It is unspeakably revolting behaviour on the part of your juniors. I am informed, and since it is not denied I have to assume the information is reliable, that a junior officer, a woman, is currently careering around Northern Ireland making policy on the hoof, taking it upon herself to decide that a young man's life is not important. Do you begin to see, Wilkins, the colossal arrogance of such a posture? I won't have it, that shocking behaviour, and I am minded to order the disengagement of the Security Service from the province . . .'

'I really think . . .' The small voice, Ernest Wilkins so mild.

'You'll be given your chance to defend the indefensible when I've finished. You will do me the courtesy, Wilkins, of hearing me out. If the Security Service believes that it is not accountable, as are the police and army, then a very rude shock . . .'

A schoolboy going home. He had lost his season ticket in the playground. His headmaster had given him the money to buy the necessary train ticket. The boy shouted through the hatch the name of the station where he lived.

A middle-aged secretary travelling to visit her mother, and requiring a return ticket to come back to the capital in the morning. She was weighed down with the gifts that would cement success on the small family birthday party. She stood behind the schoolboy.

A young account executive employed by a major advertising agency of Central London. He was heading north for a client dinner and would make his preliminary presentation in the morning. He held his closed lap-top computer in one hand, his mobile telephone in the other and shouted the news to his wife as to where he was. He waited behind the middle-aged secretary.

A retired army officer who had been given a lift into town in the morning and was now making his own way back to the country. He rolled on his heels. Great willpower to have taken himself away from the company of colleagues and a worthy lunch and an open bar at the Cavalry Club. He reckoned that if the schoolboy and the middle-aged woman and the yuppie didn't shift themselves, if he didn't get his ticket and decamp soonest to the urinal, then he'd wet his trouser leg.

A West Indian boy, bright in the plumage of his French-manufactured leisure suit, dropped a beef-burger's wrapping into the rubbish bin . . .

An impatient queue. The departure board flickering new departure times.

None of them would see the disintegration of the rubbish bin.

The light flash.

None of them would hear the hammer blow of the explosion.

The thunder roar.

The flash and the roar would be seen, heard, by the masses on the far side of the station and on the middle ground of the concourse, before the pressure blast flattened them against walls and to the ground.

They were the battlefield victims.

They were a schoolboy and a secretary and an account executive and a retired army officer and a young West Indian.

They were the enemy.

They were broken, split, mutilated.

After the light flash and the thunder roar came the monsoon fall of glass shards, and then the pain quiet.

Across the concourse the dust settled on Jon Jo Donnelly's bomb.

*　　*　　*

'. . . the Security Service may feel, because of the very vague nature of its terms of reference in Northern Ireland, that it has been given the nod and the wink to involve itself in areas where the police and army, quite rightly, feel inhibited to tread. If the Security Service feels that then it has placed itself on shifting sands, false foundations. My inclination is that the time has been reached for a sharp lesson to be learned . . .'

The Prime Minister broke off. There had been the faintest knock at the door, barely heard by Ernest Wilkins. The aide's shoes slid silently across the carpet. A notelet was passed. There was that shiver of annoyance on the Prime Minister's face, not a man who could take interruption. He read the message and the door closed on the aide.

The colour was gone from him.

His eyes closed momentarily.

He seemed to rock.

Ernest Wilkins waited on him.

'Oh, God . . .'

Held his peace.

'. . . the wicked bastards . . .'

Gave him time.

'. . . Bomb at Marylebone, at least three dead, many injured, no warning, no chance . . .'

It had been the intention of Ernest Wilkins to let the storm blow itself over before he had launched himself. He would have allowed the Prime Minister's anger to exhaust itself before offering defence of the Service's operations. He took the cue.

His voice was gentle, so reasonable. 'That'll be Jon Jo Donnelly, sir. You'll remember when the name was last talked of, and the suggestion that the man be

327

encouraged to return to his home, because there we would stand a greater chance of trapping him. I said then that I would be working on it, that you should leave it in my hands. There's a young woman in Northern Ireland, I don't think it wise you have her name, one of my best. Donnelly comes from the mountain country of Tyrone. I tell you, sir, in the greatest confidence, we have an informer inside that community. He is our informer, sir, not the army's and not answerable to the police. At our instigation there have been meetings inside the Provisional IRA, East Tyrone Brigade and Army Council level, that should, we hope, earn the recall to home territory of Donnelly. The informer, I don't think you need that person's identity, will tell us of Donnelly's return and give us the location of his hiding place. That young woman, sir, so heavily criticized by the ill-informed, has taken very grave risks to her personal safety to take us thus far . . . Oh, yes, what you should be told, our informer, vital to us, was threatened last week with exposure. We felt it necessary, for the greater good of the greater number, to divert the threat . . .'

'I want that bastard, that Donnelly animal, dead . . .'

'Of course, sir. I never doubted that, sir.'

He seemed to Ernest Wilkins to be in pain. 'God, that bloody awful place . . .'

'And much worse there, sir, when it's not left to the professionals.'

'Do what's necessary.'

'If I might say so, sir, a very wise attitude.'

Outside in the corridor, Ernest Wilkins paused to wipe the first sweat beads off his forehead. He thought he had done well, really rather well.

328

In the evening, the undertaker brought home the body of Patsy Riordan.

The open coffin was laid on trestles in the front room. The boy's face had been cleaned but a patch of hospital gauze covered that part of his jaw where the killer bullet had exited.

His mother sat stone-faced and dry-eyed beside the head of the coffin. His father stood near to the door with a filled whiskey glass in his hand. Some neighbours came and took tea or a small glass and muttered embarrassed condolences. They were the few.

Patsy Riordan had been executed for touting.

The few paid their respects, the majority gathered in the village bar.

'Should she have come by now?'

There was the sharp look into Bren's face from the cardboard city man. 'You work with her, I don't.'

'Please, I don't need any bloody sarcasm. I'll repeat my question. Should she have come by now?'

The cardboard city man said, 'I'd have expected her an hour or two back, but you can't tell with her.'

They played cards, the cardboard city man and Jocko and Herbie. The night duty had taken charge of the computers and the banks of radio equipment. Outside the rain beat the windows and the wind whined in the telephone wires.

Bren waited. And he promised that he would never let Cathy Parker, alone, loose out there again.

They had rowed through the evening. Siobhan had finally followed Mossie into the bedroom to hiss in a

329

spat and hushed voice that it was right for her to go to Mrs Riordan's home.

He had a feeling, small, for what he thought was right; a feeling, sometimes, for what he knew was wrong. He thought it was not right, that it was wrong, that his Siobhan should be away down to the Riordan house.

'You can't, not after what was done.'

'It's respect for her.'

'You'd be a sham.'

'It's respect for the family.'

'I'm not going with you, I'd not have the face.'

'I was never asking you to be with me.'

'I don't know how you'd have the face.'

Siobhan said, cunning, 'It'd cause more talk if I didn't, and she's a good and decent woman.'

It had been the usual way that they argued. They found the corners of the bungalow, away from his mother, out of earshot of the children. They had been silent through the tea, him asking the children to ask their mother to pass him the brown sauce, her asking his mother to ask him whether he wanted more chips. His mother and the children wouldn't have known that they rowed over whether Siobhan should attend the house of a shot tout.

He sat on the bed. The fight was gone from him. He looked to her for comfort.

'Will us ever be forgiven for what we've done?'

He saw the hard set of her mouth, it was a new mouth for her to wear. 'Get paid, don't we?'

He repeated what she'd said, the bitterness in his voice. 'Get paid, don't we?'

'You'll wait outside, they'd not be expecting the

likes of you, there'll be none like you there . . . and we'll go after and take a drink.'

It was accepted. He could never fight her and win. The only time that she had not won her way was when they had returned from Birmingham to his mother's bungalow. Only the once. Every other time they fought, she won. They came out of the bedroom and he let her slip her arm round his waist, like it was a sign to the children and to his mother that the hidden problem was solved. If it had been he that was shot, if it had been Mossie Nugent killed for touting, then he reckoned that Mrs Riordan would have called for her respects. The lie burdened him, he thought the weight of the lie grew each day he woke.

He gave her time to change, the dress she wore often for Sunday Mass. He helped his mother with the washing of the plates and pans, and then he romped and larked with the kids and built bricks for Mary.

Mossie drove to the Riordan house.

If the boy had been shot by the army, if he had died in the ferrying of a bomb, then the lane in front of the house would have been filled with cars. The cars would have stretched a quarter of a mile in front of the house. He had been executed by his own. There were six cars parked outside the Riordan house. If it had been the army that had done him, or his own bomb, if he had been the volunteer 'tragically killed on active service', then the neighbours would have flown black flags from their upper windows. The neighbours showed what they thought, front-room curtains open, lights blazing, televisions blaring. He parked away from the house. He let Siobhan walk a hundred yards. He sat alone in the car and he smoked a cigarette.

Shit, and he was his own man. Shit, and he had the laugh on all of them. None of them knowing, all of them ignorant, that Mossie Nugent was his own man. The smile played at his lips. It was when he could cope best, when he was alone with himself and the night was around him, when he had the laugh on all of them. There was the rap at the window of his car.

He saw the OC's face, grinning. He wound down the window.

'Surprise . . .'

'Missus gone in, I'm not. We's going for a drink after. You're not going in?'

'I am not. Just seeing who is, like to know.'

'She's a respected woman . . .'

'You heard it from London today?'

'Big bomb, no warning, I heard.'

'Jon Jo's coming.'

Mossie said quietly, 'Is that right?'

'Jon Jo's sent for.'

'That's good.'

The face was gone from the window. She hurried down the road towards the car, skipping between the rain puddles. She sagged into the seat, and the breath was out of her. Siobhan said that terrible things had been done to the boy and that his chin bone was half blown away. Mossie didn't answer her. She said that Mrs Riordan was a brave woman and that her husband was scum and drunk and bad-mouthing his son. Mossie started up the car. She said that she didn't care about the money. He reversed away up the lane to the junction. She was crying, and she asked him how long it would go on, the killing. He told her to clean her face and he drove towards the village bar.

The bar was full, like it was Friday evening or Saturday night. He pushed his way through with Siobhan holding his hand and letting him lead. If Patsy Riordan had been shot by the army or blown away by his own bomb then the bar would have been empty and the drink would have been taken at the Riordan house. The bar was in celebration because the body of a tout had been brought back by the undertaker. Loud music from the speakers and the steady chime of the fruit machine and belly laughter and shouting. He found the corner of a bench, room for Siobhan and if she pushed then room for him when he was back from the bar. He wormed forward towards the bar counter. He was a big man in the Organization and that was known to every man and woman in the bar, not what he did but that he was important. His shoulder was slapped, his hand was shaken, he was made welcome. The pint for himself, the gin and bitter lemon for herself, and a drink for Bernie behind the bar. Back to where she sat. A place made for him to sit. The bar swam with noise and smoke.

Mother of God. It was her.

Sitting across the far side of the bar.

He saw her and then the pitch of the bodies between them hid her.

He saw her again. She seemed to have a map in front of her.

She drank from a Guinness glass.

He jabbed the stomach of the young man beside him.

'The girl across the bar, who's she?'

Nearly gone, pissed up. 'Australian, Bernie said,

car's broke, waiting for a mechanic to come out. Be
lucky . . .'

Christ, she'd no right . . .

Shouldn't have been there . . .

He felt the cold shiver in his body and the music and
the laughter belted in his ears.

He saw the red gold of her hair.

Chapter Fifteen

It was the moment the music died.

It was the moment between the laughter bursts.

It was the moment that the gap in the bodies had opened and he could see across the bar. He could see her face quite clearly and there were the pouch bags at her eyes and her shoulders were hunched, like she hadn't slept.

It was the moment that Bernie, from the bar, shouted across at her, 'Heh, Miss, no sign of the mechanic you're waiting on . . .'

Mossie sat with his pint glass in front of him and not more than an inch of it drunk. The OC was at the bar, and along from him was the Quartermaster, and on a stool was Hegarty with the dog curled at his feet.

Mossie saw her. She looked up. She seemed to blink, like she'd been far away.

'. . . No sign of him.'

She called back, 'Never mind, he'll be . . .'

Eyes turning to her, snaking at her, and the rich English cut of her accent hanging in the bar.

Her voice, like the record had changed, like she'd bitten her tongue, like she was awake and alert. Her

335

voice like the Australians from the television. 'Yeah, well, won't be much longer. He said he'd come, but thanks . . .'

And the music played. The machine belted Country and Western from the speakers. But no laughter to go with the music. No-one in the bar looking at her, not even Mossie who dared not stare across at her. He saw the OC move. The OC was at the side of the Quartermaster. The OC whispered urgently into the Quartermaster's ear. The Quartermaster was slipping from the bar, drink abandoned, and had his hand on the arm of a young fellow and was talking at him urgently. And Hegarty was tugging at the OC's sleeve and his sharp finger stabbed in her direction.

Mossie quiet and into the hair that fell over Siobhan's ear. 'Don't say nothing, don't do nothing.'

'Does they know?'

'Just shut your face.'

The OC was moving. He was drifting along the bar. Short exchanges, fast unheard orders. Shit, and why didn't she move? He watched the OC. Christ's sake, why didn't she go? He looked to the door. Two of the men that the OC had spoken with stood across the door. Her knees would have been locked and her mind would have blanked out, too feckin' scared to move or to think. He felt the pulse of his heart. The OC spoke only to the men he could rely on, the men who took his orders. See nothing and hear nothing and know nothing, the creed of Altmore. All the others, who would see and hear and know nothing, backed from the floor of the bar to the walls and the tables and benches and chairs at the side, and all that could had their backs to the young woman with the gold red hair . . .

The OC was bent over Mossie's shoulder. 'She's Brit army, surveillance, Hegarty's seen her on the mountain.'

Mossie said, shrugged, 'Hegarty's not the full shilling. I wouldn't break anyone's neck on that daft bugger's say so.'

The OC insisted, 'Saw her up on Logue's Hill, with a weapon, and a soldier with her.'

Mossie said, anxious, 'Be careful. If she's a Brit, she'll have back-up.'

Bernie behind the bar was bawling that it was time when it was twenty minutes to closing, and draping the cloths that dried the glasses over the pump handles of the beer, and yelling that it was time for good folks to be getting home, and reaching up to throw the switch that killed the music. The quiet in the bar, and the OC looked back to Mossie and jerked his head for Mossie to follow him. It happened fast . . . The OC and the Quartermaster and two of the young fellows that the OC had spoken to, strong and hard, round the table where she sat. Mossie couldn't see her. The crash of a glass and the scrape of a table tipping over. Mossie saw Hegarty leaning on the bar and his face was expressionless, and the dog slept at his feet as if nothing would wake it. Fifty men and women in the bar, crouched over tables at the walls and seeing nothing and hearing nothing and knowing nothing. He saw the gold red of her hair amongst the mass of them and they dragged her towards the door.

*   *   *

Bren paced.

A telephone rang. Jocko languidly lifted it, just gave his name and listened. He replaced the telephone.

Jocko said, 'The governor down in Dungannon. She should have cleared out of his area by now, hasn't called through. That's all.'

The cardboard city man lounged, his chair tilted, his boots on the table. 'We'll stay on . . .'

There was the OC and the Quartermaster holding her, and two of the young fellows. She seemed to go easily.

Siobhan was sheet-white beside him. 'What's you going to do?'

'Wait here, love. Don't move.'

It was automatic to Mossie. His life was compartments. On the mountain he was the man of the Organization. He was her man, Cathy Parker's, he was Song Bird, in the darkness of car parks off the area, in the night blackness of farm gateways and road lay-bys away from his home. He had been called. He started to push himself up from the seat and there was the strength of Siobhan's hand on his knee as if she tried to hold him down. It was necessary for him to belong, it was his survival that he was a part of them. He knew that he hurt his Siobhan but he pulled her fist from his thigh. There was the pleading in her face and the pain screwed her mouth. Nothing said. When he had her hand off his thigh then it was limp. The palm of his hand scratched on the single small diamond of the ring he had given his Siobhan for their engagement. She would never understand. He stepped forward. He edged past the men and the women who would see and hear and know nothing.

338

She grabbed at his coat and he broke her hold. He went toward the door. The prayer was in his mind, that it would be fast. If it were not fast . . . If it were not fast then Cathy Parker, Miss Parker, the bitch, would talk . . . If she talked . . . He swung his poor leg. He passed old Hegarty, sitting on his stool, supping his beer, dropping crisp flakes down to his dog.

He walked out into the night.

They were at the back of the parking place . . . There was no back-up. Christ. Now he could only pray that it would be fast . . . They were behind the cars and near to the shadow shape of a tractor, grotesque shapes, dancing in the high light thrown from the gable end of the bar. The Quartermaster and one of the lads held her, and Mossie saw the whip of her head going back as the OC punched her. Where in God's name was the young man, the one that minded her and didn't speak? Her arms were pulled back and the punches were going into her. They didn't shout questions, like she was not softened enough, and she didn't scream her cover back at them, like there was no point. He stood by the door of the bar. It was where the compartments of his life merged. He was Mossie Nugent, Intelligence Officer, and he was Mossie Nugent, Song Bird, and he knew he would lift not a finger, nor raise his voice, to aid her.

'Are you not going to help the boys?' the grate of old Hegarty's voice behind him.

Mossie said, 'They're not needing help. It's four of them, and a bit of a girl.'

'She's a Brit spy.'

'So you've said . . .'

Blows going into her, and a boot onto her knee or

339

her shin. He wondered if she'd seen him. He was rooted. There was old Hegarty's sharp whistle and the dog came back off the grass to heel. He knew that the Hegarty house had been searched more often over the last twenty years, and in the campaign before that, than any other house on Altmore, and he knew that fifteen years back Hegarty had taken a bad, bad, beating from the police and been an old man then.

'She was just an idiot to be here,' old Hegarty said, and was away up the road, not waiting for the end.

Mossie watched. He thought she was about to go down. If she went down, she was done for. There was the punch into the stomach that seemed to bend her and he thought that if she had not been held then she would have gone down. He told himself that there was nothing he could do. She should never have been there . . . It was when he knew that she was about to go down that she seemed to pull the Quartermaster's arm across her face. His shout slashed the night air.

The Quartermaster lost his grip on her, staggered away clutching his bitten hand. So fast, the movements. Her free hand swinging the short hook into the throat of the one who held her other arm. The OC threw himself at her. The beam of the high light caught them. They thrashed, rolled, struggled, on the ground, and all the time the OC was swinging at her to beat her head back onto the gravel. Again, so fast . . . The OC was pitched onto his stomach. Her knee was into the small of his back. His right arm was twisted up towards his shoulder, and there was the crack of his wrist breaking and then his moan of pain.

The crowd was behind Mossie. They had spilled

340

from the door. They would have seen what he saw. There was a young man backing away from her and the fear of her glistened in his eye. There was the OC writhing. There was a man down and with his legs flailing haphazard strikes into the gravel. There was the Quartermaster bent over the pain of his hand and hugging the shadow safety of the fringe of the light. The young man, backing away, shouted which was her car, and he had the power over the crowd, and there was a slow surge towards the green Astra, until it was surrounded. She rocked on her feet. Mossie thought her strength had gone. He stood with Siobhan beside him and he watched her. She reached inside her coat, and pulled at her sweater and there was the glimpse of her white skin and suddenly the dark outline of a pistol.

Mossie saw the petrol cap of the car thrown up over the heads of the crowd, and there was the flash of a match and the crowd started back, and the flames burst across the car, shafted through the interior of the green Astra.

He could see her face, he could see the set of her chin.

She walked towards him and she held the pistol loosely against the seam of her jeans. The car burned behind her. No-one blocked her way. There was blood dribbling from her lip. She was silhouetted against the flames. He thought it was only the will-power that kept her on her feet. She walked deliberately, as if each step was a challenge. She looked into the face of each man and woman that confronted her. She looked through Mossie. He saw the blood running down her jaw and the pain in her face and the strength that

341

carried her on, and out into the road. She walked, slowly, never hurrying, away down the road and into the night.

The radio operator's head ducked, the concentration immediate. The woman scribbled on her pad.

Earphones off. 'Emergency, 242's signal . . .'

The man behind her on the radio racks swinging the dials in front of him.

Jocko and Herbie grabbing weapons from the floor, running for the door. Feet pounding on the staircase.

The second operator hurrying across the area, thrusting the paper with the co-ordinates into the cardboard city man's hand.

Bren dragged, then pushed, down the stairs, out into the night sprinting for the car where the engine already roared.

A helicopter scrambled from the Dungannon barracks pad.

A meal left unfinished by the crewman. A poem left unread by a Lynx pilot. A plate abandoned and a book discarded open on the Mess table.

An officer should never be seen to run by the men he commanded. Colonel Johnny strode the corridor from his office to the Operations Room.

Herbie drove. He was expert. Along the motorway and overtaking on the outside and the inside. Through the town, past the darkened shops up Church Street, skirting the square, plunging down into Irish Street, and then away through the housing estate and out past the town's golf course, and climbing for the mountain. Bren didn't speak. The cardboard city man was beside him, and Jocko in the front had plugged a headphone into the equipment in the glove compartment, and occasionally he muttered the code signals to Herbie that were gibberish to Bren. Short of Donaghmore they screamed on a corner and raced past a man out walking his greyhounds and the dogs stampeded for the verge, and through Donaghmore they had to swerve to avoid a staggering drunk and were close enough to hitting him for Bren to shield his eyes. The car bucked, rolled, at the speed . . . He thought of her. She was the young woman who was closed, secret, hidden from him. He would have said that he could understand, after a fashion, every man and woman that he had worked with in the Service. He could spot greed, vanity, ambition; he could locate motivation; he could identify courage and cowardice. Greed, vanity, ambition, were perpetually in the show cases of the office in Curzon Street. Motivation was what he thought that he had bred for himself, and he had seen others at the recruits' seminars who had more of it than himself, men and women that he sometimes passed in the corridors, sometimes sat with in the canteen. Cowardice and courage he had seen on the endurance courses that the new intake had been subjected to . . . She had no greed, vanity, ambition, that he had seen. Her motivation was hidden from him. He reckoned her without cowardice and courage was what she would have sneered at . . . He wondered if she were dead . . . He wondered if she were captured.

Fear tumbling in his mind. If she were dead, if she were captured, they would skin him, the cardboard city man and Colonel Johnny and Hobbes and Mr

Wilkins, even Rennie who had cold-shouldered her. The man who lost Cathy Parker. Fear for her ate at him. The car surged on the road. Jocko held the earphone tight against his head, then swung round and gestured for the cardboard city man to look ahead. They were both bent down, the cardboard city man and Bren, heads together and peering through the windscreen.

He saw the helicopter. The helicopter was high above them and there was the beam of its searchlight powering down, and the red flashes of the navigation lights.

No word said in the car, and there was the clatter of the cardboard city man and Jocko arming their weapons.

Herbie had slowed. The windows were down, the weapons jutted out into the night air. There was the battering roar of the helicopter's engine splashing the interior of the car.

The road wound. A rabbit ducked to safety in front of their wheels.

Bren saw her.

She was on the forward edge of the light that shone down in a narrow cone from the hovering helicopter.

She was walking in the centre of the road. The white light was behind her. The light caught the road and the hedges and petered away in the fields. A crowd walked in step with her seemingly held back by the furthest edge of the light. It was as if the crowd shepherded her away from their homes and their mountain. The voice, staccato, amplified, beat at Bren's ears. '. . . Keep back. Do not go closer. If you go closer I will open fire. Keep back . . .' Behind her was the helicopter's light and behind the light was the crowd. Bren understood. The light would dazzle the crowd, burn out their eyes, she would be only a vague shape to the crowd that followed her. '. . . Keep back. You have been warned. I shall open fire. Keep back . . .', the metallic resonance of the voice above. None of them in the car spoke as they closed on her. Once her knees seemed to sink under her and she half pitched forward and then had to push herself up. Her face was shadow but the light caught at her hair. The car stopped. Herbie reversed hard into a gateway and the wheels spun on mud as he powered the three-point turn. She was thirty yards from them. There was the grunt from Jocko, and then he was speaking, hushed, into the radio microphone. The cardboard city man out, and Bren scrambling to follow.

He ran to her.

There was blood at her mouth. Her right eye was almost closed. Her mouth was bruised, a scraped graze on her temple. He took the pistol from her. The cardboard city man on one side and Bren on the other, and tugging her away, running with her back towards the waiting car. Bren had his arm round her waist to take the weight of her, and it was nothing.

She fell into the back of the car. Bren on one side and the cardboard city man on the other. She was sandwiched between them, head down. Bren looked back once. He could see the shape of the crowd, held against the light barrier. They went away fast, and before he wound up the window he heard the helicopter's engine gaining power for altitude. He felt the shiver of her body against his. Dear God . . . he had thought he might have found her dead.

The cardboard city man said, 'Nothing serious?'

She shook her head.

'You're a bit of a mess . . .'

The grin cracked her face. 'Some of them are worse.'

Bren held her hand, as if he hoped that would give her comfort.

Herbie drove, like there was no tomorrow, for the military hospital at Musgrave Park on the outskirts of Belfast.

Word spread in the night of an incident on the mountain.

Hobbes was told. 'Right, thank you. Tell her that I'll speak to her in the morning . . .'

Colonel Johnny was told. 'The Good Lord smiles on her. Tell her we're so pleased.'

Rennie was told. 'Getting too old, starting to be sentimental. Tell her not to be so bloody stupid again.'

Word spread in the night of an escape from the mountain.

The Quartermaster dabbed antiseptic on his bitten hand. 'Wasn't me to blame . . . but credit to the wee cow, credit the hardness of her.'

The OC felt the rivers of the pain as the doctor from Omagh bound the broken wrist. 'Was our fault because we bloody played with her, like she was just a bloody woman.'

The young man lay in Casualty in Monaghan town and the words whistled from deep in his bruised throat. 'Why didn't they bring the gun faster? You's has to shoot a woman like that.'

Mossie sat with Siobhan in front of the guttering

fire. 'It was like they were all frightened of her. Even before the helicopter came, it was like they didn't dare go close to her. She'd have shot them down, right to the last bullet . . .'

She slept on her back.

Bren was beside the bed on the hard-backed chair and all the time, through the night, he held the small hand in his.

He held her hand even when the nurses and the doctor came into the small room to check her. He ignored the disapproval of their glances, and their hostility when their eyes lighted on the pistol that he had placed on the low table beside him.

The first grey light smeared through the window blinds. He heard the coughing spit of the Military Policeman on the door. He looked down at her face, cleaned and calm. Her hand rested in his, unresponding.

He had thought he had lost her.

The afternoon paper said that anti-terrorist squad detectives were swooping on known haunts of Irishmen. More than twenty Irishmen had been taken into custody for questioning. All over the country, it said, landladies and the owners of boarding and guest houses were being quizzed about Irish lodgers. According to police sources, the identity of a prime suspect was known and the biggest manhunt ever mounted in the present terrorist campaign was under way. The newspaper said that a school soccer match had been cancelled in respect for a pupil, dead. A secretary on her way to her elderly mother's birthday party was dead; a man, his wife seven months pregnant, was dead. The flag at London's Cavalry Club hung at half-mast in tribute to a one-time Desert Rat, a many times decorated veteran, dead; a 22-year-old West Indian social worker, in intensive care, fought for his life.

Jon Jo turned the pages of the newspaper.

Photographs of the wrecked concourse. Condemnation of the killings from political and religious leaders in Britain and in the Republic.

He always read the newspapers after an attack.

He heard the slap of her feet on the pavement. There was the grate of her key in the door. The whine voice of her neighbour.

'The police were here. I said you were at your basket class.'

Jon Jo moving on stockinged feet to the window.

'What for?'

'It was on the radio yesterday, they want to know where all the Irish are. I rang them about your lodger . . .'

'You'd no call to do that.'

'But you weren't here when they came. I told them he was here, gone, here again. They waited an hour in my kitchen. They said I was to tell you to ring them as soon as you were in.'

'I'm ringing no-one.'

'They'll be back.'

He heard the front door slammed.

He peeled back the carpet and lifted the loose plank in the flooring and took everything out, his lists, his passports, the weapon, the ammunition. He emptied each drawer, and the wardrobe. He worked as silently

348

as he could because he listened for the brake of a car and the ringing of the bell. He filled his suitcase and his tool bag. She would have been too lightly built for him to hear her coming up her thick-carpeted stairs. They were all oiled, all the door fittings in the house. When the door opened behind him, he was aware of the light from the landing, he was on his knees in front of the chest of drawers and the gloves were on his hands and he was wiping every inch of wood with the cloth that he kept in his tool bag to clean his hands. He turned.

'Time I was gone, missus.'

'Going without telling me?'

The wide and bright smile that she loved, that she spoke of. Thinking fast. 'Heard from a mate, over on the Continent, says it's all played out in London. The place for work is Germany or Holland.'

'The police called, they're checking everywhere there are Irish lodgers. What do I tell them?'

'Just doing their job, you tell them what you know.'

She looked at him, and at the packed bags, and then at the newspaper on the bed, the photograph of a happy schoolboy.

'If I were to go downstairs, ring the police . . .'

'You've no cause to be afraid of me, missus. I'd not touch a hair on your head.'

'Why should a schoolboy have had cause to be afraid?'

'Because . . . because . . . how long's a piece of string, missus? Where does it start? It's like when you walk in a bog field. It sucks at you. First it's the ankles, then the knees, then the thighs, then your waist. It takes you down.'

349

She kneeled on the floor beside him. His head was against her shoulder. The tears ran from his eyes and onto her blouse.

His voice choked, he asked her would she make him a cup of tea.

He finished the wiping of the room.

The kettle was whistling on her stove as he let himself out through the front door. He walked down the pavement with his grip and his suitcase and his tool bag, not looking back.

The Secretary of State blustered, 'But you gave me your word.'

The Prime Minister flushed, 'I gave you a preliminary opinion.'

'You swore to me that you'd toast them.'

'I've learned of a new world that you cared not to inform me of.'

'You've reneged on your . . .'

'Before you put yourself irrevocably on the road to resignation, you will be so patient as to allow Mr Wilkins to give you the benefit of some recent intelligence, some other aspects of the whole picture. Mr Wilkins.'

So Ernest Wilkins had his turn.

There were a few brush strokes of embellishment. Started with Jon Jo Donnelly. All justified by the capture of Jon Jo Donnelly, or if capture were not possible . . . a dropped voice, a matter not necessary to be explained. The story of a young woman. Oh yes, women had a role to play. A young woman who had been through all of the endurance courses on the Brecon mountain range, pushed to the same limits as any male. A young woman who had been subjected to the same tests of marksmanship at Aldershot and close-quarters unarmed combat as any man. A young woman who had been trained to the highest levels of surveillance and counter-surveillance procedures. A young woman who had nurtured the most valuable player in the Source Programme . . . He explained, going slowly as if talking to fools, that a young woman could move in areas where it would be suicidal for a man to attempt to follow. He listed the Service pedigree of a young woman. Recruitment, proven experience, bravery that would not and should not ever be acknowledged. A young woman who would within the next two hours be released from hospital. He listed wounds, injuries, abrasions. He spoke of the rumour that the vine carried, a bitten hand and a broken wrist and a battered windpipe, and a crowd that had been held back by a single young woman, half kicked to death, who weighed 8 stone 3 pounds and measured 5 foot 4 inches in height.

Ernest Wilkins, hands held in diffidence, said, 'It's your decision, gentlemen. Do you want Jon Jo Donnelly, or do you not?'

The Secretary of State, doubt in his voice, said, 'I have warned you . . .'

The Prime Minister said, 'Unleash the pack on him. Run him to ground.'

Ernest Wilkins hurried back to Curzon Street to send the necessary signals in confirmation of a programme now authorized.

Called back.
Ordered home.

The tang of the mountain in his nose.

The touch of his wife against his body.

The feel of the hand of his boy.

Jon Jo took the train west, to Plymouth, for the early sailing of the ferry to the Spanish port of Santander.

A gun dumped, a parcel of explosive ditched, a carton of wires and timers and detonators and papers discarded.

Called home. Ordered back.

The trail of his trade was behind him, scattered when he had replaced the telephone at the station call box. Joy enough for him to have shouted . . . Going back to Altmore . . .

She sat primly at the edge of her seat. She was shown the photograph, as she had been shown it by the constable when he had called. She confirmed that the photograph and her lodger were the same. It was easier than she had thought it would be. She wore a close-knit woollen cardigan and she had buttoned it to her throat so that there would be no sign to the detectives who questioned her of the damp stain of the tears that had been wept against her shoulder. She repeated what he had told her, that he would go to London, fly to Holland or Germany, look for work. They told her his name, and they told her what he had done. He had been a fine man to her, and he could have killed her, and she tried to sweep from her mind the image of a smiling schoolboy as photographed in the first edition of the afternoon newspaper . . . It was like it had been yesterday, the clear and recent memory to her, but it had been five weeks before, and he had been in the bathroom and she had come to the room to bring clean bedding and the photographs had been on the table beside the bed. A handsome woman and a small boy. The boy in the photograph was younger than the boy in the newspaper, and there was the stretch of a mountainscape behind the woman and the boy. She kept her question until the end, until the detectives were about to leave.

'Such a good and decent man, so helpful to me, and so cheerful . . . How could he hate so much?'

And no answer given her.

'She should go home,' Bren said.

'That's out of the question.'

'She's exhausted. She was exhausted before this happened. She made a mistake.'

'There's a job to finish,' Hobbes said.

'She's not in a fit state. She was damn near killed.'

'Brennard, when I need your advice running my department I'll seek it out. And it might help you to know that London's latest has Jon Jo on the move.'

'There's a whole bloody army here, it doesn't have to be her . . .'

The flare of anger from Hobbes. 'You don't understand anything, do you? We did the work – not the army, not the branch, not E4 – and we'll finish it. Have you got me?'

Bren played the prime card. 'She has to go home, she's compromised. It's my decision as to when the risk becomes intolerable. I can't change the jockey in mid-race. Just be thankful the big decisions aren't yours.'

They were in the corridor and away from the door to her room. They were beyond earshot. She came out

of the door, past the Military Police guard. There were
two nurses with her and the doctor. Bren saw it: the
nurse touched her elbow as if to support her and
the help was shrugged off. Vintage Parker. She was
in the same clothes they had found her in on the road
under Altmore mountain. She walked stiffly. Hobbes
went to her, Bren hung back. Hobbes kissed her
lightly on the cheek, as if he were a distant relation.
She didn't say goodbye to the doctor, she didn't offer
her thanks to the nurses. Hobbes led, Bren followed.
She stumped awkwardly between them towards the
front door of the building. She was paler than usual
and the colouring round her eye was brightening. He
saw the mud on her jeans and the dirt on her T-shirt
and the rips in her anorak. They walked outside. In
the late afternoon light they stood in the car park
and she asked about her car and was told it had been
recovered during the night, that the radio had been
destroyed by the fire, no problem. Hobbes told her
that London believed that Donnelly was on his way
back. Bren didn't see any pleasure on her face, only
the tiredness and the pallor and the colour of the
bruising. Hobbes told Bren to drive Cathy home and
went his way.

He took her back to her flat.

He stood at the open door.

She walked across her living room to her bedroom.

He wondered if she had known, while she slept
through the night and the morning, that he had held
her hand. He could feel still the gentleness of her
sleeping hand.

'Pick me up in the morning,' she said, and the
bedroom door closed behind her.

Chapter Sixteen

It was the story that the small boy loved best, the story that had no ending.

'When he had jumped the gorge, when he had escaped from the dragoons, Shane Bearnagh had to make the long way round the mountain of Altmore to avoid the troopers. They were furious at their failure to trap him, and they burned fodder barns and slashed the legs of the few cattle that the Catholic people had. More troops were sent for, from Armagh and from Omagh, and they searched all over the mountain. But the great mountain and the wild land behind, on either side of the road to Pomeroy, held its secret. It was no longer safe for a large group of men to be with him. Some deserted, some he asked to leave because he could not feed them.

'Hard times for Shane and his wife and his little boy. It was more difficult for him to bring them food, more dangerous for him to light fires to cook what little he had. It was impossible now for him to stop the coaches that came up the mountain from Dungannon on the long road to Pomeroy and Omagh and then to Derry, because all the coaches were escorted by the dragoons. They lived mainly from eating wild berries, it was a great treat for him to find a stray sheep and kill it and cook. His beard grew, he was the wild man of the mountain. His wife and his little boy never complained of their life, and on the times when Shane would try to persuade her to go back down the mountain to her family, his wife would refuse. The poor people from the town would sometimes come up the mountain with food and fresh clothes for his wife and his boy, but they took great risk when they did so. If they were caught then their homes were burned and men would be thrown into the gaol in Armagh.

'The reward for information leading to Shane's capture was increased, but the people stayed loyal to him because they believed he was the last man in all Ireland to win the fight against the English who they hated. But the English were patient, they waited for a traitor. There were some down below the summit who knew which caves were used by Shane Bearnagh, under which rock crags he sheltered with his wife and his little boy. The English waited . . .

'There were two journeymen tailors. They travelled the road from Dublin to Derry. They could repair the dresses of the fine ladies in their mansions, they could make grand suits for the English gentlemen. They were not from Altmore . . . It was winter, there was snow on the mountain. There were no berries to be eaten. There was no stray sheep to be killed because all had been taken down to the farms on the lower ground. Shane was starving. He had left his wife who was thin to the bone, and his little boy who cried at night from hunger. He took the great risk of coming to the road to find food for them. The journeymen tailors had horses and a donkey that they led behind them and that carried the clothes from which they made the suits and dresses, and their needles and their threads. They gave him food, but there was evil in their hearts. They gave him a small amount to eat and they fed him sweet words. They said they would be back in an hour with more, enough for him to take to his wife and to his boy. There was greed in their hearts. They thought nothing of the patriot. They thought only of the gold and silver pieces they would earn from the English.

'They came to a check point, where the dragoons searched all travellers. God rot them . . . They told the dragoons where they had seen Shane, and they said they had told him they would be back within the hour. Evil men, the lowest of the low, traitors . . . The dragoons found Shane and they rode their horses off the road to chase him and ride him down. At first he could hold them off. He had the long-barrelled musket with which he was a fine shot. He would stop and fire, and run, and load again, and fire, and run again. They were frightened, the English dragoons, they had no cause to die for, they were far from their own homes. But to keep them back he must shoot, and each time he fired on them so the small pouch where he kept his musket balls was lighter.

'All through the afternoon they chased him. The exhaustion grew in him. He was without food, without water, and running from men on horseback. He fired his last shot, and he ran. Each time he fired they came closer to him. He had no more shot for his musket . . . Shane tore the buttons from his coat. Now, he rammed the buttons down the barrel of the musket. They were just buttons that he fired at them, but still they feared him, they would not dare to approach him. He fired the last button from his coat. He stood on a high boulder. He was alone on his mountain. They circled him. The dragoons were all around him. He could see the road far off, and on the road were the journeymen tailors who waited for their reward. He could no longer defend himself . . .'

'Did they kill him, Ma? Did the bastard English kill the patriot?'

'It's time for your light to be off if you're to be good for school in the morning.'

Ronnie, just about to go in, heard the voices, checked, dropped his hand from the door, and listened.

Charles would do the watch duty the first night, and Bill would do the second, and then Archie would do the third, then Charles again . . .

Charles protesting: 'We're throwing a thrash for the eldest, her birthday.'

Bill complaining: 'There's a college concert and Harry's on the cello.'

Archie arguing: 'Long-standing dinner engagement, been fixed for ages.'

He heard Ernest Wilkins, the man who was walked over, the man whose temper was always secured.

'I don't think in his present mood, with the importance of the operation currently being launched by the Service, that your Director General would take kindly to backsliding, but you are at liberty to try him . . . Good, excellent. We'll be taking over the EO room in an hour when the domestics have scrubbed it through.'

Jocelyn heard, and looked out of his office to check it, Ernest Wilkins striding down the corridor and whistling the theme to 'Carousel', and there were two ladies with mops and buckets and clean sheets and laundered pillows working over the Emergency Operations room, and there was a Curzon Street engineer carrying into the EO room enough radio equipment to fit out a frigate, and an apprentice

358

behind him festooned with telephone handsets and cable.

It would have been four years, maybe longer, since Emergency Operations had been manned round the clock.

'What I heard,' said Jocelyn to Ronnie, 'it's Ernest's finest hour. He's enmeshed the PM. He's got Charles and Bill and Archie sleeping on the job . . .'

'When did they not?'

'No bloody joke . . . Poor old Mr Donnelly, I'd say he's a bad bet for insurance.'

They went down the corridor. They looked into the EO room where the engineers tested the radio and confirmed the phone lines. There was a full-face picture of Jon Jo Donnelly, life-size, on the wall above one of the two iron-framed beds, and on the pillow of that bed was a pair of folded, ironed, pyjamas.

On the upper deck of the big ferry boat Jon Jo leaned on the rail. The salt was in his lungs, the wind cleaned his throat, the air scoured his cheeks. Winter stars above him, and the swell of the waters of the Biscay below him. He felt freedom, and the love that a man has for the going home from work hard done.

The dawn had not yet given way to day when death came again to the mountain.

He was ambushed halfway between Donaghmore village and the start of the mountain climb. Death was carried by a burst from a Sterling sub-machine gun and two aimed rounds from an FN rifle.

The milk cart was slewed across the road. The driver's window was smashed. A body was slumped over the steering wheel. Blood seeped in the cab. A foot was rooted down onto the accelerator pedal and the drive wheels spun wildly in the rain ditch.

A car, stolen by Protestant para-military sympathizers, would later be found, burned through, at a picnic site on Lough Neagh, and later still a statement would be issued in the name of the UVF claiming that the dead man had been a known Republican activist.

Dead in the cab of his milk cart was the man who believed that he had no living enemy.

The widow of Pius Blaney stumbled, dazed, around her kitchen to make tea for the priest. She urged him to let it be known that she wished for no retaliation, that Pius, the softest-hearted man you could find in all Ireland, he would have wished for no retaliation.

The corpse in the mortuary not yet cold, a post-mortem examination of gouged bullet tracks not yet completed.

The OC met Mossie Nugent.

The urgency spilling in him, the eyes gleaming. 'I want a target.'

Mossie stalling. 'Would you not do better to wait for Jon Jo, not go rushing?'

'I want a target and quick.'

'I'll think on it.'

'You'll do more . . .'

'It takes setting up . . .'

They sat in the OC's car. The OC had intercepted him on his way to work. The fingers below the plaster on his wrist were swollen sore, resting on the wheel.

'You got a problem, Mossie?'

'I got no problem.'

'Why the bloody cold water, why the bloody ice?'

'I was just saying . . .'

'Why d'you kill what I want, Mossie?'

The eyes searched him. Same eyes, same strip search, as in the barn.

'There's no call for you's and me to quarrel, Mossie . . . We wait a few days and the mountain will say the Organization is soft. You let those Prod feckers kill Pius Blaney on the mountain without an immediate response we can pack the whole war in. I don't need a Jon Jo back to tell me that. Give me a target, Mossie, and quick.'

Mossie said, 'There's a UDR bastard, drives the bus from Stewartstown. He carries a gun, but he'd never reach it . . .'

'Too small. For Pius Blaney, people'd want something better.'

'There's a place where they've put patrols down from a Puma. The helicopter's used the same pad two times in the last month. Could stake it . . .'

'Needs six men, needs a heavy-calibre, you could be waiting for ever. I want now.'

'There's a Catholic in the Special Branch in Dungannon. He's Browne . . .'

'Do us great.'

He gave an address. He listed two sets of car registration plates. Detective Sergeant Joseph Browne. He gave the name and the address and the make of the car.

'How'd you do it?'

'What's it to you, Mossie?'

The eyes cut him. Mossie was getting out of the car.

'Just asking . . . just talking.' Mossie gave his OC the

full smirk. 'And I wouldn't be wanting to see another disaster like there was with that wee woman.'

He was the master of the Task Co-ordinating Group meeting. They had no alternative, Hobbes was in the chair. The major and the Assistant Chief Constable and the colonel and Rennie of the Branch and the Assistant Under-Secretary, they could only listen.

'. . . This is a Five operation which we will direct. When we require help we will request it. Any short-fall in co-operation will be reported immediately to London and then to the Prime Minister's office. We believe that Jon Jo Donnelly has already left mainland Britain. In our view, he will return quite shortly to his home territory, to Altmore mountain. From midnight an area with a radius of five miles from his home there will be declared Tactical Out of Bounds. There will be no military or police movement inside the area without my express permission. Overall direction of the operation against Donnelly will be handled from Curzon Street. I will have my people on the mountain and they will have discreet support. They will wait for Donnelly, and when the time comes a hit force will be moved in. This is the way it will be. Questions . . . ?'

Bren, sitting behind Hobbes, watched the faces. Acid-cold stares, and no questions. Not finished, not quite, bleeding the last blood.

'. . . In London, they want Jon Jo Donnelly's head and I aim to give it them.'

He shuffled his papers together. Bren saw the smirk on his face. And he saw the dry smile of the major who would provide the back-up, and the dented pride of the Assistant Chief Constable, and the suppressed

362

fury of the colonel, and the frustration of the Assistant Under-Secretary who already knew that his master had been overruled. Rennie sucked at his pipe, he shut his briefcase, and leaned towards Hobbes, out of earshot of the others.

'You're an arsehole, Hobbes, and sending her back onto Altmore makes you simply a bigger arsehole . . .'

He had been on the upper deck all through the night. He felt that the sea air had purged the memories, the fear of mainland Britain. He had used one of the British passports to go through the port immigration. He left the ferry boat behind him, where it dwarfed the fishing fleet that was clustered under the shelter of the harbour wall. Donnelly took the bus from Santander to the airport at Bilbao. He felt freedom within his grasp, and his Attracta and his Kevin, and he felt the joy grow in him that a man has in the going home from work hard done.

They stood by the cars.

Hobbes said, 'Just get over to her, and the both of you start moving.'

'She told me to pick her up this morning, I think she should be allowed to rest . . .'

'When she needs a nanny then I'm sure she'll ask for one. In the meantime look at yourself, get a bit of drive into your system.'

Hobbes walked away from him. Bren went to his own car. The radio came on as he switched the ignition.

A milk delivery driver, Catholic, shot dead by gunmen, Protestants . . . Christ, what a bloody awful war to be a part of . . . All the funerals going through his mind that were daily catalogued on the local television. A dog handler, and his Alsatian trotting behind the hearse with the police coat on its spine. A soldier, the union flag and his beret on the coffin carried by the bearer party from his platoon. The little escort behind Patsy Riordan's family, furtive as if they hoped their presence didn't give offence to those who had taken his life. A taxi driver in Belfast, his cortège made up of the cabs of his fellow Protestant workers. An English scaffolding erector, murdered for working at the new police station in Strabane, and his wife on sedation and eight months pregnant and supported by family who wouldn't have known where Strabane was . . . The war he was a part of.

Some had been warned that they were targets, most knew only generally that they were at risk.

The detective sergeant sat with the other plainclothes police. He was opposite the Press seats, close to the witness box, side on to the dock, half facing the Lord Chief Justice, and he was already nodding. Crumlin Road, No.1 Court, always had the central heating turned up as if the Lord Chief Justice had been imported from the Caribbean, not Carrickfergus. He was there to see Brady go down, and preferably for a tenner. Some of those that he saw, between the moments that his head dropped, would have been warned of specific danger, more would just have accepted the general risk to their lives. Judges were shot by the PIRA, defence lawyers were shot by the Protestants, the prison officers guarding the dock were detested equally . . . He was the man who had turned his back on his history, his family. He worked for Protestants. His wife of three years, Catholic upbringing, lived with their eight-month-old baby amongst Protestant neighbours.

Detective Sergeant Browne wore his pistol under his coat. Policemen were allowed to carry their guns into court.

He dozed because he had not slept, the baby's teeth, and close to him was the exhibits bench for the case against Brady, and laid on the bench were a Kalashnikov rifle, a Remington rifle, and a Luger pistol, and their ammunition, all wrapped in plastic bags, killing weapons.

He had heard on his car radio of the murder of Pius Blaney, the milk-cart driver. There would be reprisal, Detective Sergeant Browne knew it. It was inevitable.

He drove via the Department of the Environment office. The message was on the answerphone. He transcribed it and then rang Cathy. He spoke to her recording machine which didn't answer him back, heard him out.

Bren walked into the city centre, through the security gates and down Royal Avenue, and into a florist's and chose four dozen amber and gold chrysanthemums.

He drove out to her flat. The radio said Pius Blaney was sixty-four years old, a man who had publicly and all his life rejected violence, who was respected by Catholic and Protestant customers alike. He caught himself thinking, well, they would say that, wouldn't they, and resolved to ask Colonel Johnny next time he saw him what was the truth about Pius Blaney. And would someone be saying the same thing one day about Jon Jo Donnelly, farmer, respected by all his neighbours, devoted family man, violence an anathema to him . . . Mr Mossie Nugent, painter/decorator, a pillar of the community, no known association . . . 'Responsibility for the murder of Mr Blaney has been claimed by . . .' Bren snapped off the radio. Shut out the madness that was the real world. Wasn't ready for this real a world. Hadn't learned the code yet. Mr Gary Brennard had no known association. Mr Gary Brennard, Bren to his intimates, needed a known association. Needed it one or two hundred light years from Belfast, for starters.

He took the stairs three at a time, carrying the flowers and wondering if she'd accept them.

Bren rang the bell. He waited. He rang the bell again. A man in a pinstripe and with an attaché case came out of a flat on the same landing and stared at Bren, seemed to quiz him. He might have been a Five man or a 14th Intelligence man or a Special Military Intelligence Unit man. On the other hand, he might have been an accountant, a sales rep, a bank deputy manager, and he might have rejected violence all his life . . . There had to be another life, another world. Did accountants, sales reps, bank deputy managers believe there was hope for this world? The man smiled at him, and went down the stairs. He kept his finger on the bell.

Just reflex, he tried the handle. The door opened for him.

He called her name. On the floor were her anorak and her shoes and her jeans and her sweater, a not very straight path to her bedroom.

366

He crossed the room.

Bren pushed the bedroom door.

The curtain was not drawn, the curtain had been left open. The light flooded the room.

She lay on the bed.

She held her pillow against her. Her eyes were open. She stared at the pillow and the wall ahead of her. The bedclothes were rucked half over her body.

Bren knelt beside the bed. He put her open hand on the flowers and closed her fingers on the stems. The flowers shared the pillow with her. He took her other hand from the pillow and he held it between his own. He saw the blood red of her eyes and the rose pink of her face. He thought that if she had slept then she had cried herself to sleep. Beside her hand, beside the flowers, beside the pillow, was the low table on which was the light and a handwritten letter and her pistol. A firm feminine hand, he thought it would be a letter from her mother, he thought it would be everything safe like his own mother's letters would be, everything that a mother scared half out of her wits would write to her child who was covert in Northern Ireland. He moved the pistol to the floor, so she could see the flowers, not the pistol.

'You're a bastard . . .' she said, 'for coming here, finding me.'

There was no strength in her hand. He saw the bloodshot eyes and the bruising. He saw the scars on her temple. Bren put his arm gently under her neck and he lifted her head and shoulders and he held her against him. He tried to kiss, softly, the bruising and the scraped scars. Her head was against his chest.

A small voice. 'I hadn't been so frightened, not since

I was a child. The cat brought a rabbit into the kitchen. The rabbit was alive. The cat held the rabbit by the throat. What frightened me was the fear in the rabbit's face, it was a big animal, nearly as big as our cat, but it was so frightened that it just let itself be killed by the cat . . .'

His fingers were in the short cut of her hair. He kissed her mouth, where the hand had punched the blood from her lip.

'. . . It was only when I thought I was going to die that I fought them. I'd given up, and I don't know where it came from. It was the last chance I had. It's all about fear . . . I shouldn't have been alone, it was my fault. It wasn't your fault . . . Cathy Parker, not a nerve in her body, she'll go anywhere, not a nerve in her bloody body. I'm the living, walking, talking bloody legend. It's what I live with, that they'll get to find that Cathy Parker is just scared stiff. I went there for myself. It was only bullshit, it was to show myself that I could take it, cope with being so bloody scared that I could shit myself. Fear of failure, that's what drives you on. You have to keep proving it, testing it, that you're not scared. You said I'd make a mistake. I did, bloody fool, I showed them my voice. I was just so tired . . . and the bloody legend'll go on . . .'

He held her close against him. He kissed her cheek where the fist that had worn a signet ring had belted her.

'. . . Do you understand?'

'There has to be hope.'

'They shouldn't know.'

Bren said, 'There has to be light for us.'

368

'I couldn't survive it, not if they knew the legend was a bloody sham.'

'I want a future for us.'

'You wouldn't tell them, Hobbes and Colonel Johnny and the boys?'

He thought of them. Hobbes, who supplied the tourniquet of pressure, and who talked of Five's show, and who had only shaken her hand and kissed her cheek without emotion. Colonel Johnny, sad and caring and loving her as an uncle would a favourite niece. The boys, gruffly worshipping her and driving up the mountain in controlled silence and not knowing whether they were heading straight for a free-fire ambush situation, the cardboard city man and Jocko and Herbie.

'Not theirs, it's our business.'

There was at her broken mouth something that he had not seen before. It was the trace of shyness. Her eyes, red, pouched, squeezed between bright bruising, dropped. She kissed him back.

Bren said, 'If there is no hope and no light and no future then there is no point, no bloody point at all, in us being here . . .'

She kissed the words away from him. Then she pushed him gently back. She threaded the coat from his shoulders, and pulled the sweater over his head. She unbuttoned his shirt, pushed it off his arms. She loosed his belt, she reached to prise away his shoes and his socks. She reached up to the curtains and pulled them closed, and stiffly drew off her T-shirt. She took the flowers in her arms and lay down with them. He took off his trousers and his

369

shorts. She reached up a hand to him. She pulled him down onto her. There was the wet cold of the stems on the sheet. Her shoulder crushed the chrysanthemum blooms, amber and gold. The petals merged in her hair, gold and red. The nakedness of her against him.

'I love you, Cathy Parker . . .'

Her legs close around his, pinioning him. Her mouth brushing his, welcoming him.

Later, she made him tea. Later, she went to the living room, and as he lay on his back he heard his message to her, that Song Bird wanted a meeting. Later, she took the battered flowers and put them in a water jug and carried them back to beside her mattress. Later, when she was dressed, he heard the sounds, metal on metal, as she loaded the magazine into her pistol. Later, he had called to her that an emergency operations room was in place at Curzon Street, and that it was thought Jon Jo Donnelly was travelling back to the mountain.

He had told her that he loved her and she had not replied. But she had kissed him after she had made the calls and loaded her pistol, and heard him out.

She stood in the doorway of the bedroom. The calm was once more in her face.

'I love you, Cathy. I will never let you be alone again. I believe in the hope and the light and a future beyond this bloody place.'

'Come on, my pretty boy, let's go to work.'

'He comes back, we nail him, you go home.'

'Let's just take it one step at a time.'

*　　*　　*

370

The flight for Geneva left Bilbao airport, carrying Jon Jo Donnelly, travelling as James McHarg, on the wide route back to the mountain.

The Commander said, 'You say he's gone . . . well, all I can tell you is that the ferry ports, Channel and east coast, have been put on a high state of alert, and all the airports, and all the Irish routes, and there's not sight nor sound of him.'

Wilkins was the closed door. 'Is that so?'

'His landlady was adamant that he was headed for Germany or Holland . . .'

'Of course, what I would expect.'

'I'm going to crank Dublin up, just in case he's dumb enough to go direct . . .'

'I wonder if that's wise. I don't think so. Where are they now, their transferable goal posts, on the extradition issue? Close to the halfway line? I wouldn't think it necessary to involve our Irish colleagues. I recommend the matter be resolved on our own grounds.'

'It's your funeral . . .'

Ernest Wilkins smiled. 'My funeral or my party, we'll have to wait and see.'

He despised senior policemen, and disguised his feelings under a bed of humility and politeness. They were such different men. He thought the policeman, the Commander of the Anti-Terrorist Branch, would retire to the boardroom of a major industrial company and augment a good pension with a fat salary. He, himself, and the office clock and the sherry gathering for colleagues in the Director General's office were beckoning, would slip away after thirty-two years of service to a Cornish cottage, to oblivion. There would be no bar-fly anecdotes from Ernest Wilkins, only the closeted memories of the young men and young women that he had sent into the field.

With obsequious courtesy he escorted the Commander to the side-door exit of the building, then hurried back, not waiting for the lift, up the stairs to the Emergency Operations room. He was told Song Bird had rung for a meeting. He was told Parker and her minder were on the move. He felt a rare flush of excitement . . . he would detest the Cornish cottage and oblivion.

'. . . they's going to do a hit, a policeman.'

Cathy incisive. 'His name?'

'Browne. Detective Sergeant.'

'Working out of?'

'Dungannon barracks, Special Branch.'

'When?'

She was riding him, taking him, roughly, under her control.

'I don't know.'

'What do you mean, you don't know?'

'Wasn't told.'

'Why weren't you told?'

'They're keeping everything feckin' tight.'

'Where then?'

'Don't know that either.'

'What *do* you know, Mossie?'

'I gave you his name.'

'Tell me when.'

Mossie said, 'Want to do it fast. Want to hit him

372

while the anger's hot on the mountain. There was plenty of love for Pius Blaney.'

Bren saw that Mossie couldn't keep his eyes from her face. He stood to the side of the quarry, a little away from them. Some of the time he listened closely, and most of the time he watched the road at the quarry entrance and the rim of the steep bank. The back-up was somewhere up the road, with difficulty squeezed on the telephone from Rennie.

'Heh, miss, you did well out there. But, Jesus, you frightened me. Can you's do your drinking in some other bar now?'

He heard her light laugh. 'How are they, our friends?'

'It was the OC's wrist you broke, and you half bit off the Quartermaster's hand, the lad's in hospital . . .'

She gave him a new telephone number. Bren watched. A fox was slipping by the top of the quarry wall. He heard Donnelly's name. The fox stopped and stared at him, the intruder. He heard a sum of money mentioned. The fox darted away.

'Miss, if there's patrols and things there, if it's obvious they've been touted . . . it can come back to me.'

She slapped his shoulder. 'Just get on home, Mossie. I'll take care of you.'

Mossie's car, no lights until he was well down the road, skidded away. He put his hand loosely on her shoulder. She let it stay there, only a moment, then shrugged it off.

Bren heard her mutter, 'Shit, why the hell did he have to tell me?'

373

Chapter Seventeen

She was her withdrawn and distant self. She had told him when they had come back from the meeting with Song Bird that she needed to sleep and given him a peck on the cheek at her door, told him when she would collect him. She had been full of the cold business of the morning and he had tossed through the night, alone in his bed, where the words of hope and light and a future had pierced his mind.

They were round Hobbes' kitchen table, dabbling with cornflakes and toast and coffee.

'It's just a problem we could have done without, but it won't go away, and it has to be addressed.'

Cathy said, 'The nub of it is Song Bird's physical security.'

'The nub of it – let me put it in a slightly different way – is that, to protect the policeman, do we endanger our Song Bird?'

Cathy said, 'Saturate the area round the policeman and you might just as well send up a barrage balloon trailing a message "Come in Mossie Nugent, your time is very nearly up."'

'I don't think I can be hearing you right, Cathy.'

'You said it was a problem, I've not disagreed.'

There was the quiet round the table. The neon beamed down on them. It was still grey outside. There was a curry take-away carton on the draining board and an empty wine bottle. Bren wondered, in the silence, how much Hobbes minded that his wife was not over here with him.

'You're saying the policeman's nothing more than a nuisance . . .'

Cathy said, 'No, I'm not saying that. I'm saying that in a finely calculated arrangement of priorities, which I by God didn't ordain, Song Bird comes first.'

It was a policeman's life, a man's life.

Bren was about to burst. The anger steamed in his tiredness.

'Hell of a shame he told you . . .'

Cathy said, 'But he did, and I told you . . .'

Bren's finger jabbed alternately at Hobbes and Cathy. Past breaking point. 'Jesus, this is not a bloody board game, this is just goddamn stupid. This is a man's life . . .'

Hobbes cut him off. 'What's your difficulty?'

Bren shouted, control gone. 'It's not a difficulty, it's a man's life.'

Cathy said, 'But it's Song Bird's life.'

Bren's fist slammed onto the table. 'It isn't one or the other. You have no choice but to protect DS Browne. You have no choice but to protect Song Bird. *That's* your obligation. You're not God, sitting in bloody judgement . . .'

'Steady down, young man.'

Cathy said, 'Put the lid on it, Bren.'

'Sorry, Cathy, this isn't the sort of thing you put a

lid on. I was a party to Patsy Riordan being fingered, I have learned and it will not happen again. I will not wash my hands of a policeman's blood.'

Hobbes looked across at him, not even bothering to be angry. 'You're like the whole dismal crew of them in London. Nobody wants to accept that it's a *war* here. They're just pussy-footing around, getting in the way of the real fighting . . . Bloody delicate it'll have to be.'

Cathy seemed to understand what he meant, seemed satisfied that a compromise had been reached. He didn't, couldn't, know whether he had saved the life of a policeman at Dungannon, or whether he had simply made a bigger idiot of himself than before. She had slept alone in the bed where he had loved her. Cathy sipped at her coffee. She stared past him into the lightening day. He had been on her bed and loved her and he knew nothing of her beyond what had fallen into his hands in the one moment of weakness.

Hobbes was telephoning Rennie, making an appointment for them.

The wind off the runway caught at his face, and he rejoiced at it.

They had come in over the sea to the north of the city, swung over the coastline of the villages and the inlets and the tiny harbours, broken through the bottom of the low cloud to see the sharp green of the fields, then banked for the airfield. He had been gone close to a year. Passengers steamed around him, hurrying away towards the car-park area. Home . . . It was where Attracta was, and little Kevin. A hand on his sleeve. It was a girl who met him. He thought she was nervous of him. She drove. She took a perimeter road round the edge of the city, and she looked in her mirror often enough to have been on a driving test. He thought that she had been told not to speak to him. She took him to a house in the Tallaght estate. It was what he loathed, grey houses on grey streets under a grey sky. Where there had been grass there were kids' bike tracks and tinkers' horses and mud.

She pointed to a house. She was away before he had reached the door. They were waiting for him in the house. The greetings were in Irish. A young man and an older man. He had met them before, didn't know their names. He was told the girl had gone for petrol. He was told of a new team going onto the mainland . . . The war going hard in the Six Counties . . . New blood needed on the mainland, and new blood needed in the North . . . He was told of discord in the Organization, of the chasm between those who wanted to fight on and those who wanted to cut and run for the negotiating table . . .

'It's what the Brits are working at, dividing us, splitting us, weakening us. Soft words to deceive, and there are some, the eejits, who are believing them,' the older man said.

'It's said that if we haven't won in twenty years then we're never going to. I say if the Brits haven't won in twenty years then they're never going to. They're losing, and I'd say they've started to know it. Hurt them, Jon Jo, so's they scream,' the young man said.

He was told that there was a heavy-calibre machine gun in a cache on Altmore, and that he would have use of another. There was an RPG7, never fired, and

377

eight warheads. There was 83-lb of Semtex, and more when it was wanted. There were automatic rifles, sniper rifles and handguns. There was what he needed, and there were men who would follow him. He should live rough and he could do that 'cause he was Jon Jo Donnelly and the mountain was his. Jon Jo told them of problems on the mainland, and neither of them wanted to know, said that was all in the past for him. He complained about the communications, the criticisms, but they slapped his back and said he'd done a fine job, not to worry himself about the recent slip-ups, they weren't going to be held against him. Sandwiches were fed him, and drink was given him. He was to set the mountain on fire, this was the now, and the year in England was over.

But he asked the question. The question had been in his mind all through the last night in Geneva, in his mind all through the flight via Zurich to Dublin.

'I'm taking it there's no touts on Altmore?'

'There was one . . .' the older man said.

'. . . and he was blown away,' the young man said. 'Altmore's clean.'

Jon Jo said, 'You'll hear them screaming, all the way down here, you'll see the fire, if there's no touts.'

He was doing the late shift, noon till eight.

He kissed his wife and he kissed their baby's forehead.

The car was in the drive. He had already taken the car out of the garage and gone down the avenue to the shop for her. He was always careful. Detective Sergeant Browne had checked underneath his car at the start of the day. He kept a doormat in his garage and a light on an extension lead. He laid the mat on the concrete and knelt on it and craned under the chassis. He had looked under the centre of the car and then under the hidden wheel spaces. He looked behind the wheels on the other side.

They kept themselves to themselves in the housing estate, Catholics among Protestants, only on nodding terms with their neighbours. It would have been known that he was a policeman. It was the life he had chosen, and she had chosen to share it with him. The door was already closed on her as he slipped the key into the ignition. She never watched him drive away. She had told him once, not recently, but soon after they were married, that she sometimes went to the bathroom after she had heard the car drive away and threw up into the lavatory.

He was careful about his routine.

Detective Sergeant Browne went to work.

Mrs Wilkins had responded to her husband's decision to sleep in the Emergency Operations room with regular bulletins to his PA on the immersion heater and the apparently unending quest for a plumber. Wilkins had put down the telephone on her, banged it down in ungovernable impatience. His PA was at the door. Why on earth had she put the call through? He was wanted in the EO room. He hurried down the corridor. God, how was he supposed to know where a reliable, and not extortionate, plumber could be found? . . . Archie handed him the secure fax message.

He gutted Hobbes' report. Through the open window, open because Archie smoked and Charles complained, came the steady drone of inner London's traffic. A policeman's life known to be at risk, targeted by the PIRA, an informer's cover more or less on the other end of the same see-saw at hazard. There was a delicate trailing plant on the window ledge, a gesture of homeliness installed by Bill. A risk and a hazard getting in the way of the whole damn business. Archie's eyes questioned him. Ernest Wilkins was the man who had promised the Prime Minister . . . He had never been in the field. He was Curzon Street Man. And he had been a Leconfield House man before the move down the street to the new premises. Collator rather than hunter.

'Could demolish the whole thing,' Archie said. 'Could put us down the plug hole.'

He felt age creeping up on him. He sent young people, men and women, into the field. He understood so little of what actually confronted them.

Archie said, 'Can't for the life of me see why they didn't keep their mouths shut, let things roll.'

Wilkins said, 'I don't think the Service could survive it, if it went wrong.'

Archie muttered, 'Any war throws up casualties, stands to reason. I suppose they've gone native and got too close to things. That's what usually happens.'

Wilkins sat at the table. He started, with his penknife, to sharpen pencils. He whittled away, assessing the worth of the life of a policeman.

Rennie exploded. 'You ask anyone who knows, not inside your pathetic little point-scoring division, any soldier that's done proper time here. He'll tell you the RUC should be the only ones handling informers.

We have the skills, we have the patience. We're not looking for a bloody victory parade. We may have to wait two years for an arrest, to put together the evidence that'll stand in court, but we can wait. We're not fast-fix heroes . . .'

Bren thought every detective on the floor must have heard him and that, no doubt about it, was his intention.

'. . . The sooner you are out of here then the better I am pleased. In Christ's name, what did you think you were doing, Cathy? You sit on a police target for fourteen hours – fourteen bloody hours. I, and the likes of me, I could have been knocking on his wife's front door. Fourteen hours you sat on the information that a police officer's life was in danger. What am I supposed to say? I don't know where I'll find the charity to forgive this of you . . . For starters, when we get to Dungannon, it'll be you that I line up to explain to DS Browne that for fourteen hours you pissed about with his life. See if he understands your point of view. See if he's any more charity than I can manage . . . It's our war, we know how to fight it, and we don't want clever bastards playing with our lives. You're dead in this province, Miss Parker . . .'

She looked him square in the face. 'We pay the bills . . .'

'Don't think you can pull the strings behind my back, young lady. And don't you go thinking that I cared when I heard you were gone missing, that you damn near got yourself killed. Don't think that I was fussed . . .'

Cathy touched his hand. 'Thanks.'

*   *   *

At the Dungannon barracks two constables had been detailed to provide Detective Sergeant Browne with immediate close-quarters protection. They were waiting for him. His superior, the Detective Inspector of Special Branch who had taken Rennie's call, had set in train the process of transferring DS Browne and his wife and child. Two detectives in plain clothes, women, armed, had slipped discreetly into the house, like friends calling for a coffee morning, to guard her and the baby and to help her with the packing of essentials.

Why wasn't DS Browne on the radio in his car, the Detective Inspector had asked of DC McDonald? Malfunctioning, in repair, been reported, should be in working order tomorrow.

The motorcycle had been stolen in the early hours of the morning in the Creggan estate of Derry, away to the west. It had not been seen on the motorway that linked Lisburn to Dungannon, but now it was at the wide roundabout at the end of the motorway, between Derrycreevy and Moygashel. Many motorists and lorry drivers saw the motorcycle on the Donnydeade side of the road, and saw the two men in their black leather gear and their crash helmets, bent over the engine parts. The messages came to them by portable radio. The first that the car had turned out of the avenue and onto the main road. The second that the car was turning onto the motorway. The third that the car had not used the alternative route from the motorway turn-off at Tamnamore, that it was coming the safe way, the fast way. They had the make and the colour of the car and the registration. A van driver, carrying building equipment, saw the two men finish their repairs and straddle the 500-cc motorcycle and gun the engine. The car came steadily into the round-about. The motorcycle powered forward, drew level with the policeman's car.

There was the dark line of the high ground ahead. They were east of Crossmaglen and west of Fork-hill. The girl had said that it was the one that she knew best. Himself, he would have gone far to the west, almost to the Atlantic seaboard, before crossing the border, but he couldn't fault the girl's choice. There were no patrols, no roadblocks. The border was only a bump and a lurch from the car. They crossed where the army had cut a ditch ten years before, where ten years less a couple of days ago the local people had filled the ditch in again. The lurch of the car told Jon Jo that he was home.

He saw a helicopter far away, a high speck. He saw the watchtowers of the Brit army on the hilltops. He saw the dark purple of the winter-scarred heather and the old gold of the bracken and the worn green of the fields. He settled back against the seat. He wound down the window and let the cold air rip into his face. The tension slipped from him. Jon Jo Donnelly was back among his own.

The car had gouged twin tyre tracks through the grass verge and down the bank. Bren stood beside the driver's window. The glass had gone with the gunfire. He stood and stared at the face of the man who had been shot. She had come and she had looked at the dead, cold face and she had gone back to her car that was parked behind Rennie's. Rennie's driver was out of his car and smoking hard.

The back of the head was smashed to hell and gone but the face was recognizable. A young man's face, and the moustache that all policemen in the province seemed to need. His tie was neatly knotted at his throat still and the shirt was soaked in blood. Bren stood a few feet away and Rennie was at his shoulder. He stood back because the Scenes of Crime men, white overalls, were already at work, and the photographer. Subdued voices all about. Necessary stuff about camera angles and spent bullets, one of them chipped and, oh aye, out of shape, embedded in the inside of the front passenger door.

They had come off the motorway, following hard on Rennie's car, swept the roundabout, past the football pitches, been short of the rugby club, when they had seen the rotating blue lights on the cars and on the police Land-rovers. A policeman saluting, leaning down, explaining to Rennie, and Rennie had been out of his car and walking briskly back to them. They might be interested, they might care to follow him. Cathy had walked down the bank behind Rennie and had withstood his terrible silence, not rejecting his fury, not denying the blame he was determined to wound her with. She had absorbed it and she had gone back up the slope to the car. Bren knew nothing worthwhile to say. There seemed to be no anger around him. Too soon for that. Too much to get on with. It wasn't them, this time it was another poor bastard. He thought they had seen it all before, and would do it all and see it all again. He stayed until the men in black suits brought the plain wood coffin awkwardly down the steep bank. He turned away. He didn't want to see the body manhandled out of the car.

He stood at the top of the bank and he gulped for air.

Cathy had her arms folded across her chest, watched him.

'I'm sorry,' Bren said.

Rennie's voice was utterly flat. 'That's very good. I'm very gratified that you're sorry. I'd be sorry if I'd sat on something for fourteen hours and not thought through the consequences. We could drive back to Lisburn and you could say the same thing to a young woman, that you're sorry, and you could help her change her baby, and you could tell her that for four-teen hours you slept on a little bit of information that had happened your way. Would you like to do that?'

He wondered if Rennie were about to hit him, if the big fist were about to belt him. The men in the black suits came past him, mud on their polished black shoes. Bren shook his head. 'I don't think I've the strength . . .'

'To face up to the consequences? No, not many do. They leave that to other people.' And without a glance at Cathy, he went to his car, slammed the door, and was gone.

Cathy said softly, 'You have to hack it, Bren. There's no other way.' He saw the defiance on her face.

He saw no love in her, only her strength. He loved her and he felt his fear of her.

He was always tuned to the BBC's Radio Ulster when he worked. The BBC didn't have the good music but it had the news on the hour. The news carried the condemnations:

The Secretary of State – 'a bestial and pointless crime . . .'; the MP – '. . . this dreadful murder of a young man who had the courage to stand up and be counted . . .'; a bishop – '. . . every decent-minded person will be revolted by this killing, this disgusting sectarian killing . . .'; and the Chief Constable – '. . . the force I have the honour to command will not for one instant be intimidated from its duty by the men of violence who prey on our society . . .'

Mossie heard them all. His hand shook and the brush strokes wavered. The bitch had let a policeman be blown away to keep him in place. No doubt on it. She had had all of a night and a morning to clear the policeman off the patch, and the policeman was dead. There was the trembling in his hand and he told the foreman that he was sickening with the 'flu, and that he was packing it in for the day.

The kids not yet returned from school. His mother was out, thank the Christ. Mary was asleep in her cot.

He told Siobhan of his power and saw the shock spread across her face.

'They'd do that for you . . . ?'

'For me to get them Jon Jo.'

'Does it frighten you?'

'Half out of my skin.'

Jon Jo Donnelly had been the big man on the mountain. He had been the man the kids whispered of and the man the girls eyed. He had been the man that the soldiers hunted. When Jon Jo had been on the mountain then no policeman and no soldier had felt himself safe. Mossie knew all the tales. Donnelly with the heavy-calibre, and with the culvert bomb, and with the long-barrel sniping rifle. There had been a big man in South Derry, and another down in Fermanagh, and another from Cullyhanna near the border in Armagh, all shot down, and there had been Jon Jo Donnelly. It was the stuff of stories.

'How much'll they give you?'

'Don't know.'

'It'd be thousands?'

'Sure to be.'

As if the walls had ears, they sat against each other on the settee, they whispered to each other. The guilt bled him further with each of her questions, and she held his arm in both her hands.

'If he's so important to them . . .'

'He's all they talk about.'

'To make it worth losing one of their own, has to be thousands.'

'Be decent money.'

'When does we get out of this feckin' place?'

'There's never a way out for a tout . . .'

He told her what the life was. He knew what had happened to others. It always started fast. The flash of the bleeper. The interception of a hit car. Troops and police round the house, and sweet precious nothing of time to pack and get the kids together or drag them out from class, and the stampede out of the area. Eventually to England, chased through the military section of Aldergrove and onto an RAF transporter. A pair of semi-detached houses in some nowhere town in England. The minders sleeping next door, and spending their waking hours, their duty shifts, always with the family, always answering the telephone when it rang, always reading any mail, always with their guns. Go shopping and the minders drive. Go drinking and the minders buy. God knows how the children got schooled. Can't work because the minders don't allow it. Can't row because the minders'll break it up. Living on top of each other, suffocated. They all wanted to come back, he told her. They all ended the same way, scribbling letters to the priest pleading to be allowed back. And, sooner or later, they all came back, and they all ended in the ditch with the dustbin bag over the head . . .

'So what's the money for?'

'It's so's she can own me better.'

It had been his decision, and she had gone with it, that the car should be minimum four miles further back from when they had last been to the hide. The car was off the road in forestry halfway to Pomeroy. It had taken them two hours and twenty minutes to reach the hide, fast going in rough country, in darkness.

She talked softly in his ear, but she rambled, not the Cathy of before. '. . . if it hadn't been Browne it would have been someone else. They have the targets all drawn up. If we'd blocked Browne there'd only have been another target. They're never short of targets . . . They're so bloody clever. He'd have looked for the bomb under the car, and he'd have looked for a strange vehicle in his road, and he'd have stayed off using the back lanes. He'd have done everything right . . .'

He didn't want to hear. He could see all too clearly the white face of the dead policeman. He wanted her quiet.

'. . . So bloody good at the unexpected. They hit him where he just couldn't anticipate, and there's no defence for one man driving a car against two men on a motorcycle. That's where we lose, can't you see it? We're the procedure people. We have the duty rosters and the computers and we have the set-out way of doing things. They don't. The Provos don't have a software system, they don't have banks of library folders, they make it up as they go along. We've never found anything approaching an archive system, yet there are people out there who know as much about how Colonel Johnny's battalion operates as he does himself. They don't have Operations Rooms and telexes and faxes, they hardly ever use the telephone. They don't have manuals. It's stone-age stuff, and they're running us ragged.'

'Let it go, Cathy.'

The cattle were on the move in the field below the hedgerow where they were dug in. He thought she was talking because the strength was cracking.

'You have to understand that, because then you know the way to fight them. Company formations, battalion units, brigade groups, all with the back-up, the civilian clerical workers and the Personnel section and the electronics, that's not the way. That's the structure that ties down half your force guarding installations, putting up fences and watchtowers and cutting yourself off from the war. God knows what the percentage is of people over here who are just *indexing* the war. You can't index war and keep up with it, any more than you can index fog. I don't suppose Clausewitz said that but if he'd been in Northern bloody Ireland, he'd have said it alright.'

389

'Cathy, will you shut up.'

'We have to learn, and learn sharp. We have to fight body to body, at close quarters . . .'

'I want you to shut up so that I can concentrate.'

He felt her stiffen away from him, but there was nowhere for her to go. They lay together in the hide. The cattle were drifting in convoy up the field towards their camera's position. They were dark shapes, ships in the night, in the grey haze wash of the screen. He zoomed the lens back so that he could see the advancing cattle. He panned off the cattle. He searched the hedgerows down near the farm house. He focused as tight as possible on the outbuildings. He wondered how she would be, if the legend was taken from her. He wondered if she would last an hour, a day, a week, if her strength cracked. The cattle were coming forward. He raked the hedgerows and the outbuildings again. He looked for the shadow figure on the move. A light rain was falling. The hood of his anorak was up, but the water had started to dribble on his face. It was what he was paid to do, it was his bloody job of work. The picture was lost, then found again. There was the faint squelching of the hooves across the field, there was the bulk shape of a bullock on the screen. There were the big eyes, and then the snort of the nostrils. He saw the tongue stretch to envelop the picture image. He stared at the screen, at the misted blur.

'Shit . . .'

The picture was gone again. He could break cover, he could get into the field and chase the animals away from the camera . . .

'That is the goddam limit . . .'

In a stinking hide, in the pissing rain, wanting to use the plastic bottle and urinate, out in God's own death country, and the bloody tongue of a bloody bullock had licked the Night Observations Device lens, smeared it . . .

'That is beyond belief . . .'

Her lip brushed his cheek. 'Try not to be pompous, Bren, it doesn't suit you.'

She snuggled back against him.

'It's the hum that attracts them. Nothing you can do about it. Sheep are worse. Cattle'll move on, sheep'll stand round your camera all day. Ask any of the farmers on Altmore to find a hide, and they'll put sheep in the field, three hours and they'll know where it is. Cattle get bored.'

He turned his body. They were entangled. He smelled the clean and natural breath of her. No toothpaste, no garlic, no tobacco, because they were in the hide.

'What'll happen to us, Cathy?'

'That's not for now.'

'What's our future?'

'That's for after Donnelly. Until then there isn't a future.'

She wriggled out of the hide. He heard the faint sounds as she moved away up the hedgerow. They wouldn't understand, the Curzon Street crowd, not even Mr Wilkins, none of them would understand what it was to lie up in a hide and watch for a man to come home to his wife, and to know the man was for killing or capturing. That was Cathy's world, and she didn't bloody share.

Away to his right there was the lowing of a bullock.

The cattle moved on, in search of the sound. And then the image was clear again. Clearer than before. Cathy Parker, Night Observations Device lens polisher to Her Majesty. When she came back, she pushed herself down into the hide. There was the sweet warmth of her against him.

Bren whispered, 'What do you want? Do you want him dead, or do you want him alive?'

No answer.

No reply.

He stared at the darkened farmhouse and the black outline of the farm buildings.

It was as he had left it. There was the gap in the wire that he remembered, tied up with twine. There was the hole in the hedge where the old dumped tractor wheel had broken the thorn down. There was the bog mud behind the barn. He circled the farm twice.

Home.

He came to the buildings very slowly, bent double. He had come down from the mountain where he had made his sleeping place. Crawling the length of the hedge behind the field that backed onto the buildings. He was soaked to the skin. There was a dull light in the hall, where it had always been at night. Crawling again by the barn and the low stone wall that protected the patch where Attracta grew her vegetables he could stay beyond the range of the light. He passed the frame of the swing that he had concreted into the back yard for Kevin. He came without sound.

Suddenly, from the kennel, the raucous and angry barking. Jon Jo whistled low. The barking died. The

dog came to him. He knelt in the pitch darkness and
he rubbed his hand on his dog's throat, and the dog
lay on his back and thrashed his tail.

The key to the kitchen door was in the kennel,
where it had always been.

'The dog barked,' Cathy said. 'Jon Jo's dog.'
  'You meant it?'
  'What did I mean?'
  'That it has to be body to body, at close quarters?'
She mocked him. 'You going to be around?'

Chapter Eighteen

She had not slept well since the first house search, and hardly at all since they had come the last time with the helicopter. The dog had barked and that had pulled her from what sleep she had found. It was past two o'clock on the luminous clock radio at her bedside.

Attracta knew every one of the house's sounds. She knew where the bats nested in the roof, where the mice ran in the walls, and which floorboards creaked under pressure, worse since the soldiers had ripped them up.

She heard the scrape of the key in the kitchen door.

She stiffened upright in her bed. There was the murmur of a voice that carried softly up the stairs. She kept a short length of gnarled blackthorn under the bed and her hand reached down to it. There was the scratching noise of the dog's paw nails on the kitchen linoleum. She swung her legs off the bed and she eased her weight onto her feet and she stood beside the bed holding tightly to the weapon. Again the murmur, like a command, and then the steady approaching sounds on the stairs. The sleep had drained from her. She was alone in the house, with the small boy, just with the blackthorn stick. If she screamed then only Mossie Nugent might hear her, and his bungalow was a hundred yards away. She faced across the room and watched the slash of dull light from the landing that came through the opened door . . .

The dog came first. The dog bounded at her in pleasure. The shadow figure came after the dog.

'It's me, love.'

The voice she knew, she loved. The voice that was in her dreams, the voice that was in her mind when she was driving to the school, going to the shop, going to the barn to get fodder for the cattle. The fear spilled from her. The blackthorn clattered onto the floor. The dog jumped in excitement at her then turned back to the figure in the doorway. She felt only a great weakness overwhelm her.

He held her in his arms. She shivered away from him as the wet mud of his clothes pressed against her nightdress but he pulled her back and against him. His face was rough, for days unshaven. The dog was leaning against her legs. Only at the first moment did she hold back, then she crushed herself against him, against the slithering mud of his clothes. The anguish ebbed from her. She kissed his mouth, she felt the drive of his tongue between her lips and teeth.

She held his head in her hands. She looked up into the shadow of her man's face.

'How much time have you got?'

'Till when?'

'Before you have to go?'

'I've come home . . .'

'How long?'

'I've come back home. It's to stay.'

She held the cheeks of his face and his hands were on her hips and their bodies were apart. The wet and the cold of the mud had seeped to her skin. Her head shook. Surely he knew? He was as she remembered him. Perhaps thinner, perhaps with less weight in his arms. It was all so obvious to her.

'You can't stay, Jon Jo. They's searched the house three times in two months. They'll be listening to the phone. The post takes an age, I think they open the letters. They watch for you.'

'I'll lie up.'

'It's not safe for you here.'

'I'll lie up on the mountain.'

She fell away from him. She could feel the love and the warmth of him, and the yearning. She sat on the bed. She huddled her arms around the chill of her shoulders. There had been soldiers in this very bedroom, their sneering and hostile faces. Three times her house raped. And in little Kevin's room, great bastard brutes in their protective armour, with their guns and their sledgehammers and crowbars.

'You can't come back . . .'

She felt him flinch.

'. . . It's just daft to think you can. They'll know you're here in a day, everyone'll know. You think there's secrets here? Jon Jo, no, no. There's no way you can come back . . .' She felt his hands come to rest on her arms. '. . . I couldn't take it, Jon Jo, to know that you're back.'

'It's you I came back to, love.'

She tried so hard not to cry. She heard the whisper of her words.

'I could take it when you was away, because I didn't know where you were, not each hour, each day. I knew what you'd done. I knew what you did because the soldiers came. It was awful, but I could take it . . . If you were out on Altmore, then I'd worry each living minute . . . They'd not have shot you dead on the mainland, here they'd shoot you. I couldn't take that, Jon Jo. Don't you see . . . ?'

He said, 'It's all I dreamed of, coming home to you and Kevin . . .'

'You were better gone, that's God's truth, you were better away. You want to know, I'll tell you . . . The Devitt boy was shot by the soldiers, two others with him, he's buried not two weeks. He was touted. The Riordan boy was taken in, young Patsy, and he was killed for touting. That was idiot. Patsy Riordan was simple, he knew nothing . . . You hear what I'm saying, Jon Jo. There's a tout on the mountain. That's why you're better away . . .'

'They told me Altmore was clean.'

'What do they know, that would kill Patsy Riordan? I went to the Devitt boy's wake, Jon Jo. They shot him down, but they had finished him with a bullet in the head. I saw the wound, everyone did. They wanted us to see the wound . . . It'll be the same for you, Jon Jo, the army'll shoot you like a dog and they'll finish you with a bullet in your head, and it'll be a tout's word that kills you. That's God's truth . . .'

'If there's a tout I'll find him.'

She said, 'You're best gone.' She hated herself.

'I thought you'd want me back.'

She had thought it through so many times, Jon Jo's homecoming. Him back at the farm and her loving

397

him. Her man at his home again and their loving and their laughter. She had never thought that she would tell him that he was best out of the house, far far away. He seemed to reel from her. She didn't know how she could have said it more kindly.

He was gone out of her bedroom and not looking back at her. The dog was at her feet and eyed her, his tail was bent between his legs, uncertain.

Jon Jo held the boy in his arms. The boy babbled in fear, as if still in the grip of a nightmare.

'You shouldn't be here, Da . . . if the journeymen tailors see you, Da . . . they'll tell the dragoons . . . they'll ride on the mountain after you, Da . . . all your bullets'll be spent . . . the dragoons'll hunt you and ride you down . . .'

'Where did he get this shit?' he snarled at her.

All the misery welling in her, all the pain. She thought the boy was waking, that his dream would finish.

'It's a story . . .'

'It's just shit.'

She cried out, 'I was trying to tell our son that a man could die for what he believed in. You weren't here to tell him. I was here, I was with him, I was waiting for the priest to call. I was trying to tell him, in my way, the future of his father.'

He passed the boy to her. She saw only the great sadness in Jon Jo's eyes. Little Kevin clung to her.

She said, flat, 'Whoever it is, they'll take money for naming you, Jon Jo, as they always did on Altmore . . .'

He was gone through the door.

She was left in the silence of the night with the fright

of the child waking in her arms and the cowering dog at her feet.

'Did you see something?'

'I can't be sure . . .'

'Either you saw something or you didn't.'

'I don't know.'

'Where did you think you might have seen something?'

'At the side of the barn, I thought something moved.'

'But not sure?'

'If there was anything, it certainly isn't moving now. It probably died of exposure.'

He panned the camera back and forth across the grey mist of the fields and inched the image along the dark outline of the hedgerows. He saw nothing move. With the naked eye Bren could see the light burning in the farmhouse, and further away another light in the bungalow. He wondered if Mossie Nugent slept. His teeth started to chatter.

'You're right,' Cathy said. 'God, it's so cold.'

He could take her in his arms, he could warm her. But he stared into the screen, slowly traversed down the field, and back, slowly, on the path between the bungalow and the farmhouse, and back. He saw nothing.

The cardboard city man folded the map. Herbie stubbed out his cigarette. Jocko slipped the earpiece from his head, coiled it and put it back with the radio in the glove compartment. They were two miles from the farmhouse, by the most direct route. A foul place to be holed up for a long night on Altmore. The call had not come. The night watch was over. Herbie drove the car away.

Ernest Wilkins woke to the clamour of the alarm. He had been thirty years away, reliving the spat between Five and Six over the surveillance operation on Peter Kroger's place . . . damn good operation, the more so because Six had wanted in and had been seen off. None of their business . . . It was eighteen minutes past six.

Archie sat at the table smoking a Sobranie in a holder, his overcoat across his shoulders with a scarf round his neck. The electric fire was on, both bars burning.

'No calls?'

'Nothing.'

'Well, it's early days.'

'If you say so.'

It was his first waking thought, nobody at Curzon Street cared but himself. He could not at first find the slippers he had stowed under the bed. He reached inside his overnight bag for his washing kit.

'Don't you understand, Archie?'

'I understand, Mr Wilkins, what is happening in Northern Ireland. I have yet to grasp, I confess, why in the very heart of central London we have to camp like Boy Scouts . . .'

Wilkins put on his dressing gown, and said, patiently, 'Parker and Brennard will track their player to his meeting with Donnelly. This Donnelly is a psychopath who will kill without hesitation if he thinks he's at risk. Parker and Brennard will get close

400

enough to identify him. Where they will find him, I can't and they can't know. They may be able to call on the reserve and they may not. If not . . .'

'Christ, you haven't actually told Parker to . . . ?'

Wilkins paused in the doorway. 'Parker will do what is necessary.'

'That's not our game, Mr Wilkins, that's the Gun Club's job.'

'If it goes wrong, then it'll be damage limitation in a hurry.'

Archie said, 'If it goes wrong then Parker and her toy boy will be in rather poor shape.'

'Well done, Archie, you finally grasped it.'

He went off down the corridor to the washroom, to shave and wash his socks. Oh yes, if it went wrong Parker and Brennard would be in rather poor shape. And yes, there would be huge potential damage to be limited. They would be coming off the mountain just about now. If they could spot the man at his house and whistle up the military, so much the better. If they had to use Song Bird to take them forward all the way to Donnelly, so much the worse.

He had complained yesterday to House Services about the lack of hot water. It was lukewarm again. He shaved carefully. They ought to be safely back in Dungannon by now.

She swung hard into the gateway of the Mahon Road barracks. Bren had his ID card up for the sentry to see, but Cathy just waved and the soldier smiled his greeting and the barrier was lifted. He followed her to the Five building, up the stairs.

The room was alive already, men and women at the

401

computers and the radio operators craned towards their dials. The man, Jimmy, was coming across the area with a tray of coffee mugs and he grinned at Cathy and offered his cheek for a fierce, short kiss. Bren saw it, her belonging. Jimmy carried the coffee on towards the corner, and Bren saw that the back-up had beaten them home, Jocko and Herbie in their sleeping bags on the floor. The cardboard city man, as usual, was tilted in his chair with his huge stockinged feet on the table. He watched the wild cheerfulness of their greeting for Cathy. The cardboard city man was up on his feet, crashing away the chair, hugging her as if she was back from the other side of God knows where. Herbie was crawling out of his bag, sagging boxer shorts and white legs and gripping her hand. Jocko was pushing himself to his feet, his bag still hanging to his waist, and Cathy giggling and un- zipping him. Everyone was laughing. Bren stood back. She was amongst her own. He had been some- thing to her when she was frightened half to death. Now she had no need of him. Bren said that he would get the coffee and she didn't seem to hear him. He went out into the corridor, to the cupboard at the top of the stairs where the fridge and the kettle were. More laughter from behind the swing doors. Jimmy stood beside him.

'You'll be wanting the tray, herself and you and me and a couple more on the radios. Did you have a good night?'

'Who are they, for God's sake? We saw bugger all.'

'Your back-up? Didn't they tell you? No, they're not the best with the social graces.'

Bren said evenly, 'I don't seem to get told much . . .'

'It'll come, don't push it . . . The tramp is Sir David Wainwright, Baronet, Grenadier Guards, had the Military Cross for some do on the road to Nasirayah in the Gulf, rich as Croesus, soldiering's just a hobby . . . Herbie's on his sixth tour here, five kids at home, they're all Northern Ireland babies, there'll be another when he's posted back, super gardener, takes all the prizes round here with his onions. Jocko's the Military Medal from Oman on his first tour abroad. He's a great talent with his water colours, only drawback is that they're all of the Brecons. I've a couple at home.'

The kettle was boiling.

'And who are you?'

Bren said, 'Oh, I'm nothing. I just trail around after Miss Parker.'

'It's meant kindly.'

Bren spooned the coffee into the mugs. 'And who's she?'

'I doubt any of us know that . . .'

He poured the boiling water.

'. . . and I doubt any of us'll give up trying to find out . . .'

He picked up the tray.

'. . . You're a lucky man to work with her.'

Bren carried the tray back into the work area. The cardboard city man was hunched forward in his chair. Herbie still wore just his boxer shorts and Jocko was back in his sleeping bag, on his knees, and they looked at the map spread out on the low table. Cathy was between them, sitting cross-legged, and Jocko had his arm on her shoulder. The map had red pencil squares, and each square a letter on it. He passed her a mug of coffee.

403

She was talking and the smile beamed on her. '. . . he'll have the bleep on him and that'll come through to here. Jimmy'll look after that, but that's only in case we've lost him. We hope to be closer in than you. If all goes well we'll have Song Bird and Donnelly in sight . . . Thanks, Bren . . . If it's possible we'll whistle you in. If not . . .'

She didn't have to finish it. Bren stood cupping his coffee in both hands. If it was not possible to whistle up the firepower then it would be down to the two of them. He could see it on all of their faces. They didn't rate him.

'Shouldn't be a problem,' Bren said.

Cathy said she was going for a shower, and he was asleep in a borrowed sleeping bag before their three-hand card game had begun.

It was the way he had worked from the beginning.

He alone knew where it was. The cache had been well made. The inside of the dustbin was bone dry. Stowed in the dustbin were plastic farm bags, tied at the neck. Inside the bags were a Kalashnikov rifle, heavily greased, cartons of ammunition and magazines, two hand-guns, a drogue grenade, a black balaclava, camouflage denims, a pair of boots which he had oiled before they went into the sack and which were soft to the touch now, and a thermal sleeping bag. They were all dry, all as he had left them in the dustbin that he had sealed with masking tape. Jon Jo changed swiftly into the camouflage denims and pulled on his old, familiar boots, and then taking what he needed, repacking the rest, he resealed the bin and rebuilt the cover over the pit. Working fast, summoning up the urgency, because that was the way to suppress the wrenching disappointment of his homecoming.

First, he told himself, identify the tout. Second, he told himself, kill the bastard, kill the killer of old Mrs Riordan's boy, of Vinny Devitt. He would take pleasure in killing the tout. And then, then they would sit up off their arses in Dublin. The sky above Altmore would be, by Christ, on fire.

Old Hegarty, sitting motionless in the gorse with his dog, saw Donnelly fill in the pit, replace the stones over the dustbin, saw the rifle in his hand, saw him slip for cover.

He'd had his breakfast, he had sat on the toilet, he had been given his lunch box. His mother was still in her bedroom, and the children were all over her and squabbling. Siobhan opened the bedroom door. He was on his knees, half into the wardrobe. Must have been the sounds of the children, fighting, that were magnified through the suddenly opened door. She saw the bald patch on the crown of his head, his white paint-stained overalls, then the fright on his face as he swung round.

'What's you doing, Mossie?'

He held it up, the bleeper box, for explanation.

'But you don't take it.'

She saw him tremble as his teeth bit at his lower lip.

'You reckon he's back?'

She watched him force down, fumbling, the wardrobe floor.

'You'll lead them to him?'

405

He had the buttons of his overalls unfastened, and he was working at his belt and his zipper, and he had the elastoplast beside him.

'. . . God, if he knew . . .'

He strapped the bleeper box high under his crutch.

'He'd kill you. He'd kill the both of us, if he knew.'

She followed him out of the bedroom, and down the hall. She watched him go to the car with the lunch box in his hand. It was for money they could not spend. He had not said goodbye to his children. He had said not a word to her. He drove away without a sign.

She was in the bathroom and washing the baby. The OC told her he was going out. She never asked why and she never asked where he was going to. He told her that he didn't know when he'd be back. He might have told her, but he didn't, that he had business with a man in Coalisland. He closed the door behind him and locked it with the mortise. He'd had the new locks put on all the doors since the summer, since the Protestants had been to the village bar with their guns, and he now kept his car always in the garage, and there was a new lock on the garage door. They weren't much, the precautions he by himself could take against the Protestant gunmen. One precaution was already taken, the message passed by a Nationalist councillor to a Protestant councillor, giving the cast-iron guarantee to the UVF that every last one of them in their command structure would be singled out, shot down, their homes burned over the heads of their slags and their brats if one hair on the head of any of the Brigade officers of East Tyrone was harmed.

And his own private treaty was that for as long as

he commanded East Tyrone, no UVF officer of a comparable rank would be a target.

He unlocked the swing-back door of the garage, heaved it over. He switched on the light.

'Get it off.'

He froze.

'Shut it off.'

He saw Jon Jo Donnelly in the camouflage gear and a woollen cap rolled up onto his forehead. It was an order, and he obeyed it. He snapped the light off.

'Pull the door down.'

The door screeched on the runners as he dragged it down.

The OC stood his ground. There was the flash of a match in the darkness and the glow of a cigarette and the smell of the tobacco.

He said it nervously, 'Great to have you back, Jon Jo.'

'Good to be back.'

'You going well, Jon Jo?'

'I'm going alright.'

'Anything you be needing . . . ?'

'I heard there was a tout on Altmore.' The voice was ice-cold and the cigarette burned and wavered in front of the OC.

'I did what I was supposed, I brought the security in, I handed it to them.'

'Didn't hear me criticize you, did you? Just saying that I was told there was a tout on Altmore.'

'The security pulled the Riordan boy in, they did him.'

'What did he confess to?'

'Don't know.'

'You didn't see what he confessed to?'

'I wasn't shown anything, nor heard a tape.'

'Did you think it was the Riordan boy?'

'I don't know.'

He saw the cigarette flake to the floor. He heard the scrape of the boot on the concrete floor of the garage.

'When you pulled the security in, did you tell them you thought Patsy Riordan was a tout?'

The drip of the voice. No emotion, no surprise, no regret. He had only once been on an operation with the man, and he hadn't known he would be there until the last minute, and he'd been on the 50-calibre, feckin' incredible, not a bloody soldier bastard daring to show his face over the wall on the Altaglushan Bridge.

'I didn't . . . it was after the Devitt boy was shot by the SAS, and Jacko from Pomeroy and Malachy from Coalisland. Only Mossie Nugent got clear . . . It had to be a tout.'

'When you called the security in, who did you think was the tout?'

'It was Patsy was done.'

'What did you think?'

He blurted, 'I thought it was Mossie.'

'Who named Patsy to the security?'

The OC said, quiet, 'Mossie did . . . but I'm telling you that, Mossie's no tout. We did a policeman yesterday, a branch man. I told Mossie the evening before and we did him the next morning, late. He hadn't been warned. Couldn't have been Mossie . . . but when the Devitt boy and Jacko and Malachy were shot I didn't see how's Mossie could have run clear from the guns, him with a bad leg . . .'

408

He heard the voice in the darkness ahead of him. 'Important man, a tout on Altmore. They'd play big stakes for an important man.'

'What'll you be wanting of me?'

'That you hold your tongue.'

There was the light tread of the boots. There was the swing of the back door of the garage. He waited until there were no more sounds, only the wind on the garage roof. He saw that the back door had been jemmied open. He had been in the house and he had heard nothing.

It had been taken from him, the command of the East Tyrone Brigade. Mossie had told him that he would still be OC after Jon Jo returned, but the command had been lifted from him. There had never been any arguing with Jon Jo Donnelly. He pushed the broken door closed.

While they did a check-list Jimmy fussed around them, and the cardboard city man and Jocko and Herbie were kitting up. Thermal underwear, light-weight boots, camouflage denims, balaclavas, mittens. They had swilled out their mouths and there would be no more cigarettes, and there had been no soap used. Their faces were smeared in the camouflage cream that broke the outlines and blunted the skin colour.

Bren felt the pressure growing on him. Plastic bottle and the silver tinfoil and cling-wrapped sandwiches.

The short-barrelled rapid-fire Heckler and Koch rifles, with the long-range sights and image intensifiers; the heavyweight Browning 9-mms and shoulder holsters; the radio that would fit into the rucksack; the cellular telephone; the ammunition magazines, four loaded for each of the rifles, and three loaded for each of the Brownings; binoculars; medical kits which she had not allocated to them before. He thought of his mother and father, feet in front of a winter fire, television on and her knitting and him reading the evening paper, and their not knowing what their son did, and how they would cope with a visit from Mr Wilkins if it didn't work out. His jeans were dank from the previous night's soaking and mud bath, not yet fully dried out even after a day's break on the radiators, his shirt was grimed, his sweater smelt.

Bren looked up. Across the far side of the area was the bank of television sets. Second from the right, third rack from the bottom, the view of a farmhouse and a bungalow. The back-up was ready to leave.

The man, Jimmy, said, 'Good luck, all, don't worry on it and just know that we're here through the night. And if it's tonight then give the bad boy one from us . . .'

The Quartermaster swore, told his woman he'd drink taken, couldn't drive. His woman told him it had never made a fig of difference before, that he was to go and collect the girl from her friend's, that any decent father would think more of picking up his daughter on such a night than filling his gut with drink.

He lived on the edge of the village. His garage was filled with the new linoleum he was to lay in his kitchen and the new units. His car was out in the road because he hadn't bothered himself when he had come home to get out and open the gates and bring it

410

onto the driveway. It was dark out on the road because the soldiers saw to it that the street lights were kept off, and bloody dangerous it made the road for women and kids and the elderly . . . A faint light only, from the gap in the curtains of the front room.

The figure came fast from the shadow of the hedge opposite. He saw the bulk of the man's body and the dark of his face and of his clothes. He thought he was about to wet himself. If he hadn't been petrified still, mind swirling on the Protestants, then he'd have turned to run.

He heard the light chuckle, like the man in the darkness knew he was scared half to death.

'Heh, it's me, it's Jon Jo.'

'Shit, you . . .'

'It's Jon Jo, and I'm back.'

The Quartermaster wiped the sweat off his forehead, felt the rubbery weakness in his legs. 'Jesus, you give me a turn . . . Jon Jo, feckin' great to have you back, big man.'

'Good of you to say that.'

'How's you, how's Jon Jo?'

The Quartermaster knew that Jon Jo Donnelly was thirteen years younger than himself. He could remember his own slow advancement through the Organization, and he could remember the shooting star that had been young Jon Jo before he had gone away. Right from the day of his recruitment going his own way. Calling for a weapon to be brought to him, or for explosives, never discussing and never justifying, his own man. The Quartermaster wouldn't have dared say so, but the way Jon Jo Donnelly treated those around him was like dirt. He had been told once

411

that Jon Jo had gone to shoot a UDR man the far side of 'gannon, and he'd found on his way to the hit a policeman, off duty, walking his child on the roadside, and he'd shot him instead, and finished him between the eyes with the kiddie half over him. A feckin' hard man, and the world a safer place with him on the mainland.

'I heard there was a tout on Altmore.'

The Quartermaster gulped. 'I know nothing . . . but they took the Riordan boy.'

'Did you reckon Patsy Riordan could have touted?'

'Honest?'

'I'm asking what you thought.'

'I thought the boy was an idiot,' the Quartermaster blurted. The rain spat on the shoulders of his jacket and the legs of his trousers. It was quiet around them. He could hear the television from next door. He thought that if Jon Jo Donnelly were back then the killings would go harder, and the army would sit heavier, and that the Brigade officers would be dragged from their houses more often for the cells at Gough Holding Centre. He hated the cells, and the detectives, and the snipe of the questions and the curl of the cigarette smoke, and the hammer of the doors locking and closing, and the high bars on the windows.

'You keep your silence.'

'You don't have to worry about me, Jon Jo.'

'I wouldn't ever worry about you . . .'

And he was gone. The Quartermaster's knees shook. He reversed his car and thumped the kerb opposite and the rain pelted into the windscreen and

412

twice he cut the verge as he drove to get his daughter from her friend's.

Hegarty crossed the bar to him. The dog followed the old bastard to where Mossie sat alone. Mossie thought it a crying shame that the dog's coat wasn't brushed to rid it of the burrs and the knots. Hegarty leaned across the table, stale tobacco breath in Mossie's face.

'He's back, Mossie, I's seen him,' he whispered.

'Who's back?'

'Jon Jo's back.'

'That's not safe talk.'

'I's seen him on the mountain. I's seen him where he left his guns before he went away.'

'That talk's not good for you.'

'I's not afraid. Just telling you that he's back,' and he shuffled himself back to the bar and his drink.

The light flashed. Bren wriggled to pull the headset over his ears. He had the pencil light and his biro and the pad of paper. It was Jimmy. Song Bird had telephoned that Jon Jo Donnelly was back, living rough on Altmore. Cathy was half across his body, reading the message.

'About bloody time,' she murmured.

Bren thought of how, one after the other, Hobbes would hear, Rennie would hear, and Wilkins would hear and he might even clap his hands and say that it was all going according to plan. And there, in that sodden, freezing hide, on the edge of the great God Almighty plan, Bren thought, what he minded most about was the sweet weight of her against his right

413

side. Digging into the left side of him, where they could be reached, were the rifles, on safety. The back-up thought he would just be the bloody gun-bearer for her. He didn't know whether they were right.

'When this is over . . .'

'Oh, for Christ's sake.'

'You are coming out of here . . .'

'Not again.'

'Even if I have to take you kicking and screaming . . .'

'Do piss off.'

'I am going to put you where you are safe and where there is a normal life to be lived. I am going to do that before it is too late for you. I love you . . .'

'Watch the bloody screen,' she said.

He stared at the farmhouse on the screen, at the light from an upper window on the back yard. He saw nothing move. He wondered if she would think the more of him if he shot Jon Jo Donnelly.

Chapter Nineteen

He lay on his back.

There was the glow and the wetness of her body against his.

Jon Jo Donnelly and his Attracta after the collapse of love-making. It was what he had cried for during the months away. She nestled against him. He was back and he was home.

It should have been beautiful.

She hadn't talked to him of danger, she hadn't demanded of him when he was leaving. He had the new route into the farmhouse, in the shadow of the lean-to where the logs were stacked, and through the larder window that she had left unlocked, squeezing inside. If the house were watched then he would not be seen because he did not have to use the back door and the front door that were obvious. She hadn't questioned him about England, not about a schoolboy and not about two schoolgirls.

It should have been wonderful.

There had never been a tout on the mountain. There had been touts in Belfast and in Derry and in Newry and in Lurgan. There had never been a tout identified on Altmore . . . When he had been home, before he had gone away to England, there had twice been a suspension of operations because of tout fear. After the search up beyond old Hegarty's home, a mile beyond him, where the cache had been found with the RPG7 and the two rifles and nothing other than information could have taken the soldiers to that corner of a field. After the controlled explosion of a culvert bomb on the Ballygawley road, in place three days, and no military activity prior to the helicopter coming over, repeated sweeps, with the electronics, there had been the second tout hunt. It was four years back and it was two years back, and each time the outsiders had been called onto the mountain to sift for evidence. Nothing decided, nothing proved, but the unit had been stood down each time for a month, and the outsiders had moved among the volunteers with their sharp questions . . . Who knew of what operation? Who had been told? Who knew the locations of the caches and the identity of targets . . . He had been questioned himself by a bald bastard with a squint and a Derry accent. There had never been a tout found on the mountain. He knew the way of touts. There would be no scramble to clear a unit from an area, not the way the handlers directed their player. They chipped at an Active Service Unit, a man here and a man there, lifted, a weapon here and a made-up bomb there, recovered . . . He knew about the money and he knew about the threats. He knew that men were trapped with money and bludgeoned with threats. He knew how the handlers gained their players . . . There was no mercy for touts. There was no sentiment. Touts were for killing.

He lay on his back and she was cuddled close to him and sleeping, and the poison of a tout on the mountain filled his mind.

'Can you not sleep, Jon Jo?'

He kissed her.

'Thinking.'

'You don't have to be gone, not yet.'

'Thinking on what you said.'

'What did I say?'

'You said there was a tout on the mountain, you said that's why I was better away . . .'

'Who knows you're back?'

'There's just two. The OC and the QM, it's all.'

'If it wasn't wee Patsy, who might it be?'

Her fingers played in the hair on his chest. Her nails furrowed in his skin. There were some who took women when they were away, and one had gone in London to whores. There were some who screwed the girls that were in the ASUs over the water. He had never met the woman or the girl that matched his Attracta. Never wanted to. He felt the soft blackness of her hair on his shoulder.

'Mossie Nugent was looked over. It was Mossie that named Patsy.'

There was quiet wonderment in her voice. 'Mossie's been a good friend to us. He's done all the painting and papering for us. Plus the electrics when it all fused. I give him eggs, and Siobhan, because Mossie'll not take money from me . . .'

'It's Mossie that's pointed at.'

'I'd give my life to Mossie and know it were safe. I'd give him your life . . .'

'I'm just telling you what I'm hearing.'

417

'What'll you do, Jon Jo?'

'It's not right, it's not for talking about.'

There was the anger of her breath against his skin. 'He's been my friend.'

He started up. He heaved himself onto his elbow. He looked down at her. 'What's that mean?'

'When you weren't here, and Kevin and I were alone for bloody months on end, Jon Jo, he was my friend.'

'But . . .'

'But nothing – would you kill him, Jon Jo, my friend?'

'If it was him . . .'

'Would you kill him for touting, or would you kill him because when you were away he was my friend?'

Her fingers held tight in the hairs. The pain stung him. He had been a boy when Mossie Nugent had first gone to gaol. He had been a child and first learning to kick the gaelic ball from his hands and to swing the hurley stick. He could remember when Mossie had gone down for Possession and he could remember the talk in the village when Mossie had been arrested again in the Free State. He had been the volunteer, the kids hanging at his ankles and the old men buying him drink in the bar, when Mossie Nugent had come back from England. Clever, sharp, good at what he did, and Jon Jo had thought him an arse crawler. Clever at setting up, sharp on his reconnaissance, good at his planning, and an arse crawler because he always wanted to be praised . . . He could not remember when, in three years, Mossie Nugent had fired a rifle nor when Mossie Nugent had detonated a bomb . . . And now Mossie Nugent was Intelligence

418

Officer and knew each move and knew each target. The man was in his mind, with the shambling walk from the injury that was always the excuse for not firing, not detonating.

Jon Jo said, 'He has a bad leg.'

'He fell off a ladder, everyone knows that.'

'And he ran from the SAS feckers who shot the Devitt boy and Jacko and Malachy . . .'

'You'd kill him? Wouldn't matter what I said?'

He said, heavy, 'Touts is for killing. Doesn't matter who they are, doesn't matter what friends they have, they're for killing . . . Time I was gone.'

When he was out of the bed he pulled the sheets and blankets back over her. The fear of the tout had broken the loving. He dressed in the darkness and he sensed that she had turned away from him. When he was dressed he picked up her nightdress and carried it to the bed, and put it underneath the bedding to warm it for her. He kissed her and there was no response from her. Last thing, he lifted the Kalashnikov rifle up from the carpet and held it loosely in his hand as he stood at the door and looked on her.

He went to stand by Kevin's bed, to kneel and kiss the boy's cheek and then he went out through the kitchen where he took the food that she had made him, through the larder window, under the shadow of the farm buildings, through the cover of the hedgerows, up into the mountain. He would sleep, and after he had slept he would think on a meeting with Mossie Nugent.

He listened to Hobbes on the secure telephone. The voice was distant and without emotion. He'd taught Hobbes. Hobbes was his creature.

'. . . Yes, I confirm it, they're back and they've their heads down. The weather? Well, it's foul, it's like it always is. They've the right clothing, they're well dug in. I appreciate it isn't a picnic, but it's what they're trained for, Ernest. They've a meeting scheduled with Song Bird, sometime in the middle of the day. They had the camera on the farmhouse all night, saw nothing, not sight nor sound of him. The dog didn't even bark. He's there, somewhere, that's certain. It's only a matter of time.'

Wilkins stood in the Emergency Operations room and held the telephone tight against his ear. He was shaved, showered, and dressed. His concession to a crisis was that his suit jacket was on the hanger at the back of the door and his waistcoat was unbuttoned and held together by the chain of his watch.

'You're not pushing them too hard?'

'They know they'll get a good kick from me if they don't manage the business, Ernest. She's in great form, as you'd expect. She's satisfied with Brennard, says he's standing up well. Actually, that's like getting an Oscar from her . . .'

'There is the back-up.'

'It's our show, Ernest, and if we can manage it on our own then that is how it will be, that's what I've told her. Quite frankly, I hope we piss all over those policemen.'

'Safety must come first.'

He put the telephone down. Bill was doing the duty watch, and had been late in with all the familiar excuses about roadworks on the Hammersmith flyover . . . If it went wrong, if it wasn't safety first and it failed, then, by God, oh yes, Hobbes was for the jump, oh yes . . . and for himself, if it went wrong, the Cornish cottage, and the endless damp, and oblivion.

'He's back, Mossie, and I'm chancing my neck telling you.'

'Why's that?'

'He's like a mad bull, all strung up. He's not the Jon Jo I knew.'

'No reason for me to be feared of him.'

'He's talking about touts, he's asking about Patsy Riordan.'

'That was settled.'

'He's asking whether Patsy Riordan was the real thing.'

'What's that to me?'

'He's on the mountain, it's like it's festering in him, that there's a tout. He won't move till he's satisfied.'

'Why's you telling me?'

'This is friend's talk, Mossie. Get yourself the hell out of here if there's things you can't answer. Watch yourself, God knows where he'll come from, but don't be there if you can't take the questions.'

'I can answer anything,' Mossie said.

He walked back to his car. The OC wound his window up and powered away. Nugent climbed back into his car. The Reilly girl was on her Da's tractor behind him, filling the road with the trailer. He waved at her. Old Reilly had always wanted boys and he'd to make do with girls, and they all of them drove the tractor like it was a feckin' Ferrari. She squeezed the tractor and the trailer away past him.

The OC had been waiting for him. They all knew when he went to work, what time, and they all knew the route he took. The place in the road was a sharp dip and old Reilly never could bother himself with the hedge trimmer and the thorn and holly grew high on each side. The OC had chosen the place to intercept him where he would not be seen, not by a watcher on the mountain. He sat in his car. He felt the fear gathering round him. Tomorrow was the monthly pay day. Five hundred pounds to a Building Society account held in the name of Mossie Nugent.

But if the bitch didn't help him to run then there was nowhere for him to run to.

He drove to the Housing Executive renovation on the west side of Dungannon. The fear in him was a screw, and tightening.

Hobbes' stage.

The Task Co-ordinating Group listened.

He felt the hostility from around the table and relished it.

'He's on the mountain, gentlemen, he's where I said he'd be. It's only patience that's required now. Sooner, hopefully not later, he will call for my Song Bird, and that will lead my operatives forward, with the support of back-up . . . I don't want any fancy ideas about a military or a police operation onto Altmore. You'd need a flight of helicopters and two brigades of infantry to search that place, and you'd have to step on top of him to find him. We're doing it the right way, gentlemen. Perhaps today, perhaps tomorrow, we'll have him. Are there any questions . . . ?'

Rennie said, 'He's good, is Jon Jo. You blunder in

and corner him and he'll fight like hell. I hope, Mr
Hobbes, you've told that to your *amateurs*. No, I don't
have any questions because I have a funeral to be
getting to . . .'

She led him down the stairs of the Five area. He'd slept
after his shower, didn't know whether she'd slept. He
thought she looked great, whether she'd slept or not.
There was the brightness back in her cheeks and the
bruise on her eye was going fast and there was the lush
colour in her hair. He thought she looked great and
that it didn't matter, not to him.

They went out through the door. The cold hit them.
It was his reflex, to take her arm and steer her round
the rainwater puddle. It was what any young man did
for any young woman. She looked at him. It was days
since he had seen it, the shyness trace.

'You alright, Bren?'

'I'm fine.'

'Did you sleep a bit?'

'Sure, seemed like for ever.'

Cathy said, 'You shouldn't take it hard, Bren . . .'

'Skin of a rhino, Miss Parker.'

'It's just that . . .'

'It's not worth talking about.'

'Are you understanding?'

'Starting to.'

'It never works . . .'

Bren unlocked the car and held the door open for
Cathy. 'Manual of Office Romance, Security Service
Eyes Only (Attention of Field Staff), Page 29,
Paragraph 8, Section 3, Sub-Section C: *Don't*. Full
point. Got you, Miss Parker, loud and clear.'

She bent down into the car. 'It gets in the way,' she said.

He leaned over. He kissed her on the cheek. 'Can we talk about something else . . . ?'

It was a hotel up the road and beyond the round-about where Detective Sergeant Joseph Browne had been shot to death. Jimmy had booked the room. The back-up was to be Rennie's men. He thought there would be a team in the car park . . . He reckoned there would be a second team in the lobby of the hotel, watching the front doors and the corridors off to the bedrooms . . . He drove into the car park of the hotel. The room was booked, the courier had been sent down to do the check-in and take the key and the key had been given to Bren. He took Cathy's arm again and hurried her across the car park.

They were the couple, good-looking boy and fine-looking woman, hurrying to a hotel bedroom with a DO NOT DISTURB sign on the door.

The wrist of the OC throbbed under the plaster cast.

For four hours he had waited in his car outside the terrace of homes that the Housing Executive were renovating.

On the stroke of one, on St Anne's in Church Street, when the men on the site would have been breaking for their sandwiches and flasks, he had seen Mossie Nugent go to his Cortina, peel off his overalls, and drive away.

He didn't know what he looked for.

He followed, as he had followed him to work.

Lunchtime, and the hotel's parking area was well filled, cars and delivery vans, but he found a

424

space from which he could see Mossie's car.

There were so many explanations. Could have been checking for work. Could have been booking for family lunch. Could have been . . .

He settled in his car to watch the main doors that had swung shut on Mossie Nugent's back.

She played the bitch. She had the curtains drawn behind her and the young fellow with her was standing across the room's door. He was sat on the bed. She played the bitch because she was above him, looking down on him, and all the time there was the guy behind . . . He was only the tout, only the paid man . . .

'You have the bleeper, we can locate the bleeper. Three signals is for when you are on the move, and we can track that. Two signals is when you meet him, have him right there beside you, and we move forward then. It has to be your decision as to when you think it is right for us to close, and that's one longer signal. It may be us that closes or it may be the back-up, depends on the circumstances. When we close, if you see us, you don't give any sign of recognition.'

He was scared and she gave him nothing to sustain him. Staccato instructions.

He spoke soft, below the music of the radio that had been tuned in when he went into the hotel bedroom.

'He's a powerful man. He can be the devil.'

'You'll be fine, Mossie, and I'll be watching for you. Wear your red jacket.'

'If I don't get home, if I'm called from work,' head down, sheepish, 'it's at home . . .'

425

'Work clothes, red anorak, or your white overalls. Nothing else.'

He sat on the bed with his head bowed. He would do as she told him . . .

'Yeah, right, but how does I give you the signal, whatever?'

'Where is it?'

He felt the blush. He pointed. There was the cheerful grin of her.

'Got an itch, haven't you? Got a bloody awful itch, right? Got to scratch your balls, yes?'

He stood. She watched him. It was as if he amused her. He put his hand down into his pocket and his fingers went through his handkerchief and the loose change and the car keys and he pressed down through the pocket's material. He felt the cold outline against his skin and then the raised button.

Mossie said, 'What's the money?'

It was his last throw. It was what he had wound himself up to demand of her. Couldn't go back, not to Siobhan, couldn't go back and tell her that he didn't know what the money would be. Alright for her, rich bitch. He'd done a house once, in Birmingham's Edgbaston, he'd been on the team of decorators, sub-contract, and the house had had a hall that was bigger in the floor space than all the bungalow where he lived now with Siobhan and his mother and the four little ones, and there had been the daughter of the house who spoke the same as the bitch. She seemed to laugh at him.

'You get plenty.'

Braver, because he'd have Siobhan up his arse. 'How much?'

'You get ten thousand,' she said, and it was as if that wasn't a figure that was big to her.

'And I get out, right?'

'Who knows, Mossie, who knows.'

He heard the door behind him click open. He turned. The man behind him had leaned out of the door and was checking the corridor. He heard the drone of a vacuum cleaner.

The man said, 'On your way, Song Bird.'

The bitch said, 'Scratch them hard, scratch them often.'

He went out into the corridor, empty. The bitch, she hadn't even wished him luck.

She said she was going shopping. His Ma had been shopping the day before. She said she was going shopping again to Dungannon. He knew the secret. He had held the secret all day at school as to why his Ma had to go again to buy more food. He liked it that his Ma trusted him with the secret. She said that he was a grand boy and that he should, again, take the fodder up to the Mahoneys' field to the bullocks. He had lain in his bed all of the previous night, with the blanket high over his head, and still he had heard the muffled footfall on the stair. But he had been asleep if his Da had come to him . . . He said he would take a bale of hay fodder to the bullocks in the Mahoneys' field, and he had felt the distracted kiss of his Ma on his forehead.

He saw Mossie Nugent come through the swing doors. He would have driven out after him if it had not been for the way his Intelligence Officer glanced twice to the right, and then to the left, like he was checking, then scurried for his car.

He sat low in the seat. He wore a cap on his forehead. He could see through the grime of the bottom of the windscreen. He was careful. He watched Mossie drive away, and turn on the road for Dungannon.

It was the hair on a woman's head. It was red gold. She came fast out of the doors of the hotel, and a young man half ran to keep up with her. Red gold hair. He saw her and he knew her. He saw her in the shadow light of the bar's car park where they'd held her, where he'd punched her, kicked her. His eye line was over the bonnet of his car. She ran to her car and the wind and the spitting rain plucked at the red gold hair and she never looked around her. He saw her as she had flung herself at him, as she had pitched him over, as he had felt the pain explode in his wrist, as he had rolled over and seen the gun in her hand. Their car went fast out of the car park. A van moved. Sudden, quick, a van driving out, and he had noticed no-one go to the van. Mossie gone, and the young woman with the red gold hair gone, and a van gone behind them, had to have been the back-up. There were two more coming out of the hotel. They had the fresh faces and the cut hair and the trimmed moustaches, they were the pigs and they could never hide themselves.

He had seen the break-up of a meeting.

The OC sagged back in his seat.

The enormity of it belted him.

A meeting, a player and a handler, a tout and a Brit with back-up.

Holy shit . . .

He waited a full ten minutes. He drove away and went through Dungannon and passed the Housing Executive renovation site and saw the car, and knew Mossie Nugent was back at his work.

Jimmy came to the shoulder of the woman who monitored the racks of television screens.

'What on earth . . . ?'

'It's the cattle. They're all round it. Focus is all wrong, that's not tree trunks, that's their legs. Lovely looking beasts they were when they were further away, it's the Limousin cross with Herefords.'

The light had just been switched on.

The greyness was falling outside the windows distorted by the anti-blast covering.

Cathy slept in the corner of Colonel Johnny's office. Bren watched the telephone. Herbie was squatted on the floor with his back against the wall and he said nothing and had a seed catalogue to read, and every few minutes, as if that was the big decision in his life, he took his pencil and licked it and entered another order on the sale sheet. Jocko had a small sketch pad on his knee, sat on a straight-backed chair, drew Cathy. Bren couldn't see the work, only the delicate short stabs of his crayons, and there was the bored look on his face that said it might just as well have been a bowl of apples. The cardboard city man, clothes older and more torn and more filthy than Bren had seen them before, had his right boot and his right sock off and carefully, rapt in the work, he darned the heel of the sock.

429

Shortly they would move off.

He sat and he watched the telephone. He thought that he was incomplete. He couldn't sleep, he couldn't grow vegetables, he couldn't draw nor paint to save himself, he couldn't darn because he had never been taught. Sometimes he paced, sometimes he gazed out of the window at the perimeter arc lights of the barracks over towards the pad where the helicopters came and went, always he watched the telephone and waited on it.

There was a new item for the check-list. Their equipment was in the corner, against Cathy's shoulder, and with the equipment was now a box of flares and the pistol to shoot them.

He wondered if they were frightened, any of the rest of them . . .

The dog circled him, and snarled. He lashed a kick at it. He saw the hatred of the little savage, but it wouldn't come closer, not while it had a sight of his boot.

The OC hammered on the door. There were no lights in the farmhouse. He hammered and he waited. He heard no voice and he heard no footstep, only the barking of the dog.

He shouted her name, and he shouted the boy's name. He hit the door again with his good fist, and then because it had crept closer he kicked again at the dog.

Attracta would surely have told him where he might find her man.

The darkness was gathering on the mountain above him. He turned away. He swore at the dog and backed

430

towards the front gate and when he shut it after him then the dog launched itself at the gate. He drove back down the lane and saw that Mossie's car was not yet in the drive in front of the bungalow.

The cattle were gathered at the top hedge where the field gave way to the mountain slope. He stopped. He put down the bale and waited to catch his breath. He shouted, a piping reedy voice, for the bullocks to come to him. His Ma always said that he was not just to dump the bale and cut the twine and spread the hay, he was to get the animals to it, so that they ate it before the rain was into it. He felt the cold. The darkness was closing. He yelled into the wind for the animals. He could see them at the far top of the field. He gritted his teeth. He wondered where his Da was, if his Da watched him. He heaved the bale up again, onto his thin shoulder, and the taut twine cut at the palms of his hands. He staggered under the weight of the bale. The cattle were shapes in the greyness ahead of him. He hoped that if his Da watched then that his Da was proud of him. He squelched across the field. He slid on fresh manure, fell to his knees, picked himself up, lifted the bale again.

Little Kevin crossed the field. The breath sobbed in his lungs. The wind stripped his face, tousled his hair. He slipped again on a smooth stone that he had not seen. He struggled forward. If his Da were watching from the mountain then his Da should not see him cry.

He reached them.

He cut the twine. He kicked and dragged the pressed hay from the shape of the bale. The bullocks ignored him. He pushed his way, all his strength and

431

he had no fear of them, into the heart of the bullock mass. He drove them apart. He saw where they had gathered.

The last of the light caught the brightness of the lens.

He was on his hands and knees and the wet of the grass was through his clothes and the mud smeared him that had churned from the bullocks' hooves. He crawled forward. He saw the lens glass set in the heart of the old moss-covered log that had always been in the hedgerow, long as he could remember. His finger moved to touch the glass, and in his ears there was the suppressed hum of power, like a bulb at home, like when his Ma said that a bulb was going down and needed changing. He crawled into the hedge and he scraped in the earth under the hedgerow of thorn and he found the cable that led into the furthest end of the log. All his strength, everything remaining to him, he tugged at the cable, two hands, he pulled the cable clear and the plug.

He ran for the bottom of the field, for the Mahoneys' lights. Ahead of him were the outline shapes of the farmhouse and the bungalow that had been watched by the hidden eye in the log in the hedgerow.

He ran as if for his life, and his Da's life. He ran as if the dragoons chased in pursuit, gasping, sobbing, running.

'Shit . . .'

Jimmy hurried to her.

'. . . I only went for a pee. It's like it's cut off.'

There was the snow storm on the screen in the centre of the rack of television pictures.

432

Jimmy said quietly, 'That's awkward, leaves us rather blind.'

She heard the fist beating at the door, and the boy's cry. She was doing the children's tea, and Mossie's plate was beside the stove and his food covered, waiting on his return.

'I'm coming, I'm coming . . .' She wiped her hands. She went to the front door.

He was so small, Attracta's boy. He caught at her sleeve. He couldn't speak. He was soaked through and mud-streaked. His breath came in great pants. A proud little beggar he was most times. He was pitiful. She took him into the hallway. Siobhan crouched down in front of him.

'Now what's the matter, Kevin?'

The boy babbled. She tried to catch the gist. She understood something, not everything.

'. . . They've a camera . . . they's looking at us . . . I went to tell the Mahoneys, I shouted through the letter box to them, they bolted the door on me . . . there's a camera up there . . . the cattle found it me, they were round it, it's in a log, it's looking at us . . . I broke it, I broke the wire to it. The camera watches our house, looking for my Da. My Ma's gone to get food for my Da on the mountain . . . It's so they can come for him, it's so's the dragoons can hunt him down. The journeymen tailors'll tell them where they saw him, and then the camera eye will find him, and the dragoons'll come for him . . . It's how they find all the patriots, with touts, journeymen tailors . . .'

And her Mossie was late home for his tea, and Jon Jo Donnelly was on the mountain, and a camera was

433

aimed at the farmhouse, and a small boy stammered the story of touts. Her kids were fighting behind her, and her Mossie was late home, and the talk of the small boy was of touts. She banged on his mother's door. She shouted through the door that it was no time for resting, and she should see to the little ones' tea. She pulled on her coat. His mother was at the door of her room, half dressed, her teeth out. Would she look to the kids?

Siobhan said soft to the boy, 'I'll take you up home. I'll wait up home with you till your Ma's back.'

Little Kevin said, spent, 'The journeymen tailors'll tout on him, it's the touts'll get my Da . . .'

She took him out into the night. She held tight to his hand. The wind off the mountain blew against them. Guilt and shame battered her, as the wind hit her. It was for money. She led the boy back up the lane. It was only for money. When the boy stumbled in his exhaustion Siobhan picked him up and carried him.

Bren had the car started.

Cathy was running, and the boys behind her.

Herbie into his car, and the engine sweetly pounding.

The guns on her lap and the rucksack. The camouflage cream on her face. The wild joy and excitement in her eyes.

The cardboard city man was at her window. 'You're alright, Cathy?'

'Great.'

'Just give us the word.'

She squeezed his hand.

'No fucking about, Cathy.'

The cardboard city man sprinting to join Herbie and Jocko.

He drove out of the barracks, swerved to avoid the sentries. Cathy had the earpiece in.

Cathy said, 'This is what's new . . . We've had the triple signal four times now. They're clocking him. Took them time, silly arses, to get the fix right. They've got that sorted. They've got a good signal now. First signals were bloody awful. He's gone up on the Donaghmore road, then on for Gortavoy Bridge, that's Corrycroar . . . they'll have to do something about seeing to the bloody signal, it's not good enough, not having the proper signal . . . He's taken the left at Corrycroar. He's not hurrying himself. Well, doubt I would in his shoes . . .'

'Where'll that take him?'

'Top of the mountain.'

'How far?'

'Three miles, three and a half.'

'Can we find him up there from the bleeper?'

'Hope so.'

'You promised him.'

'Had to . . . He wouldn't have gone if I hadn't.'

He turned to her, a fast glance. 'It's not a game, you know . . .'

Cathy said, 'Everyone's scared the first time, Bren.'

He swerved up through Donaghmore village. The close village lights were behind him, just the darkness ahead beyond his headlamps and the further pinpricks of the farmhouses and bungalows that spread across the slopes and above them the dark

435

mass that was the wilderness and the killing ground. Cathy heaved the rucksack onto the seat behind. She had the map open across her knees, and on top of the map she was loading the magazines into the two rifles.

Chapter Twenty

Mossie went along the back road behind the lip of the mountain. He drove down the lane that was rutted with winter weather, he splashed slowly over the pot-holes. He had come past the turning to Cornamaddy and past the back road to Inishyegny. It was where he had played as a boy, amongst the trees and the broken walls of what had once been a fortress for the English. The bleeper box cut into his groin. Twice he was hooted from behind, and once he saw the driver, speeding past, turn to give him the finger for going so slow.

There were times when Mossie felt the excitement, the blood drive, when he performed for the bitch. For her he could walk on water. There were times when he felt the exhilaration of the double twist of his world. He could push aside mountains. Now, the excitement and exhilaration were buried. He went by the falling lane that slipped steep on the slope to Crannogue, where the stream tumbled between the reservoir lakes. He had answered the call, as the bitch had known he would.

The foreman had come from his portacabin office

behind the row of homes being renovated for the Housing Executive. He would have blasted any other worker for having a personal call come through to the site office, but he knew Mossie had been to prison, twice, and he knew what for. He would not know whether the stick was broken or the man was still involved, but he had seen the respect and the wariness of those of his workers who came from the same community as Mossie Nugent. The foreman wasn't going to cross a man who might be senior in the Organization.

'He said he'd meet you up by the Back Bridge, up Altmore Forest, some time past six, said you'd know who he was, wouldn't give me the name, cocky frigger. He said you was doing rabbits with lamps. He said to be sure you was there . . .'

He had gone on with his painting. He had left at the normal time. He hadn't rung Siobhan and he hadn't rung the number that would go through to the bitch's people. He might have been watched, and he might not. The man had been more impatient than curious. Not a bad excuse. Fine good rabbits on Altmore, and money to be had for them in the village. It was only sensible to think that he might be watched, followed.

He had pressed the button, hard, three times, when he had left the work site, and again before he was past the Golf Club, again going through Donaghmore and again at Skea Bridge. Damn near pushed the button through the box when he had turned off the Pomeroy road at Corrycoar, and the rain coming. It was as if he was shouting and could hear no answer. He could only trust that they heard.

Mossie saw, on more than one occasion, lights on

the road behind him. He couldn't be sure, but he thought the lights kept the distance between them. He swore to himself because the back window was running mud and water, and the road wound and climbed. He couldn't be sure. He came to the cross-roads. His wipers were going hard, bailing the water from his windscreen. The foreman would now be in front of his fire with the rain hitting his windows, and he'd be thinking it was a feckin' awful night to be out for gun sport.

He pressed the button at the crossroads, and turned left. It was the road past the deep reservoir, leading to the Back Bridge. He pressed the button again.

He had no-one else to trust, only the bitch.

'Straight on.'

'You said he'd turned left.'

'Do as I bloody tell you.'

Bren went over the crossroads. Jimmy had said over the radio that the track on Song Bird's car showed it had gone left at the crossroads. He looked once, but the tail-lights were lost.

'Round this corner, stop. Cut the lights. Turn here. Back like a rat up a sewer. Move it, Bren.'

The adrenalin pumped in him. It would have been her little game. Lights off, hitting a stone behind as he turned, bouncing off it, scraping the tyres. He was hunched over the wheel and peering through the rain. He understood. Anyone watching the approach of Song Bird's car would have seen the lights behind, and seen them go straight on, and lost them behind the outline of the hill they called the Sentry Box. He wound down his window and navigated by the right-hand verge, going as smoothly and as quietly as he could in third, praying that no-one else would be using this road. They were back at the cross-roads. He turned right.

Cathy was hunched forward, her hands clamped over her ears, she whispered, 'He's stopped.'

'How far?'

'They reckon less than a mile . . . Christ . . .'

Bren threw the wheel over . . . Some lunatic with his dog . . . He didn't know how he had missed him. He'd bloody near put the man in the ditch. He registered the long overcoat, the woollen cap, the dog cringing back against the man's legs, and they were past him, as the man stumbled and swore, and Bren knew in an instant that it was the spycatcher from the Library in Dungannon.

'Well left, sunshine,' Cathy said.

There was her light chuckle. He thought he would rather have vomited than laugh. She reached back and pulled the rucksack through the space between their seats. She laid one of the rifles across his lap. She reached inside the rucksack and he heard the click of a switch. It would be the homing signal for the back-up. He heard her breathing, calm and controlled, as if that was the way she had been taught.

'Far enough,' Cathy said. She armed her rifle.

They were out of the car. She threw him the ruck-sack, didn't help him to sling it. She was on the move.

They were the men who waited.

Hobbes had the call from Jimmy, that they were going forward, that Song Bird was close to his rendezvous with Donnelly. He poured himself a

440

second glass. What he called, at times like this, Headmaster's whiskey.

Rennie was still in his office. He said he would telephone Dungannon and put Scenes of Crime on stand-by as soon as he had finished cleaning the graveside mud off his shoes.

Colonel Johnny stamped away down his corridor to alert the Quick Reaction Platoon and to ask the two helicopter pilots assigned to him to begin at once the checks for take-off.

Ernest Wilkins had the call on the fifth floor of Curzon Street high above the evening traffic clog of the rush home and pushed aside the tray from which he had eaten the Stilton salad brought by Bill from the canteen, and felt an old and tired man.

It would be the next call that they waited for . . . to tell Hobbes he had won or failed, to tell Rennie he had been right or wrong, to tell Colonel Johnny whether he should hug that sweet super girl or speak a quiet prayer for her, to tell Ernest Wilkins whether it was Downing Street in triumph or the Director General's office in failure.

Each man in his own place, quiet and waiting for a telephone to ring.

Mossie stopped the car and killed the lights. He climbed out of the car and he slammed the door shut. The rain in the wind spattered on his face. The cold bit into the cotton of his work overalls. He peered into the darkness. He strained his ears. He could see the parapet of the bridge and the trees all round. He could hear the wind and the sigh of his fast breathing and the tumble of the floodstream on the rocks under the bridge. He left his windcheater in the car. No way he was going to obscure his white overalls. He put both hands in his trouser pockets, one hand through the slit at the hip of the overalls and down into his trouser pocket with his handkerchief and his change, and his finger rested on the button of the bleeper box. He thought the elastoplast was loosening. Before he had left the site he had gone to the lavatory and tried to rearrange the elastoplast so that it held better. The roll of elastoplast was at home. He didn't know where she, the bitch, was. He didn't know whether the triple signals had been received. It was his instinct to stand away from the car. To be out of the car gave him . . . The light beam hit his face.

Mossie screwed his eyes shut, then blinked, then turned away from the light. He looked back into the light, into the blindness. The light wavered off him and swept the car.

''Tis you, Jon Jo . . . ?'

The light came back to him, held him. He put his left hand out to shield his eyes.

'. . . It's a fine thing that you're back, Jon Jo . . . It's you, Jon Jo . . . ?'

Never moving off him, holding him like the rabbit that the foreman thought he had come to shoot.

'Heh, can you take the feckin' light off me, Jon Jo . . . ?'

The rain was in his face. His finger was on the button. He thought that the movement of his finger would be seen.

'Put the thing off, Jon Jo.'

The light died.

Mossie pressed the button. He pressed it twice.

'Where is you, Jon Jo? Will you stop your games? Where's you at?'

Only darkness in front of him.

'I was your friend, Mossie . . .' Behind him.

Mossie turned. The wind now pricking at the back of his neck.

'My friends are for keeping, Jon Jo.'

He started forward towards the voice.

'Well, I've a problem with that friendship.'

'You've no problem with me . . .'

Sideways on to him now, the voice.

'Stay where you are, Mossie . . . There's people telling me about Patsy Riordan.'

'What's they telling you?'

'That Patsy Riordan never had the wit to tout.'

'Security said he did.'

In front of him. Mossie spun again to face the voice.

'How long did they have him?'

'You tell me, Jon Jo, you've been listening to the talk.'

'What did they do to him?'

The voice so threatening, so quiet. He strained to hear. 'How the feck do I know? I wasn't there.'

'What do you think they did to him?'

'Roughed him a bit . . .'

'That what you think they do to touts, Mossie? Gone soft in security, have they? Just roughed him?'

The voice circled him. The voice to the left of him and then behind him and then to the right of him. He no longer turned to face it. He stood his ground. His finger was on the bleeper-box button. More shit scared than he had ever been. He didn't know whether they were out there, whether they were close, or whether they were drinking feckin' coffee in feckin' Belfast. He had only her word.

'I'd have said they went heavy on him, Mossie.'

'Why don't you ask them as was there?'

'If they'd gone heavy on him, Mossie, what'd he have done?'

'I don't know, Jon Jo, and . . .'

'You don't know much, Mossie. What would *you* have done?'

'I'm not a tout, I can't say . . .'

'Let's say they're hurting you, Mossie. The pain's bad and they're telling you that's for starters. The pain's going to be worse, it's only the beginning. Then they tell you that if you cough it, if you tell them what you know, then, perhaps, it's going to be settled. That's what they do, Mossie. They give it you hard and they give it you soft, but the harder gets worse till you're crying louder for the soft. What I'm saying, when the hurting's bad they offer you a way out. You agree with me, you'd want to take the way out?'

'It's not for me to say.'

Close to him, right behind him. Mossie half jumping. The fist against his shoulder, then the barrel of the weapon cold against his skin.

'He'd talk, Mossie, don't you reckon so? He'd be messing his pants and he'd be talking. Isn't that what you'd be doing, Mossie?'

'I don't . . .'

'But he didn't. There was no confession from Patsy Riordan.'

The muzzle of the gun was off his neck. The fist was away from his shoulder. His stomach was falling, his knees were quivering. He should never have come, and he didn't know whether she, the bitch, was close.

'Perhaps he didn't confess because he'd nothing to confess to. You're a clever man, Mossie, that make sense to you? What you looking for, Mossie? I'm here, I'm in front of you. I'm not behind you . . . Are you looking for your friends, Mossie?'

'That's just daft talk.'

'Have you got some problem, Mossie?'

'Damn right. You's my problem. All your smart talk is my problem . . . I've had this shit. I don't need you telling me about the Riordan boy. I told the man from security. I was clean, clear.'

The soft voice in darkness. 'It's what I heard.'

'Well, hear this, too, Jon Jo. We've been fighting over here, perhaps you didn't read our papers when you were in England. We have a hard war here. We've got more on our plates than stupid feckin' tossers of English policemen. We've got the real war here, not the war against women and kids . . .'

'I heard. I heard you were doing well . . . And I heard there was funerals.'

'Wars go hard. Here we fight, we don't hide.'

'That's what I don't believe about you, Mossie. I think you hide a lot. If I roughed you a bit, Mossie, if I slapped you round a bit, would you slip some of what you hide?'

He was gone. He knew he was gone.

He waited for the blow, the punch, the gun barrel. It was in his mind, when the bitch had come to the police cell and torn up the charge sheet, and he waited for the fist. He thought of the meetings with her, the lay-bys and the car parks and the quarry off the Armagh road, and he waited for the boot. He had run from the soldiers, and the Devitt boy and Jacko and Malachy had been on the pavement and the gutter behind him, and the red anorak he had worn had streamed in the wind. He waited. He didn't know whether Jon Jo circled him, whether he was behind him or in front of him.

'What's touts for, Mossie?'

He sobbed the words. 'For killing, touts is for killing.'

Behind him, savage cold. 'Take your hands out of your pockets, Mossie . . .'

His finger drifted on the button. There was no strength in him. He could feel the button. He had neither the strength nor the trust to press the button.

'. . . Take your hands out of your pockets, Mossie, and put them on the top of your head . . .'

Mossie did as he was told. He always did.

'. . . Kneel down, Mossie . . .'

He knelt and the wet was on his knees, and the tears were on his face, and the box cut into his groin, and the gun's muzzle was against the nape of his neck.

'How long have you been touting, Mossie?'

He could see, but he could not hear.

Bren could see through the image intensifier on the Heckler and Koch. He was too far back to hear. He had seen Jon Jo Donnelly circling Song Bird, now he could see Song Bird kneeling and the grey-green form of the target above him. The cross-hairs were on the target. The voices were a murmur, mixed with the wind and the rain's fall and the stream's clatter, too indistinct for him to hear. It was for Cathy to do it . . . For Christ's sake, woman, do it . . . Time spiralling, the opportunity spilling down the drain. He didn't know why she didn't shoot. He lay on his stomach. The trees were around him. The kneeling figure and the standing figure, sharp in the lens at fifty paces in the clearing, close to the road and the bridge.

How much bloody longer did she want?

Her voice.

The hissed urgency.

'I'm blocked, bastard trees, can't aim, I've only 20 per cent target . . .'

He had his finger inside the trigger guard. His thumb eased the safety. He had the butt against his shoulder. He had the scope against his eye. So clear in front of him. He could see the face of the target . . . His finger rested on the trigger. Where were the boys? When it was their work, where were they?

'Do it . . .'

Jon Jo heard what he said.

Mossie said, through the tears, 'It's what they made me. They made me a tout . . .'

He had the weapon's barrel hard against Mossie Nugent's neck. The questions, they'd been easy. The answer came so feckin' hard.

'. . . You don't know what it's like when they've trapped you. You wouldn't know, Jon Jo. You's trapped, and they's the claws in you. You's can never back away.'

The answer came so hard to him. The answer was harder than anything that he had known. Mossie Nugent, snivelling, blubbering bastard, had been calling at his Attracta's. He was gone now anyhow, but the answers made it right. The answers came

447

from a man grovelling, and he was crying for mercy.

'It's your own friends. What meant anything to you? Did you take their money, Mossie . . . ?'

'Don't kill me . . . I'll go and never come back.'

The cold came again to Jon Jo. 'Would you tout on me?'

'I's trapped, don't you see?'

'You'd tout on me?'

'Oh, Jesus. It was you special that they wanted.'

He heard the plea in the voice. It was the cry for forgiveness. He had not heard a cry from two school-girls, nor from a schoolboy buying a ticket at a railway station.

The pistol shook in the grip of his hands. He understood. Staying too long. Shouldn't have come, shouldn't have stayed. Should have been in the caves by now. Should have been gone.

'I'll not hurt you, Mossie. I'll . . .'

He would shoot and he would run. The barrel was at the bone of the neck . . .

Jon Jo felt himself lifted. He was careering back. The gale punch had whipped him. He tried to hold his feet, and fell, and he tried to stand again and he slipped. No sound around him, and no movement. Tried to crawl and had no strength. And the pain had come, exploding in him.

Bren lay on his stomach. The slammed weight of the recoil had hit his shoulder. The blast of the noise had killed his ears. He followed the target through the haze of the image intensifier. His target stood again, fell again, and crawled. Bren could not move. She was at his ear. 'Christ, you cut it fine . . .' He saw Song Bird

448

crumpled in front of him, his head in his hands and his head bent down on his knees. She was shaking at his shoulder and then she punched it. 'Bloody good shot, Bren. Well done . . .' She was standing above him. He heard nothing, but he saw the flash of light behind her. The flare burst, brilliant bubbling red in the night sky. The light of the flare reflected back from the low cloud. 'Come on, old thing, don't just lie there.' And then the crisp belt of her voice into the radio.

They had been at the door of the farmhouse.

They had heard the shot, booming, echoing down off the mountain in the wind. They saw the bright blood colour of the flare.

Little Kevin was against Attracta's leg. They stood at the door and Siobhan was on the path beyond the step. They watched the tumbling dying of the flare.

Attracta said, 'My Jon Jo, he's up there.'

The taste of the tea was in Siobhan's mouth, and the warmth of the kitchen still lingered around her.

The voice of the boy babbled, muffled in the skirt against his mother's leg. 'The journeymen tailors'll get the dragoons to kill the patriot. It's the touts that'll get him. Ma, is that the end of the story?'

Siobhan Nugent went to Attracta Donnelly. Mossie's wife's arms were around Jon Jo's wife's neck. She kissed the face of her neighbour. She ran the length of the front path.

The telephone was ringing, Charles was first to it. Wilkins watched . . . Charles held the telephone against his ear, and there was the dry, droll smile on his face.

'I'll tell him, he has been very anxious to hear . . . Goodbye.'

It was the moment of triumph or the moment of failure. You never could tell with Charles, infuriating man.

'Splendid news, Ernest . . . your wife, the plumber's in at last, the immersion's working again. She thought you'd want to know so you wouldn't worry . . .'

He'd kill that woman. So help him, he'd do a life sentence for her. He slumped against the wall. His head was close to the life-size photograph of Jon Jo Donnelly. The telephone rang. Again Charles beat him to it.

'An incident on Altmore. *An incident?* Is that the best you can do? It looks to me as though Mr Wilkins could use a little bit more detail . . . Ah yes, thank you, Jimmy, a *shooting* incident. That's more like it. What shall I tell him? Three hundred rabbits believed seriously injured . . . ? You'll come back if you get an exact head count, bless you, Jimmy.' Charlie put the receiver down. 'Well, you heard what the man said, Ernest. Rather a confused picture on Altmore just at present.'

He wanted him dead. He gazed at the photograph. Too damned old for it all. The shame surged in him. He wanted him dead, killed.

He heard the voice, the command shout.

'Stay still. Don't move, Mossie.'

The eye of the night scope was on the figure. The figure crawled a few inches at a time towards the far tree line. The figure struggled to be out of the clearing. He had done it. He had cut the figure from his legs, reduced him to a crawling effort of escape. The shadows swam around him. Coming quickly and coming silently. He never took the night scope sight away from the target figure, but he saw them running, the shadows, hunched and bent. A shadow merged with her, then moved on. They were spread out, three of them. Two shadows, from opposite sides, ringing the clearing. The third shadow away from her and then forward to the still kneeling Song Bird, crouching over him. The protection had arrived. He watched the shadows, sometimes he lost them in the tree shapes, sometimes he saw them clear. Flitting shadows that closed on the target figure. He could almost have shouted out to the fallen man that the danger was on him. Bren watched in the image intensifier. Too late to warn the target. They were black in the scope, one tall and one short, one who painted water colours and one who grew onions. It was because of what he had done, and because of what she had told him to do. The shorter man going in, grabbing the weapon from the target's hand. No resistance. The second figure moving forward. It was very quick. The boot onto the small of the back of the target, the weapon pointing down. It was the moment when Bren closed his eyes, and the moment of the crash of the single shot bouncing in his ears . . . and then he heard the first stirrings of the helicopter rotors.

The light flooded down from the helicopter. Through the night scope the clearing had seemed huge, but the light from the helicopter shrunk it. Bren stood up. The Heckler and Koch hung against his leg.

It was cardboard city who had gone to Song Bird. He shouted at Bren.

'Make safe your weapon.'

They were the professionals, and they had not been there . . .

He wanted no more part of it. Cathy had the radio across her face. The body of Jon Jo Donnelly was at the far side of the clearing and in the beam from the helicopter Bren saw the hole at the shoulder of the tunic. The cardboard city man dragged Song Bird to the edge of the clearing. Herbie and Jocko were crouched over the target figure, and the rotors whipped their camouflage smocks as the first helicopter landed.

There were troops ducking from the helicopter, running under the low rotor thrash. He disengaged the magazine. He cleared the breech. He pocketed the live round. He saw Cathy stride over to Song Bird and the cardboard city man. She had to shout against Mossie's head. Bren could just hear her.

'Well done, Mossie. Sorry we left it so late.'

Bren saw the pleading on his face, just as had been when he pleaded for his life.

'You're not hurt? That's good. Get moving. Don't go straight home. Stop and get yourself a couple of pints. Make it natural. I can get you a long slow search if you need an alibi for the last half-hour. Let me know if need be, but for heaven's sake keep your head down for the next two or three days. Safe home, Mossie.' She thumped his shoulder.

Bren watched. Mossie walked away. Each stride and the strength grew back in his legs. Cathy wasn't looking over her shoulder at him. Cathy was hard in talk with the cardboard city man and Colonel Johnny, and the colonel put his arm on her shoulder and she removed it briskly and pointed to Bren. Bloody good, credit where it was due. He saw Mossie go out from the range of the lights, trudging away towards his car . . . It was what they taught the recruits on the Source Unit seminar, that there should never be emotion between a player and a handler, didn't matter how valuable was the player's talk. All by the bloody book, all the emotion stifled, strangled, chucked out of the bloody window.

Jocko was beside him. 'Good effort. A perfectly adequate shot, in the circumstances . . .'

He took the rifle from Bren, and Bren gave him the magazine and the last live round.

'. . . You did well, but it has to be down to us. You don't exist, you see.'

Jocko had one of Bren's arms, and Cathy had the other and they ran him to the open door of the helicopter.

Bren felt the shudder as it lifted off, swooped up out of the forest.

Epilogue

He would have told her that morning.

Bren would have told Cathy what he had decided.

It was a crisp start to the day, fiercely cold. The roads from Belfast to Dungannon had been gritted, but the lanes onto the mountain would be treacherous, and he was slow coming the last few miles. He had never driven through the village before and up towards the farmhouse and the bungalow. He didn't need the map because the helicopters ploughing the low cloud overhead guided him. He felt no tiredness although he had not slept. He had been sitting in the small living room of the flat, where he had been all through the night and still dressed, when she had telephoned. He had left in darkness. He arrived in the first pale gleam of sunlight.

He was numbed by the anger he felt.

At the roadblock 200 yards short of the bungalow Bren showed his ID and was waved through. He gazed into the camouflage-creamed faces of the soldiers and the smooth-shaven faces of the policemen as if from them he might read an explanation for Cathy's summons, which had told him nothing, and the blanked-off expressions gave him no clue. He drove on until he was just short of the bungalow's garden and there he was waved down and signalled to park against the hedgerow. He climbed out. He could feel the ache where his shoulder was bruised from the recoil of the automatic rifle.

In front of the bungalow was the old Cortina estate. It was slewed across the road in front of the low iron gates and the driver's door was wide open. The dust sheet was where it always was, hiding the tools of Mossie's trade. He looked into the car, through the open front door, and he saw the keys in the ignition and the frosted dew on the seat. He understood. Bren could make the picture in his mind. The car pulling up at the gate, engine on, leaving the door open as he went to pull back the gates. Coming back from the pints in Dungannon that he had been told to take, coming back after the destruction of Jon Jo Donnelly, and the men waiting for him and seizing him . . .

A policeman stepped aside.

Cathy was standing in the porch. He felt the filth on his body. She would have gone back to her home, after it was over, and she would have showered and slept, and she was in clean jeans and he could see the collar of a pretty blouse over her sweater and she had a leather jacket to her hips that he had not seen before, and her hair was mostly hidden by a scarf. Her car wasn't in the lane and he assumed that she had come from the barracks by helicopter. Her calm refuelled his anger.

'Roads slippy, were they?'

Did he care how the roads were?

So matter of fact, and then in the same low, even voice, she said: 'When Mossie got home, they were waiting for him. They must have rumbled him already, wouldn't have been enough time to have mounted it in response to what happened last night.'

'Is Siobhan alright?'

'. . . There's footsteps all round in the mud on the verge and there's two sets of tyre marks from where they were parked up and waiting . . .'

'How's Siobhan?'

Cathy looked into his face. He couldn't read her. She said nothing. She led him through the hall and towards the kitchen. He stepped over children's toys, a plastic machine gun and a half-clothed doll. He went by a framed photograph of John Paul the Second. His shoulder brushed a line of coats hanging from hooks and there was a red anorak that was paint-stained and gone at the elbow. It was turning in his mind, what he would say to Siobhan, how he would face her, whether he would abide by the creed of the handler that there should be no emotional attachment to players . . . He went into the kitchen after Cathy.

They were round the table, the children and their grandmother. The children were in their night clothes and their grandmother was dressed. The washing-up from last night's supper had not been done.

Cathy said, 'Mrs Nugent, this is a colleague of mine. Would you tell him, please, about Siobhan.'

He felt the cold settle on him, run in his body.

The children's grandmother looked up from the table. She lit a cigarette. The ashtray was half-filled in front of her. The smoke wafted into the face of the baby child that sat on her lap. 'God's truth, I had her as a loveless woman who made a misery of him. I'm not proud of it, but I'd no time for her, but she fought for him . . . She'd been all jumpy, all restless. She said there had been shooting on the mountain. She'd been to the Donnelly woman's house. The Donnelly woman's brat had been here, blethering some gibberish about cameras and journeymen tailors and touts. Siobhan had taken him home, and she stayed up to talk with the Donnelly woman and then there was shooting high on Altmore. She'd been waiting for Mossie to be home, as if she knew there was danger. She was in the kitchen when we saw Mossie's car lights. She'd gone to the front door. What I saw was first from the kitchen. She had the door open. I could see past her. There was men around my Mossie. He was out of the car and they was trying to carry him off. I never liked her, and I've shame for it. She shouted, "You take him and you take me . . ." That's what she shouted first. They had a gun turned at her and she went off down the path. I saw her kick the leg of the man with the gun. I saw my Mossie's face. I've never seen such fear in my son. She kicked that one man with the gun and she tried to hit another of them, and Mossie was struggling like it was for his life. She shouted at them, "You're not having him . . ." She fought for my Mossie. She kicked them and punched them all the time until they'd beaten the fight from her. Mossie, there was a moment he had a hand free of them, he tried to push her away . . . They took the both of them . . .'

Cathy's hand dropped, only for a moment, onto the

457

shoulder of the grandmother of the children. 'Thank you, Mrs Nugent,' she said.

Bren tried to capture, indelibly, the remnant of this family. He nodded his thanks to the old lady, he gazed, through tears welling in his eyes, at the three silent children, staring hollow-eyed at him. He blundered out into the hall. His hands found the steep rail of the steps to the loft. He held it for support. The roar of a helicopter gathered over the house.

He went to the front doorway. There were ropes and a chain snaking, swinging, down from the heli-copter and the policemen and soldiers were running the chain and the ropes under the chassis of the old Cortina estate. They wanted the evidence out quickly. They wanted to be gone, the soldiers and the policemen. The slopes of Altmore mountain were that sort of place. The one car had been allowed forward. Bren watched. It was parked close to where the uncut hedge bent under the downdraft of the rotors. He saw the priest, a big man and walking well, and never bothering to look up at the hovering helicopter, never sparing a glance at the men with the ropes and the chain. The priest came up the front path and to the door. He stood in front of Bren and challenged him to move aside. There was contempt for him in the priest's eyes, and blame. He stepped aside. He wondered what the priest would say to the mother of a tout and to the children of a tout.

Mossie's car swayed beneath the helicopter. The helicopter banked away.

Below it, the opened door of the Cortina estate, Mossie's door, flapped.

Cathy shouted, 'There's two bodies down on the

border. They're not identified yet, but it's a man's and a woman's.'

He wanted to be away from her.

Bren walked halfway down the front path. There were weeds in the flower beds and the winter debris on the grass. He turned, 'Cathy . . .'

She came to him, she stood in front of him. She looked into his eyes. The scarf on her head had slipped from the beauty of the red gold of her hair.

Bren said, 'We should never have let him . . .'

'It was his best chance.'

'I suppose you'd say that getting Donnelly made it worthwhile.'

'Nothing makes losing Song Bird worthwhile.'

'I'm going home.'

It had grown in him through the night hours, alone in his flat. He had steeled himself to the decision. Perhaps he hoped that she might fight him . . .

Cathy shrugged, 'I'm sorry, I mean that . . . You had what it takes.'

'I had nothing, and I am going because there is nothing for me to contribute. You don't think you'll be staying . . . ?'

'I'm not going anywhere.'

He flared. 'Switch on, Cathy . . . I'm here because a tout was lost and a lost tout talks. Our guy compromised. I was sent as the fast solution stop-gap. Mossie's lost, Mossie'll have talked or they wouldn't have killed him. They'll have bled him desert-dry before they murdered him. Don't you understand it, compromised . . . ?'

'Give my regards to Mr Wilkins.'

'They know your face, your work, and they know

your style. Nowhere's safe for you. Vulnerable, do you hear anything?'

'Not your worry . . . Thanks for the concern. I'll cope.'

He wondered if he fooled himself, if she would talk round Hobbes, batter Wilkins into submission, if she would be staying. He wondered if she deluded herself, if he would meet her in a corridor in Curzon Street within the month, if she would nod at him and smile and share the coffee machine, if she would ignore him. He looked into her face. He gazed down at the red-gold peep of hair jutting from under the scarf. Of course she was compromised, of course she should go home.

He thought she was beyond the reach of his love.

He would never forget . . .

Cathy said, 'We were going well, in time we'd have made a good team.'

Bren mouthed it quietly, 'I'm going home before I'm destroyed . . .'

'. . . There won't be much for you, Bren, not with you walking out of here, but then you'll have thought that through . . .'

Bren said, 'I'm going home before I am destroyed, before I know for certain that there is no light, no hope, no future. I wouldn't want to know that, not for certain.'

He reached to shake her hand. She kissed his cheek.

Bren walked away to his car. He could see up the lane. In the yard behind the farmhouse a young boy was carrying a bale of hay from the barn. The bright sunlight was on the mountain slope, catching the dead bracken.

He turned. He looked back for her. She had stood her ground beside the gate. She waved to him.

He would drive back to the flat, and pack and go to the airport. He would be in London by the end of the day. He unlocked the door of his car. He was not strong enough for life without light and hope and a future. It was her world, Cathy Parker's world, in front of him, behind him, around him.

He sat in his seat, and he leaned forward against the steering wheel. He watched a hawk circling high. He didn't understand why the hawk had no fear of the hovering Lynx helicopter above it.

He knew where she would be, later that day. She was in the eye of his mind. She would be hemmed around by her men, her people. There would be the cardboard city man, and Herbie and Jocko. There would be the guns that they carried to protect her. Near to her, but warned back from coming too close, would be the soldiers and the policemen. He saw her walking the length of the hill, going up the middle of the lane between the bare hedgerows. There would be the bodies in the ditch, dumped. There would be the dustbin bags over the heads of the bodies, and the bale twine cutting at the wrists of the bodies, and there would be the bare and lifeless feet of the bodies. When the bags had been cut away from the heads of the bodies she would look down into the faces of her Song Bird and her Song Bird's woman. She would not have shrunk from making the identification. And she would be gone from the lane, gone from the consequences of her work. It was what Bren imagined . . .

He drove away. A last time he looked, back over his shoulder, for the hawk.

The bird soared, floated, feathered.

'God keep you safe, Cathy . . .'

The hawk dived to kill, brilliant in the low winter sunlight, without fear.

THE END

THE UNTOUCHABLE
by Gerald Seymour

'The finest thriller writer in the world today'
Daily Telegraph

Albert William Packer is the supreme baron of London crime. He rules his manor with a cruel, ruthless fist. To those around him, on whatever side of the law, he is the Untouchable.

When another criminal case against him collapses, Packer turns his attention to expanding his heroin empire abroad. Where better to cut out the middle man than at the historic smuggling crossroads of Europe, the Balklans?

New men and women are drafted into the Customs & Excise unit dedicated to convicting Packer. Only one from the old team survives: the most junior, Joey Cann retained solely for his obsessional knowledge of the man who calls himself 'Mister'. When Packer leaves for Sarajevo, it is inevitable that Cann be sent after him for 'intrusive surveillance'. The brief: to bring back the evidence that will nail Packer to the wall, whatever it takes.

In London, it would have been no contest. But here on the war-torn streets of a city where justice is enforced by gangster warlords, Packer is far from home and from what he knows. Here, who will be the Untouchable, who will walk away?

'A clever, informed and worldly cynical story about arrogance, obsession and tragedy'
The Times

'A genuinely exciting epic . . . the novel has a truly memorable final chapter . . . entertaining'
Independent

0 552 14816 4

A SELECTED LIST OF FINE WRITING AVAILABLE FROM CORGI BOOKS

THE PRICES SHOWN BELOW WERE CORRECT AT THE TIME OF GOING TO PRESS. HOWEVER TRANSWORLD PUBLISHERS RESERVE THE RIGHT TO SHOW NEW RETAIL PRICES ON COVERS WHICH MAY DIFFER FROM THOSE PREVIOUSLY ADVERTISED IN THE TEXT OR ELSEWHERE.

☐	14746 X	THE MASTER OF THE RAIN	Tom Bradby	£6.99
☐	15073 8	ANGELS AND DEMONS	Dan Brown	£6.99
☐	14578 5	THE MIRACLE STRAIN	Michael Cordy	£5.99
☐	14923 3	THE VETERAN	Frederick Forsyth	£6.99
☐	14901 2	WALLS OF SILENCE	Philip Jolowicz	£6.99
☐	15021 5	THE ANALYST	John Katzenbach	£6.99
☐	14970 5	THE BUSINESS OF DYING	Simon Kernick	£6.99
☐	14584 X	THE COLD CALLING	Will Kingdom	£5.99
☐	14870 9	DANGEROUS DATA	Adam Lury & Simon Gibson	£6.99
☐	14798 2	LAST LIGHT	Andy McNab	£6.99
☐	54535 X	KILLING GROUND	Gerald Seymour	£6.99
☐	14605 6	THE WAITING TIME	Gerald Seymour	£5.99
☐	14682 X	A LINE IN THE SAND	Gerald Seymour	£6.99
☐	14666 8	HOLDING THE ZERO	Gerald Seymour	£6.99
☐	14816 4	THE UNTOUCHABLE	Gerald Seymour	£6.99
☐	14723 0	FIELD OF BLOOD	Gerald Seymour	£6.99
☐	14722 2	HARRY'S GAME	Gerald Seymour	£6.99
☐	14729 X	ARCHANGEL	Gerald Seymour	£6.99
☐	14733 8	HOME RUN	Gerald Seymour	£5.99
☐	14731 1	A SONG IN THE MORNING	Gerald Seymour	£5.99
☐	14732 X	AT CLOSE QUARTERS	Gerald Seymour	£5.99
☐	14730 3	IN HONOUR BOUND	Gerald Seymour	£5.99
☐	14726 5	KINGFISHER	Gerald Seymour	£5.99
☐	14725 7	THE GLORY BOYS	Gerald Seymour	£5.99
☐	14727 3	RED FOX	Gerald Seymour	£5.99
☐	14728 1	THE CONTRACT	Gerald Seymour	£5.99
☐	14735 4	THE FIGHTING MAN	Gerald Seymour	£5.99
☐	14736 2	THE HEART OF DANGER	Gerald Seymour	£5.99
☐	14734 6	CONDITION BLACK	Gerald Seymour	£5.99
☐	14391 X	A SIMPLE PLAN	Scott Smith	£5.99
☐	10565 1	TRINITY	Leon Uris	£6.99

All Transworld titles are available by post from:

Bookpost, P.O. Box 29, Douglas, Isle of Man IM99 1BQ

Credit cards accepted. Please telephone 01624 836000,
fax 01624 837033, Internet http://www.bookpost.co.uk or
e-mail: bookshop@enterprise.net for details.

**Free postage and packing in the UK. Overseas customers allow
£2 per book (paperbacks) and £3 per book (hardbacks).**